R Data Mining

Implement data mining techniques through practical use cases and real-world datasets

Andrea Cirillo

BIRMINGHAM - MUMBAI

R Data Mining

First published: November 2017

Production reference: 1271117

Published by Packt Publishing Ltd.
Livery Place
35 Livery Street
Birmingham
B3 2PB, UK.

ISBN 978-1-78712-446-2

www.packtpub.com

Credits

Author
Andrea Cirillo

Reviewers
Enrico Pegoraro
Doug Ortiz
Radovan Kavicky
Oleg Okun

Commissioning Editor
Amey Varangaonkar

Acquisition Editor
Varsha Shetty

Content Development Editor
Mayur Pawanikar

Technical Editor
Karan Thakkar

Copy Editors
Safis Editing
Vikrant Phadkay

Project Coordinator
Nidhi Joshi

Proofreader
Safis Editing

Indexer
Tejal Daruwale Soni

Graphics
Tania Dutta

Production Coordinator
Aparna Bhagat

About the Author

Andrea Cirillo is currently working as an audit quantitative analyst at Intesa Sanpaolo Banking Group. He gained financial and external audit experience at Deloitte Touche Tohmatsu and internal audit experience at FNM, a listed Italian company. His main responsibilities involve the evaluation of credit risk management models and their enhancement, mainly within the field of the Basel III capital agreement. He is married to Francesca and is the father of Tommaso, Gianna, Zaccaria, and Filippo. Andrea has written and contributed to a few useful R packages such as updateR, ramazon, and paletteR, and regularly shares insightful advice and tutorials on R programming. His research and work mainly focus on the use of R in the fields of risk management and fraud detection, largely by modeling custom algorithms and developing interactive applications.

Andrea has previously authored *RStudio for R Statistical Computing Cookbook* for Packt Publishing.

To Cesca, Tommaso, Gianna, Zaccaria and Filippo.

About the Reviewers

Enrico Pegoraro graduated in statistics from the Italian University of Padua more than 20 years ago. He says that "he *has experienced in himself the fast-growing computer science and statistics worlds*". He has worked on projects involving databases, software development, programming languages, data integration, Linux, Windows, and cloud computing. He is currently working as a freelance statistician and data scientist.

Enrico has gained more than 10 years of experience with R and other statistical software training and consulting activities, with a special focus on Six Sigma, industrial statistical analysis, and corporate training courses. He is also a partner of the main company supporting the MilanoR Italian community. In this company, he works as a freelance principal data scientist, as well as teacher of statistical models and data mining with R training courses.

In his first job, Enrico collaborated with Italian medical institutions, contributing to some regional projects/publications on nosocomial infections. His main expertise is in consulting and teaching statistical modeling, data mining, data science, medical statistics, predictive models, SPC, and industrial statistics. Enrico planning to develop an Italian-language website dedicated to R (www.r-project.it).

Enrico can be contacted at pego.enrico@tiscalil.it.

I would like to thank all the people who support me and my activities, particularly my partner, Sonja, and her son, Gianluca.

Doug Ortiz is an enterprise cloud, big data, data analytics, and solutions architect who has been architecting, designing, developing, and integrating enterprise solutions throughout his career. Organizations that leverage his skillset have been able to rediscover and reuse their underutilized data via existing and emerging technologies such as Amazon Web Services, Microsoft Azure, Google Cloud, Microsoft BI Stack, Hadoop, Spark, NoSQL databases, and SharePoint along with related toolsets and technologies.

He is also the founder of Illustris, LLC and can be reached at dougortiz@illustris.org.

Some interesting aspects of his profession are:

- Experience in integrating multiple platforms and products
- Big data, data science, R, and Python Certifications
- He helps organizations gain a deeper understanding of the value of their current investments in data and existing resources, turning them into useful sources of information
- He has improved, salvaged, and architected projects by utilizing unique and innovative techniques
- He regularly reviews books on Amazon Web Services, data science, machine learning, R, and cloud technologies

His hobbies are yoga and scuba diving.

I would like to thank my wonderful wife, Mila, for all her help and support, as well as Maria, Nikolay, and our wonderful children.

Radovan Kavicky is the principal data scientist and president at GapData Institute, based in Bratislava, Slovakia, where he harnesses the power of data and wisdom of economics for public good. He is a macroeconomist by education, and consultant and analyst by profession (8+ years of experience in consulting for clients from the public and private sector), with strong mathematical and analytical skills. He is able to deliver top-level research and analytical work. From MATLAB, SAS, and Stata, he switched to Python, R and Tableau.

Radovan is an evangelist of open data and a member of the Slovak Economic Association (SEA), Open Budget Initiative, Open Government Partnership, and the global Tableau #DataLeader network (2017). He is the founder of PyData Bratislava, R <- Slovakia, and the SK/CZ Tableau User Group (skczTUG). He has been a speaker at @TechSummit (Bratislava, 2017) and @PyData (Berlin, 2017).

You can follow him on Twitter at @radovankavicky, @GapDataInst or @PyDataBA. His full profile and experience are available at https://www.linkedin.com/in/radovankavicky/ and https://github.com/radovankavicky.

GapData Institute: https://www.gapdata.org.

Oleg Okun is a machine learning expert and author/editor of four books, numerous journal articles, and many conference papers. His career spans more than a quarter of a century. He was employed in both academia and industry in his mother country, Belarus, and abroad (Finland, Sweden, and Germany). His work experience includes document image analysis, fingerprint biometrics, bioinformatics, online/offline marketing analytics, credit scoring analytics, and text analytics.

He is interested in all aspects of distributed machine learning and the Internet of Things. Oleg currently lives and works in Hamburg, Germany.

> *I would like to express my deepest gratitude to my parents for everything that they have done for me.*

www.PacktPub.com

For support files and downloads related to your book, please visit www.PacktPub.com.

Did you know that Packt offers eBook versions of every book published, with PDF and ePub files available? You can upgrade to the eBook version at www.PacktPub.com and as a print book customer, you are entitled to a discount on the eBook copy. Get in touch with us at service@packtpub.com for more details.

At www.PacktPub.com, you can also read a collection of free technical articles, sign up for a range of free newsletters and receive exclusive discounts and offers on Packt books and eBooks.

https://www.packtpub.com/mapt

Get the most in-demand software skills with Mapt. Mapt gives you full access to all Packt books and video courses, as well as industry-leading tools to help you plan your personal development and advance your career.

Why subscribe?

- Fully searchable across every book published by Packt
- Copy and paste, print, and bookmark content
- On demand and accessible via a web browser

Customer Feedback

Thanks for purchasing this Packt book. At Packt, quality is at the heart of our editorial process. To help us improve, please leave us an honest review on this book's Amazon page at `https://www.amazon.com/dp/1787124460`.

If you'd like to join our team of regular reviewers, you can e-mail us at `customerreviews@packtpub.com`. We award our regular reviewers with free eBooks and videos in exchange for their valuable feedback. Help us be relentless in improving our products!

Table of Contents

Preface

You have probably heard that R is a fabulous tool that is gaining in popularity everyday among data analysts and data scientists, and that it is renowned for its ability to deliver highly flexible and professional results, paired with astonishing data visualizations. All this sounds great, but how can you learn to use R as a data mining tool? This book will guide you from the very beginning of this journey; you will not need to bring anything with you except your curiosity, since we will discover everything we need along the way.

The book will help you develop these powerful skills through immersion in a crime case that requires the use of data mining skills to solve, where you will be asked to help resolve a real fraud case affecting a commercial company using both basic and advanced data mining techniques.

At the end of our trip into the R world, you will be able to identify data mining problems, analyze them, and correctly address them with the main data mining techniques (and some advanced ones), producing astonishing final reports to convey messages and narrate the stories you found within your data.

What this book covers

Chapter 1, *Why to Choose R for Your Data Mining and Where to Start*, gives you some relevant facts about R's history, its main strengths and weaknesses, and how to install the language on your computer and write basic code.

Chapter 2, *A First Primer on Data Mining -Analyzing Your Bank Account Data,* applies R to our data.

Chapter 3, *The Data Mining Process - the CRISP-DM Methodology,* teaches you to organize and conduct a data mining project through the CRISP-DM methodology.

Chapter 4, *Keeping the Home Clean – The Data Mining Architecture*, defines the static part of our data mining projects, the data mining architecture.

Chapter 5, *How to Address a Data Mining Problem – Data Cleaning and Validation*, covers data quality and data validation, where you will find out which metrics define the level of quality of our data and discover a set of checks that can be employed to assess this quality.

Chapter 6, *Looking into Your Data Eyes – Exploratory Data Analysis,* teaches you about the concept of exploratory data analysis and how it can be included within the data analysis process.

Chapter 7, *Our First Guess – A Linear Regression,* lets us estimate a simple linear regression model and check whether its assumptions have been satisfied.

Chapter 8, *A Gentle Introduction to Model Performance Evaluation,* covers the tools used to define and measure the performance of data mining models.

Chapter 9, *Don't Give Up – Power Up Your Regression Including Multiple Variables,* predicts the output of our response variable when more than one exploratory variable is involved.

Chapter 10, *A Different Outlook to Problems with Classification Models,* looks into classification models, the need of them and they are uses.

Chapter 11, *The Final Clash – Random Forest and Ensemble Learning,* in this chapter we will learn how to apply ensemble learning to estimated classification models.

Chapter 12, *Looking for the Culprit – Text Data Mining with R,* shows how to prepare the data frame for text mining activities, removing irrelevant words and transforming it from a list of sentences to a list of words. You also learn to perform sentiment analyses, wordcloud development, and n-gram analyses on it.

Chapter 13, *Sharing Your Stories with Your Stakeholders through R Markdown,* employs R markdown and shiny, two powerful instruments made available within the RStudio ecosystem.

Chapter 14, *Epilogue,* is the unique background story made to learn the topics in a very engaging manner.

Appendix, *Dealing with Dates, Relative Paths, and Functions,* includes additional information to get things running in R.

What you need for this book

You will easily be able to sail through the chapters by employing R and UNIX or Windows. The version used is R 3.4.0.

Who this book is for

If you are a budding data scientist or a data analyst with basic knowledge of R, and you want to get into the intricacies of data mining in a practical manner, this is the book for you. No previous experience of data mining is required.

Conventions

In this book, you will find a number of text styles that distinguish between different kinds of information. Here are some examples of these styles and an explanation of their meaning.

Code words in text, database table names, folder names, filenames, file extensions, path names, dummy URLs, user input, and Twitter handles are shown as follows: "Finally, ggplot2 gives you the ability to highly customize your plot, adding every kind of graphical or textual annotation to it."

A block of code is set as follows:

```
install.packages("ggplot2")
library(ggplot2)
```

New terms and **important words** are shown in bold.

Words that you see on the screen, for example, in menus or dialog boxes, appear in the text like this: "In order to download new modules, we will go to **Files** | **Settings** | **Project Name** | **Project Interpreter**."

Warnings or important notes appear like this.

Tips and tricks appear like this.

Reader feedback

Feedback from our readers is always welcome. Let us know what you think about this book-what you liked or disliked. Reader feedback is important for us as it helps us develop titles that you will really get the most out of. To send us general feedback, simply email feedback@packtpub.com, and mention the book's title in the subject of your message. If there is a topic that you have expertise in and you are interested in either writing or contributing to a book, see our author guide at www.packtpub.com/authors.

Customer support

Now that you are the proud owner of a Packt book, we have a number of things to help you to get the most from your purchase.

Downloading the example code

You can download the example code files for this book from your account at http://www.packtpub.com. If you purchased this book elsewhere, you can visit http://www.packtpub.com/support and register to have the files emailed directly to you. You can download the code files by following these steps:

1. Log in or register to our website using your email address and password.
2. Hover the mouse pointer on the **SUPPORT** tab at the top.
3. Click on **Code Downloads & Errata**.
4. Enter the name of the book in the **Search** box.
5. Select the book for which you're looking to download the code files.
6. Choose from the drop-down menu where you purchased this book from.
7. Click on **Code Download**.

Once the file is downloaded, please make sure that you unzip or extract the folder using the latest version of:

- WinRAR / 7-Zip for Windows
- Zipeg / iZip / UnRarX for Mac
- 7-Zip / PeaZip for Linux

The code bundle for the book is also hosted on GitHub at
`https://github.com/PacktPublishing/R-Data-Mining`. We also have other code bundles
from our rich catalog of books and videos available at
`https://github.com/PacktPublishing/`. Check them out!

Downloading the color images of this book

We also provide you with a PDF file that has color images of the screenshots/diagrams used
in this book. The color images will help you better understand the changes in the output.
You can download this file from `https://www.packtpub.com/sites/default/files/`
`downloads/RDataMining_ColorImages.pdf`.

Errata

Although we have taken every care to ensure the accuracy of our content, mistakes do
happen. If you find a mistake in one of our books-maybe a mistake in the text or the code-
we would be grateful if you could report this to us. By doing so, you can save other readers
from frustration and help us improve subsequent versions of this book. If you find any
errata, please report them by visiting `http://www.packtpub.com/submit-errata`, selecting
your book, clicking on the **Errata Submission Form** link, and entering the details of your
errata. Once your errata are verified, your submission will be accepted and the errata will
be uploaded to our website or added to any list of existing errata under the Errata section of
that title. To view the previously submitted errata, go to
`https://www.packtpub.com/books/content/support` and enter the name of the book in the
search field. The required information will appear under the **Errata** section.

Piracy

Piracy of copyrighted material on the internet is an ongoing problem across all media. At
Packt, we take the protection of our copyright and licenses very seriously. If you come
across any illegal copies of our works in any form on the internet, please provide us with
the location address or website name immediately so that we can pursue a remedy. Please
contact us at `copyright@packtpub.com` with a link to the suspected pirated material. We
appreciate your help in protecting our authors and our ability to bring you valuable
content.

Questions

If you have a problem with any aspect of this book, you can contact us at
`questions@packtpub.com`, and we will do our best to address the problem.

1
Why to Choose R for Your Data Mining and Where to Start

Since this is our first step on the journey to R knowledge, we have to be sure to acquire all the tools and notions we will use on our trip. You are probably already an R enthusiast and would like to discover more about it, but maybe you are not so sure why you should invest time in learning it. Perhaps you lack confidence in defining its points of strength and weakness, and therefore you are not sure it is the right language to bet on. Crucially, you do not actually know where and how to practically begin your journey to R mastery. The good news, is you will not have to wait long to solve all of these issues, since this first chapter is all about them.

In particular, within this chapter we will:

- Look at the history of R to understand where everything came from
- Analyze R's points of strength, understanding why it is a savvy idea to learn this programming language
- Learn how to install the R language on your computer and how to write and run R code
- Gain an understanding of the R language and the foundation notions needed to start writing R scripts
- Understand R's points of weakness and how to work around them

By the end of the chapter, we will have all the weapons needed to face our first real data mining problem.

What is R?

Let's start from the very beginning, *What exactly is R?* You will have read a lot about it on data analysis and data science blogs and websites, but perhaps you are still not able to fix the concept in your mind. R is a high-level programming language. This means that by passing the kind of R scripts you are going to learn in this book, you will be able to order your PC to execute some desired computations and operations, resulting in some predefined output.

Programming languages are a set of predefined instructions that the computer is able to understand and react to, and R is one of them. You may have noticed that I referred to R as a high-level programming language. What does high-level mean? One way to understand it is by comparing it to typical industrial company structures. Within such companies, there is usually a CEO, senior managers, heads of departments, and so on, level by level until we reach the final group of workers.

What is the difference between those levels of a company hierarchy? The CEO makes the main strategical decisions, developing a strategical plan without taking care of tactical and operational details. From there, the lower you go in the hierarchy described, the more tactical and operational decisions become, until you reach the base worker, whose main duty is to execute basic operations, such as screwing and hammering.

It is the same for programming languages:

- High-level programming languages are like the CEO; they abstract from operational details, stating high-level sentences which will then be translated by lower-level languages the computer is able to understand
- Low-level programming languages are like the heads of departments and workers; they take sentences from higher-level languages and translate them into chunks of instructions needed to make the computer actually produce the output the CEO is looking for

To be precise, we should specify that it is also possible to directly write code using low-level programming languages. Nevertheless, since they tend to be more complex and wordy, their popularity has declined over time.

Now that we have a clear idea of what R is, let's move on and acquire a bit of knowledge about where R came from and when.

A bit of history

When *Ross Ihaka* and *Robert Gentleman* published *R: A Language for Data Analysis and Graphics* in 1996, they probably didn't imagine the success the language would achieve between then and now. R was born at the University of Auckland in the early 1990s. In the beginning, it was supposed to be a user-friendly data analysis tool, employed by students to perform their research activities. Nevertheless, the points of strength we will look at in the following paragraphs quickly made it very popular among the wider community of researchers and data analysts, finally reaching the business realm in recent years and being used within major financial institutions.

R language development is currently led by the R core team, which releases updates of the base R language on a regular basis. You can discover more about the bureaucratic side of R by visiting the official R website at `https://www.r-project.org/about.html`.

R's points of strength

You know that R is really popular, but why? R is not the only data analysis language out there, and neither is it the oldest one; so why is it so popular?

If looking at the root causes of R's popularity, we definitely have to mention these three:

- Open source inside
- Plugin ready
- Data visualization friendly

Open source inside

One of the main reasons the adoption of R is spreading is its open source nature. R binary code is available for everyone to download, modify, and share back again (only in an open source way). Technically, R is released with a GNU general public license, meaning that you can take it and use it for whatever purpose; but you have to share every derivative with a GNU general public license as well.

These attributes fit well for almost every target user of a statistical analysis language:

- **Academic user**: Knowledge sharing is a must for an academic environment, and having the ability to share work without the worry of copyright and license questions makes R very practical for academic research purposes
- **Business user**: Companies are always worried about budget constraints; having professional statistical analysis software at their disposal for free sounds like a dream come true
- **Private user**: This user merges together both of the benefits already mentioned, because they will find it great to have a free instrument with which to learn and share their own statistical analyses

Plugin ready

You could imagine the R language as an expandable board game. You know, games like *7 Wonders* or *Carcassonne,* with a base set of characters and places and further optional places and characters, increasing the choices at your disposal and maximizing the fun. The R language can be compared to this kind of game.

There is a base version of R, containing a group of default packages that are delivered along with the standard version of the software (you can skip to the *Installing R and writing R code* section for more on how to obtain and install it). The functionalities available through the base version are mainly related to filesystem manipulation, statistical analysis, and data visualization.

While this base version is regularly maintained and updated by the R core team, virtually every R user can add further new functionalities to those available within the package, developing and sharing custom packages.

This is basically how the package development and sharing flow works:

1. The R user develops a new package, for example a package introducing a new machine learning algorithm exposed within a freshly published academic paper.
2. The user submits the package to the CRAN repository or a similar repository. The **Comprehensive R Archive Network (CRAN)** is the official repository for R-related documents and packages.

3. Every R user can gain access to the additional features introduced with any given package, installing and loading them into their R environment. If the package has been submitted to CRAN, installing and loading the package will result in running just the two following lines of R code (similar commands are available for alternative repositories such as **Bioconductor**):

```
install.packages("ggplot2")
library(ggplot2)
```

As you can see, this is a really convenient and effective way to expand R functionalities, and you will soon see how wide the range of functionalities added through additional packages developed by R users is.

More than 9,000 packages are available on CRAN, and this number is sure to increase further, making more and more additional features available to the R community.

Data visualization friendly

as a discipline data visualization encompasses all of the principles and techniques employable to effectively display the information and messages contained within a set of data.

Since we are living in an information-heavy age, the ability to effectively and concisely communicate articulated and complex messages through data visualization is a core asset for any professional. This is exactly why R is experiencing a great response in academic and professional fields: the data visualization capabilities of R place it at the cutting edge of these fields.

R has been noticed for its amazing data visualization features right from its beginning; when some of its peers still showed *x* axes-built aggregating + signs, R was already able to produce astonishing 3D plots. Nevertheless, a major improvement of R as a data visualization technique came when Auckland's Hadley Wickham developed the highly famous `ggplot2` package based on *The Grammar of Graphics*, introducing into the R world an organic framework for data visualization tasks:

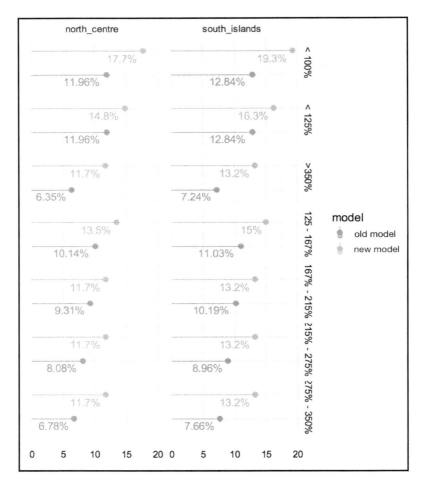

This package alone introduced the R community to a highly flexible way of producing and visualizing almost every kind of data visualization, having also been designed as an expandable tool, in order to add the possibility of incorporating new data visualization techniques as soon as they emerge. Finally, `ggplot2` gives you the ability to highly customize your plot, adding every kind of graphical or textual annotation to it.

Nowadays, R is being used by the biggest tech companies, such as Facebook and Google, and by widely circulated publications such as the Economist and the New York Times to visualize their data and convey their information to their stakeholders and readers.

To sum all this up—should you invest your precious time learning R? If you are a professional or a student who could gain advantages from knowing effective and cutting-edge techniques to manipulate, model, and present data, I can only give you a positive opinion: yes. You should definitely learn R, and consider it a long-term investment, since the points of strength we have seen place it in a great position to further expand its influence in the coming years in every industry and academic field.

Installing R and writing R code

Now that you know why it is worth learning R as a language for data analysis, let's have a look at how to get up and running with R coding. First of all, let's have a bit of clarity—installing R is different from installing an integrated platform on which to write and run R code. Here, you will learn both of these and the differences between them.

Downloading R

Installing R means installing the R language interpreter on your computer. This will teach your computer how to execute R commands and R scripts, marked with the `.R` file extension. The most up-to-date release of the R language is hosted on the official R project server, reachable at `https://cran.r-project.org`.

Once you have surfed the website, you will have to locate the proper download link, that is, the link to the R version appropriate for your platform. You will have these three choices:

- Download R for Linux (`https://cran.r-project.org/bin/linux/`)
- Download R for macOS (`https://cran.r-project.org/bin/macosx/`)
- Download R for Windows (`https://cran.r-project.org/bin/windows/`)

R installation for Windows and macOS

For macOS and Windows, you will follow a similar workflow:

1. Download the files bundle you will be pointed to from the platform-related page.
2. Within the bundle, locate the appropriate installer:
    - The one for Windows will be named something like `R-3.3.2-win.exe`
    - The one for macOS will be similar to `R-3.3.2.pkg`
3. Execute that installer and wait for the installation process to complete:

The Comprehensive R Archive Network

`Download and Install R`

Precompiled binary distributions of the base system and contributed packages, **Windows and Mac** users most likely want one of these versions of R:

- Download R for Linux
- Download R for (Mac) OS X
- Download R for Windows

R is part of many Linux distributions, you should check with your Linux package management system in addition to the link above.

`Source Code for all Platforms`

Windows and Mac users most likely want to download the precompiled binaries listed in the upper box, not the source code. The sources have to be compiled before you can use them. If you do not know what this means, you probably do not want to do it!

- The latest release (Monday 2016-10-31, Sincere Pumpkin Patch) R-3.3.2.tar.gz, read what's new in the latest version.
- Sources of R alpha and beta releases (daily snapshots, created only in time periods before a planned release).
- Daily snapshots of current patched and development versions are available here. Please read about new features and bug fixes before filing corresponding feature requests or bug reports.
- Source code of older versions of R is available here.
- Contributed extension packages

`Questions About R`

- If you have questions about R like how to download and install the software, or what the license terms are, please read our answers to frequently asked questions before you send an email.

CRAN
Mirrors
What's new?
Task Views
Search

About R
R Homepage
The R Journal

Software
R Sources
R Binaries
Packages
Other

Documentation
Manuals
FAQs
Contributed

Once you are done with this procedure, R will be installed on your platform and you will be ready to employ it. If you are a Linux user, things will look a little different.

R installation for Linux OS

The most convenient choice, if you are a Linux user, is to install the R base version directly from your command line. This is actually a straightforward procedure that only requires you to run the following commands on your Terminal:

```
sudo apt-get update
sudo apt-get install r-base
```

This will likely result in the Terminal asking you for your machine administrator password, which is strictly required to perform commands as a superuser (that is what `sudo` stands for).

Main components of a base R installation

You may be wondering what you get with the installation you just performed, and that is what we are going to look at here. First of all, the base R version comes with a proper interpreter of the most updated version of the R software. This means, if you recall what we learned in the *What is R?* section, that after performing your installation, the computer will be able to read R code, parse it, and execute instructions composed of parsed code. To get a feel for this, try the following code on your OS command line, choosing the appropriate one:

- On Windows OS (on PowerShell):

```
echo "print('hello world')" >> new_script.R
Rscript.exe new_script.R
```

- On macOS or Linux OS:

```
R
print('hello world')
```

Both of these should result in the evergreen `'hello world'` output.

Apart from the interpreter, the R language base version also comes packed with a very basic platform for the development and execution of R code, which is mainly composed of:

- An R console to execute R code and observe the results of the execution
- An R script text editor to write down the R code and subsequently save it as standalone scripts (the ones with the `.R` file extension)

- Additional utilities, such as functions to import data, install additional packages, and navigate your console history:

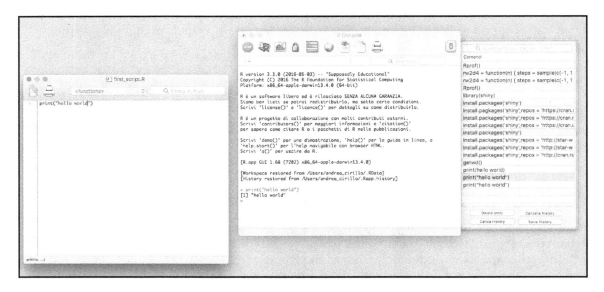

This was the way R code was produced and consumed by the vast majority of the R community for a long time. Nowadays, even though it runs perfectly and is regularly updated, this platform tends to appear one step behind the available alternatives we are going to explore in the next section.

Possible alternatives to write and run R code

We have already discussed two ways of executing R code:

- Employing your OS terminal
- Employing the development environment that comes with the R base installation

The first of the aforementioned ways can be quite a convenient way for experienced R users. It clearly shows its advantages when executing articulated analytical activities, such as ones requiring:

- The sequential execution of scripts from different languages
- The execution of filesystem manipulation

Regarding the second alternative, we have already talked about its shortfalls compared to its direct competitor. Therefore, now is the time to have a closer look at this competitor, and this is what we are going to do in the following paragraphs before actually starting to write some more R code.

Two disclaimers are needed:

- We are not considering text editor applications here, that is, software without an R console included and additional code execution utilities included. Rather, we prefer an integrated development environment, since they are able to provide a more user-friendly and comprehensive experience for a new language adopter.
- We are not looking for completeness here, just for the tools most often cited within R community discussions and events. Perhaps something better than these platforms is available, but it has not yet gained comparable momentum.

The alternative platforms we are going to introduce here are:

- RStudio
- Jupyter Notebook
- Visual Studio

RStudio (all OSs)

RStudio is a really well-known IDE within the R community. It is freely available at `https://www.rstudio.com`. The main reason for its popularity is probably the R-dedicated nature of the platform, which differentiates it from the other two alternatives that we will discuss further, and its perfect integration with some of the most beloved packages of the R community.

RStudio comes packed with all the base features we talked about when discovering the R base installation development environment, enriched with a ton of useful additional components introduced to facilitate coding activity and maximize the effectiveness of the development process. Among those, we should point out:

- A filesystem browser to explore and interact with the content of the directory you are working with
- A file import wizard to facilitate the import of datasets
- A plot pane to visualize and interact with the data visualization produced by code execution

- An environment explorer to visualize and interact with values and the data produced by code execution
- A spreadsheet-like data viewer to visualize the datasets produced by code execution

All of this is enhanced by features such as code autocompletion, inline help for functions, and splittable windows for multi-monitor users, as seen in the following screenshot:

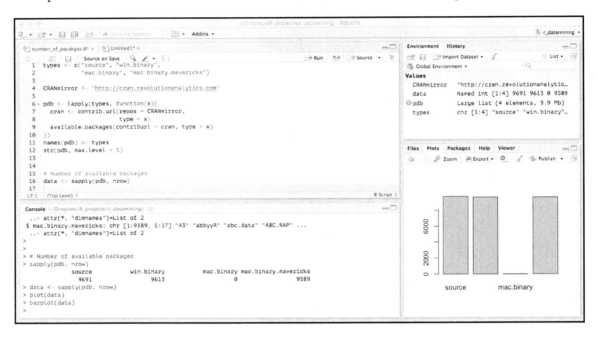

A final word has to be said about integration with the most beloved R additional packages. RStudio comes with additional controls or predefined shortcuts to fully integrate, for instance:

- `markdown` package for markdown integration with R code (more on this in `Chapter 13`, *Sharing your stories with your stakeholders through R markdown*)
- `dplyr` for data manipulation (more on this in `Chapter 2`, *A First Primer on Data Mining - Analysing Your Banking Account Data*)
- `shiny` package for web application development with R (more on this in `Chapter 13`, *Sharing your stories with your stakeholders through R markdown*)

The Jupyter Notebook (all OSs)

The Jupyter Notebook was primarily born as a Python extension to enable interactive data analysis and a fully reproducible workflow. The idea behind the Jupyter Notebook is to have both the code and the output of the code (plots and tables) within the same document. This allows both the developer and other subsequent readers, for instance a customer, to follow the logical flow of the analysis and gradually arrive at the results.

Compared to RStudio, Jupyter does not have a filesystem browser, nor an environment browser. Nevertheless, it is a very good alternative, especially when working on analyses which need to be shared.

Since it comes originally as a Python extension, it is actually developed with the Python language. This means that you will need to install Python as well as R to execute this application. Instructions on how to install Jupyter can be found in the Jupyter documentation at `http://jupyter.readthedocs.io/en/latest/install.html`.

After installing Jupyter, you will need to add a specific component, namely a kernel, to execute R code on the notebook. Instructions on how to install the kernel can be found on the component's home page at `https://irkernel.github.io`.

Visual Studio (Windows users only)

Visual Studio is a popular development tool, primarily for Visual Basic and C++ language development. Due to the recent interest showed by Microsoft in the R language, this IDE has been expanded through the introduction of the R Tools extension.

This extension adds all of the commonly expected features of an R IDE to the well-established platform such as Visual Studio. The main limitation at the moment is the availability of the product, as it is only available on a computer running on the Windows OS.

Also, Visual Studio is available for free, at least the Visual Studio Community Edition. Further details and installation guides are available at `https://www.visualstudio.com/vs/rtvs`.

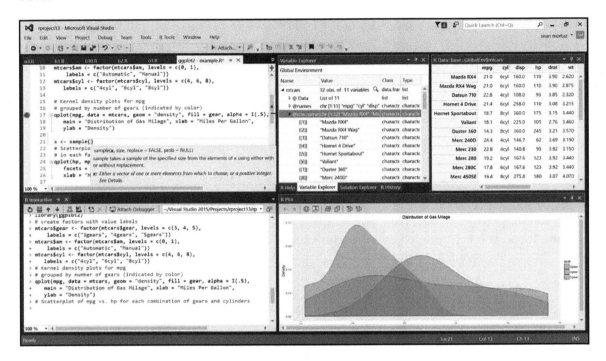

R foundational notions

Now that you have installed R and your chosen R development environment, it is time to try them out, acquiring some foundations of the R language. Here, we are going to cover the main building blocks we will use along our journey to build and apply the data mining algorithms this book is all about. More specifically, after warming up a bit by performing basic operations on the interactive console and saving our first R script, we are going to learn how to create and handle:

- Vectors, which are ordered sequences of values, or even just one value
- Lists, which are defined as a collection of vectors and of every other type of object available in R
- Dataframes, which can be seen as lists composed by vectors, all with the same number of values

- Functions, which are a set of instructions performed by the language that can be applied to vectors, lists, and data frames to manipulate them and gain new information from them:

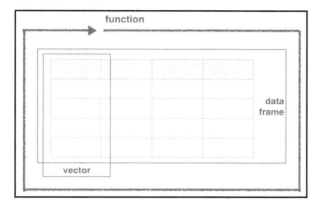

Finally, we will look at how to define custom functions and how to install additional packages to extend R language functionalities. If you feel overwhelmed by this list of unknown entities, I would like to assure you that we are going to get really familiar with all of them within a few pages.

A preliminary R session

Before getting to know the alphabet of our powerful language, we need to understand the basics of how to employ it. We are going to:

- Perform some basic operations on the R console
- Save our first R script
- Execute our script from the console

Executing R interactively through the R console

Once you have opened your favourite IDE (we are going to use RStudio), you should find an interactive console, which you should be able to recognize by the intermittent cursor you should find on it. Once you have located it, just try to perform a basic operation by typing the following words and pressing *Enter*, submitting the command to the console:

```
2+2
```

A new line will automatically appear, showing you the following unsurprising result:

```
4
```

Yes, just to reassure you, we are going to discuss more sophisticated mathematical computations; this was just an introductory example.

What I would like to stress with this is that within the console, you can interactively test small chunks of code. What is the disadvantage here? When you terminate your R session (shutting down your IDE), everything that you performed within the console will be lost. There are actually IDEs, such as RStudio, that store your console history, but that is intended as an audit trail rather than as a proper way to store your code:

```
Console  ~/

> demo()
> demo(scoping)

        demo(scoping)
        ----  ~~~~~~~

Type  <Return>   to start :

> ## Here is a little example which shows a fundamental difference between
> ## R and S.  It is a little example from Abelson and Sussman which models
> ## the way in which bank accounts work.      It shows how R functions can
> ## encapsulate state information.
> ##
> ## When invoked, "open.account" defines and returns three functions
```

In the next paragraph, we are going to see the proper way to store your console history. In the meantime, for the sake of completeness, let me clarify for you that the R language can perform all the basic mathematical operations, employing the following operators: +, −, *, /, ^, the last of which is employed when raising to a power.

Creating an R script

An R script is a statistical document storing a large or small chunk of R code. The advantage of the script is that it can store and show a structured set of instructions to be executed every time or recalled from outside the script itself (see the next paragraph for more on this). Within your IDE, you will find a New script control that, if selected, will result in a new file with the .R extension coming up, ready to be filled with R language. If there is no similar control within the IDE you chose, first of all, you should seriously think about looking for another IDE, and then you can deal with the emergency by running the following command within the R console:

```
file.create("my_first_script.R")
```

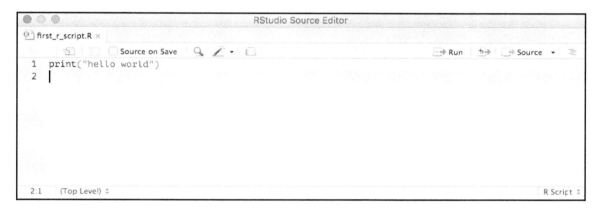

Let's start writing some code within our script. Since there is a long tradition to be respected, we are going to test our script with the well-known, useless statement, "hello world". To obtain those two amazing words as an output, you just have to tell R to print them out. How is that done? Here we are:

```
print("hello world")
```

Once again, for the reader afraid of having wasted his money with this book, we are going to deal with more difficult topics; we are just warming up here.

Before moving on, let's add one more line, not in the form of a command, but as a comment:

```
# my dear interpreter, please do not execute this line, it is just a
comment
```

Comments are actually a really relevant piece of software development. As you might guess, such lines are not executed by the interpreter, which is programmed to skip all lines starting with the # token. Nevertheless, comments are a precious friend of the programmer, and an even more precious friend of the same programmer one month after having written the script, and of any other reader of the given code. These pieces of text are employed to mark the rationales, assumptions, and objectives of the code, in order to make clear what the scope of the script is, why certain manipulations were performed, and what kind of assumptions are to be satisfied to ensure the script is working properly.

One final note on comments—you can put them inline with some other code, as in the following example:

```
print("hello world") # dear interpreter, please do not execute this comment
```

It is now time to save your file, which just requires you to find the **Save** control within your IDE. When a name is required, just name it `my_first_script.R`, since we are going to use it in a few moments.

Executing an R script

The further you get with your coding expertise, the more probable it is that you will find yourself storing different parts of your analyses in separate scripts, calling them in a sequence from the terminal or directly from a main script. It is therefore crucial to learn how to correctly perform this kind of operation from the very beginning of our learning path. Moreover, executing a script from the beginning to the end is a really good method for detecting errors, that is, bugs, within your code. Finally, storing your analyses within scripts will help make them reproducible for other interested peoples, which is a really desirable property able to strengthen the validity of your results.

Let's try to execute the script we previously created. To execute a script from within R, we use the `source()` function. As we will see in more depth later, a function is a set of instructions which usually takes one or more inputs and produces an output. The input is called an argument, while the output is called a value. In this case, we are going to specify one unique argument, the `file` argument. As you may be wondering, the argument will have the name of the R script we saved before. With all that mentioned, here is the command to submit:

```
source("my_first_script.R")
```

What happens when this command is run? You can imagine the interpreter reading the line of code and thinking the following: *OK, let's have a look at what is inside this* `my_first_script` *file. Nice, here's another R command:* `print("hello world")`. *Let's run it and see what happens!* Apart from the fictional tone, this is exactly what happens. The interpreter looks for the file you pointed to, reads the contents of the file, and executes the R commands stored in it. Our example will result in the console producing the following output:

```
hello world
```

It is now time to actually learn the R alphabet, starting with vectors.

Vectors

What are vectors and where do we use them? The term vector is directly derived from the algebra field, but we shouldn't take the analogy too much further than that since within the R world, we can simply consider a vector to be an ordered sequence of values of the same data type. A sequence is ordered such that the two sequences represented below are treated as two different entities by R:

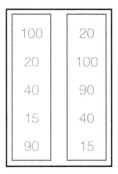

How do you create a vector in R? A vector is created through the `c()` function, as in the following statement:

```
c(100,20,40,15,90)
```

Even if this is a regular vector, it will disappear as long as it is printed out by the console. If you want to store it in your R environment, you should assign it a name, that is, you should create a variable. This is easily done by the assignment operator:

```
vector <- c(100,20,40,15,90)
```

As soon as you run this command, your environment will be enriched by a new object of type `vector`. This is fine, but what is the practical usage of vectors? Almost every input and output produced by R can be reduced to a vector, meaning it represents the foundation for every development of this language. Within this book, for instance, we are going to store the results of statistical tests performed on our data in vectors, and create a vector representing a probability distribution we want our model to respect.

A final relevant note on vectors—so far, we have seen only a numerical vector, but you should be aware that it is possible to define all of the following types of vectors:

Type	Example
numeric	1
logical / Boolean	TRUE
character	"text here"

Moreover, it is possible to define mixed content vectors:

```
mixed_vector <- c( 1, TRUE, "text here")
```

To be exact, by the end these kinds of vectors will be forced to a vector of the type that can contain all the others, like character in our example, but I do not want to confuse you with too many details.

So, now we know how to create a vector and what to store within it, but how do we recall it and show its content? As a general rule, recalling an object will simply require you to write down its name. So, to show the `mixed_vector` we just created, it will be sufficient to write down its name within the R console and submit this minimal command. The result will be the following:

```
[1] "1"        "TRUE"       "text here"
```

Lists

Now that you know what vectors are, you can easily understand what lists are: containers of objects. This is actually an oversimplification of lists, since they can also contain other lists, or even data frames inside them. Nevertheless, the relevant concept here is that lists are a convenient way to store objects within the R environment. For instance, they are used by a lot of statistical functions to store the results of their applications.

Let's show this to you practically:

```
regression_results <- lm(formula = Sepal.Length ~ Species, data = iris)
```

Without getting into regression details too much (which will be done in a few chapters), it will be sufficient here to explain that we are fitting a regression model on the Iris dataset, trying to explain the length of sepals of particular species of the iris flower. The Iris dataset is a really famous preloaded data frame included with every R base version.

Let's now have a look at this regression_results object that, as we were saying, stores the results of the regression model fitting. To find the kind of any given object, we can run the mode() function on it, passing the name of the object as a value for the argument x:

```
mode(x = regression_results)
```

This will result in:

```
list
```

Creating lists

Let's move one step back; how do we generally create lists? Here, we always use the assignment operator <-, the one we met when dealing with vectors. What is going to be different here is the function applied. It will no longer be c(), but a reasonably named list(). For instance, let's try to create two vectors and then merge them into a list:

```
first_vector  <- c("a","b","c")
 second_vector <- c(1,2,3)
 vector_list   <- list(first_vector, second_vector)
```

Subsetting lists

What if we would now like to isolate a specific object within a list? We have to employ the `[[]]` operator, specifying which level we would like to expose. For instance, if we would like to extrapolate only the first vector from `vector_list`, this would be the code:

```
vector_list[[2]]
```

Which will result in:

```
[1] 1 2 3
```

You may be wondering, is it possible to expose a single element within a single object composing a list? The answer is yes, so let's assume that we now want to isolate the third element of the `second_vector` object, which is the second object composing the `vector_list` list. We will have to employ the `[[]]` operator once again:

```
vector_list[[2]][[3]]
```

Which will have the expected output:

```
[1] 3
```

Data frames

Data frames can be seen simply as lists respecting the following requisites:

- All components are vectors, no matter whether logical, numerical, or character (even mixed vectors are allowed)
- All vectors must be of the same length

From the mentioned rules, we can derive that data frames can be imagined, and commonly are, as tables having a certain number of columns, represented by the vectors composing them and a certain number of rows, which will coincide with the length of the vectors. While the two rules are always to be respected, no limitation is placed on the possibility of having columns of different types, such as numerical and boolean:

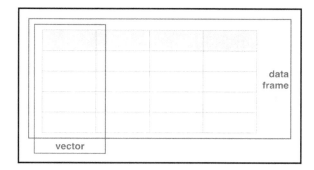

As you can imagine, data frames are a really convenient way to store data, especially sets of structured data, such as experimental observations or financial transactions. As we will come to better understand in the following chapters, a data frame lets us store an observation within each row and an attribute of any given observation within each column.

Even though data frames are a logical subgroup of lists, they have a full pack of tailored functions for their creation and handling.

Creating a data frame closely resembles the creation of a list, except for the different name of the function, which is once again named in a convenient way as data.frame():

```
a_data_frame <- data.frame(first_attribute = c("alpha","beta","gamma"),
second_attribute = c(14,20,11))
```

Please note that every vector, that is, every column, is named by the text token preceding the = operator. There are two relevant observations on this:

- Avoiding specifying the name of the vector will result in an ugly and rather unfriendly automatically assigned name, that in this case would have been c..alpha....beta....gamma.. for the first column and c.14..20..11.. for the second column. This is why it is strongly recommended to add column names.
- It is also possible to give column names composed of spaced values, such as first attribute rather than first_attribute. To do so, we need to surround our column name with double quotes:

  ```
  a_data_frame <- data.frame("first attribute" ...)
  ```

To be honest, I would definitely discourage you from going for the second alternative because of the annoying consequences it would create when trying to recall it in the subsequent pieces of code.

How do we select and show a column of a data frame? We employ the $ operator here:

```
a_data_frame$second_attribute
[1] 14 20 11
```

We can add new columns to the data frame in a similar way:

```
a_data_frame$third_attribute <- c(TRUE, FALSE, FALSE)
```

Functions

If we would like to put it simply, we could just say that functions are ways of manipulating vectors, lists, and data frames. This is perhaps not the most rigorous definition of a function; nevertheless, it catches a focal point of this entity—a function takes some inputs, which are vectors (even of one element), lists, or data frames, and results in one output, which is usually a vector, a list, or a data frame.

The exception here are functions that perform filesystem manipulation or some other specific tasks, which in some other languages are called procedures. For instance, the file.create() function we encountered before.

One of the most appreciated features of R is the possibility to easily explore the definition of all the functions available. This is easily done by submitting a command with the sole name of the function, without any parentheses. Let's try this with the mode() function and see what happens:

```
mode

function (x)
 {
  if (is.expression(x))
   return("expression")
  if (is.call(x))
   return(switch(deparse(x[[1L]])[1L], `(` = "(", "call"))
  if (is.name(x))
   "name"
 else switch(tx <- typeof(x), double = , integer = "numeric",
   closure = , builtin = , special = "function", tx)
 }
<bytecode: 0x102264c98>
<environment: namespace:base>
```

We are not going to get into detail with this function, but let's just notice some structural elements:

- We have a call to `function()`, which, by the way, is a function itself.
- We have the specification of the only argument of the mode function, which is *x*.
- We have braces surrounding everything coming after the `function()` call. This is the body of the function and contains all the calculations/computations performed by the function on its inputs.

Those are the actual, minimal elements for the definition of a function within the R language. We can resume this as follows:

```
function_name <- function(arguments){
    [function body]
}
```

Now that we know the theory, let's try to define a simple and useless function that adds 2 to every number submitted:

```
adding_two <- function(the_number){
the_number + 2}
```

Does it work? Of course it does. To test it, we have to first execute the two lines of code stating the function definition, and then we will be able to employ our custom function:

```
adding_two( the_number = 4)
[1] 6
```

Now, let's introduce a bit more complicated but relevant concept: value assignment within a function. Let's imagine that you are writing a function and having the result stored within a `function_result` vector. You would probably write something like this:

```
my_func <- function(x){
function_result <- x / 2 }
```

You may even think that, once running your function, for instance, with x equal to 4, you should find an object `function_result` equal to 2 (4/2) within your environment.

So, let's try to print it out in the way that we learned some paragraphs earlier:

```
function_result
```

This is what happens:

```
Error: object function_result not found
```

How is this possible? This is actually because of the rules overseeing the assignment of values within a function. We can summarize those rules as follows:

- A function can look up a variable, even if defined outside the function itself
- Variables defined within the function remain within the function

How is it therefore possible to export the `function_result` object outside the function? You have two possible ways:

- Employing the `<<-` operator, the so-called superassignment operator
- Employing the `assign()` function

Here is the function rewritten to employ the superassignment operator:

```
my_func <- function(x){
    function_result <<- x / 2 }
```

If you try to run it, you will now find that the `function_result` object will show up within your environment browser. One last step: exporting an object created within a function outside of the function is different than placing that object as a result of the function. Let's show this practically:

```
my_func <- function(x){
   function_result <- x / 2
   function_result}
```

If you now try to run `my_func(4)` once again, your console will print out the result:

```
[1] 2
```

But, within your environment, once again you will not find the `function_result` object. How is this? This is because within the function definition, you specified as a final result, or as a resulting value, the value of the `function_result` object. Nevertheless, as in the first formulation, this object was defined employing a standard assignment operator.

R's weaknesses and how to overcome them

When talking about R to an experienced tech guy, he will probably come out with two main objections to the language:

- Its steep learning curve
- Its difficulty in handling large datasets

You will soon discover that those are actually the two main weaknesses of the language. Nevertheless, not even pretending that R is a perfect language, we are going to tackle those weaknesses here, showing effective ways to overcome them. We can actually consider the first of the mentioned objections temporary, at least on an individual basis, since once the user gets through the valley of despair, he will never come back to it and the weakness will be forgotten. You do not know about the valley of despair? Let me show you a plot, and then we can discuss it:

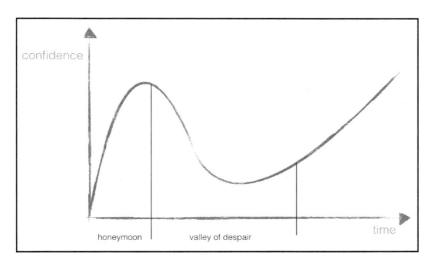

It is common wisdom that every man who starts to learn something new and complex enough will go through three different phases:

- The honeymoon, where he falls in love with the new stuff and feels confident to be able to easily master it
- The valley of despair, where everything starts looking impossible and disappointing
- During the rest of the story, where he starts having a more realistic view of the new topic, his mastery of it starts increasing, and so does his level of confidence

Moving on to the second weakness, we have to say that R's difficulty in handling large datasets is a rather more structural aspect of the language, and therefore requires some structural changes to the language, and strategical cooperation between it and other tools. In two new paragraphs, we will go through both of the aforementioned weaknesses.

Learning R effectively and minimizing the effort

First of all, why is R perceived as a language that is difficult to learn? We don't have a universally accepted answer to this question. Nevertheless, we can try some reasoning on it. R is the main choice when talking about statistical data analysis and was indeed born as a language by statisticians for statisticians, and specifically for statistics students. This produced two specific features of the language:

- No great care for the coding experience
- A previously unseen range of statistical techniques applicable with the language, with an unprecedented level of interaction

Here, we can find reasons for the perceived steep learning curve: R wasn't conceived as a coder-friendly language, as, for instance, Julia and Swift were. Rather, it was an instrument born within the academic field for academic purposes, as we mentioned before. R's creators probably never expected their language to be employed for website development, as is the case today (you can refer to Chapter 13, *Sharing your stories with your stakeholders through R markdown;* take a look at the Shiny apps on this).

The second point is the feeling of disorientation that affects people, including statisticians, coming to R from other statistical analysis languages. Applying a statistical model to your data through R is an amazingly interactive process, where you get your data into a model, get results, and perform diagnostics on it. Then, you iterate once again or perform cross-validation techniques, all with a really high level of flexibility. This is not exactly what an SAS or SPSS user is used to. Within these two languages, you just take your data, send it to a function, and wait for a comprehensive and infinite set of results.

Is this the end of the story? Do we need to passively accept this history-rooted steep learning curve? Of course we don't, and the R community is actually actively involved in the task of leveling this curve, following two main paths:

- Improving the R coding experience
- Developing high-quality learning materials

The tidyverse

Due to it being widespread throughout the R community, it is almost impossible nowadays to talk about R without mentioning the so-called **tidyverse**. This original name stands for a framework of concepts and functions developed mainly by Hadley Wickham to bring R closer to a modern programming experience. Introducing you to the magical world of the tidyverse is out of the scope of this book, but I would like to briefly explain how the framework is composed. Within the tidyverse, at least the four following packages are usually included:

- `readr`: For data import
- `dplyr`: For data manipulation
- `tidyr`: For data cleaning
- `ggplot2`: For data visualization

Due to its great success, an ever-increasing amount of learning material has been created on this topic, and this leads us to the next paragraph.

Leveraging the R community to learn R

One of the most exciting aspects of the R world is the vital community surrounding it. In the beginning, the community was mainly composed of statisticians and academics who encountered this powerful tool through the course of their studies. Nowadays, while statisticians and academics are still in the game, the R community is also full of a great variety of professionals from different fields: from finance, to chemistry and genetics. It is commonly acknowledged that its community is one of the R language's peculiarities. This community is also a great asset for every newbie of the language, since it is composed of people who are generally friendly, rather than posh, and open to helping you with your first steps in the language. I guess this is, generally speaking, good news, but you may be wondering: How do I actually leverage this amazing community you are introducing me to? First of all, let us find them, looking at places - both virtual and physical - where you can experience the community. We will then look at practical ways to leverage community-driven content to learn R.

Where to find the R community

There are different places, both physical and virtual, where it is possible to communicate with the R community. The following is a tentative list to get you up and running:

Virtual places:

- R-bloggers
- Twitter hashtag `#rstats`
- Google+ community
- Stack Overflow R tagged questions
- R-help mailing list

Physical places:

- The annual R conference
- The RStudio developer conference
- The R meetup

Engaging with the community to learn R

Now that we know where to find the community, let's take a closer look at how to take advantage of it. We can distinguish three alternative and non-exclusive ways:

- Employing community-driven learning material
- Asking for help from the community
- Staying ahead of language developments

Employing community-driven learning material: There are two main kinds of R learning materials developed by the community:

- Papers, manuals, and books
- Online interactive courses

Papers, manuals, and books: The first one is for sure the more traditional one, but you shouldn't neglect it, since those kinds of learning materials are always able to give you a more organic and systematic understanding of the topics they treat. You can find a lot of free material online in the form of papers, manuals, and books.

Let me point out to you the more useful ones:

- *Advanced R*
- *R for Data Science*
- *Introduction to Statistical Learning*
- *OpenIntro Statistics*
- *The R Journal*

Online interactive courses: This is probably the most common learning material nowadays. You can find different platforms delivering good content on the R language, the most famous of which are probably **DataCamp**, **Udemy**, and **Packt** itself. What all of them share is a practical and interactive approach that lets you learn the topic directly, applying it through exercises rather than passively looking at someone explaining theoretical stuff.

Asking for help from the community: As soon as you start writing your first lines of R code, and perhaps before you even actually start writing it, you will come up with some questions related to your work. The best thing you can do when this happens is to resort to the community to solve those questions. You will probably not be the first one to come up with that question, and you should therefore first of all look online for previous answers to your question.

Where should you look for answers? You can look everywhere, but most of the time you will find the answer you are looking for on one of the following (listed by the probability of finding the answer there):

- Stack Overflow
- R-help mailing list
- R packages documentation

I wouldn't suggest you look for answers on Twitter, G+, and similar networks, since they were not conceived to handle these kinds of processes and you will expose yourself to the peril of reading answers that are out of date, or simply incorrect, because no review system is considered.

If it is the case that you are asking an innovative question never previously asked by anyone, first of all, congratulations! That said, in that happy circumstance, you can ask your question in the same places that you previously looked for answers.

Staying ahead of language developments: The R language landscape is constantly changing, thanks to the contributions of many enthusiastic users who take it a step further every day. How can you stay ahead of those changes? This is where social networks come in handy. Following the `#rstats` hashtag on Twitter, Google+ groups, and similar places, will give you the pulse of the language. Moreover, you will find the R-bloggers aggregator, which delivers a daily newsletter comprised of the R-related blog posts that were published the previous day really useful. Finally, annual R conferences and similar occasions constitute a great opportunity to get in touch with the most notorious R experts, gaining from them useful insights and inspiring speeches about the future of the language.

Handling large datasets with R

The second weakness of those mentioned earlier was related to the handling of large datasets. Where does this weakness come from? It is something actually related to the core of the language—R is an in-memory software. This means that every object created and managed within an R script is stored within your computer RAM. This means that the total size of your data cannot be greater than the total size of your RAM (assuming that no other software is consuming your RAM, which is unrealistic). Answers to this problem are actually out of the scope of this book. Nevertheless, we can briefly summarize them into three main strategies:

- Optimizing your code, profiling it with packages such as profvis, and applying programming best practices.
- Relying on external data storage and wrangling tools, such as Spark, MongoDB, and Hadoop. We will reason a bit more on this in later chapters.
- Changing R memory handling behavior, employing packages such as `ff`, `filehash`, `R.huge`, or `bigmemory`, that try to avoid RAM overloading.

The main point I would like to stress here is that even this weakness is actually superable. You should bear this in mind when you encounter it for the first time on your R mastery journey.

One final note: as long as the computational power price is getting lower, the issue related to large dataset handling will become a more negligible one.

Further references

- **Historical R papers**: https://www.stat.auckland.ac.nz/~ihaka/downloads/R-paper.pdf
- **Interview with Ross Ihaka, R creator**: http://www.ingenio-magazine.com/r-the-ultimate-virus/
- **GNU general public license**: https://www.gnu.org/licenses/gpl.html
- **An introduction to R**: https://cran.r-project.org/doc/manuals/r-release/R-intro.pdf
- **Writing R extensions**: https://cran.r-project.org/doc/manuals/r-release/R-exts.html
- **On the tidyverse**: http://r4ds.had.co.nz

Summary

In this chapter, we started our journey in the best possible way.

We discovered what our powerful weapon is, where it comes from, and what its powers are, learning the main points of strength of the R language. We started to learn how to handle it, understanding the installation process and basic building blocks such as vectors, lists, data frames, and functions. Finally, we acknowledged the main weaknesses of R and how to reduce their impact.

In the next chapter, we will have a kind of training session, applying R to real data from our own personal data, specifically, from our banking data. Take time to recollect what you have discovered in the previous pages; you will need all of it when you take on the next chapter.

2
A First Primer on Data Mining Analysing Your Bank Account Data

It should be now clear to you why R is worth investing your time in: it is a powerful language, plugin-ready, data visualization-friendly, and all the other adjectives you can derive from the previous chapter. Wouldn't it be great to taste a bit of all of those powerhouses?

That is what this chapter is all about—letting you experiment with discovering insights from your data with R.

We are going to do this with your own data, in particular, your banking data. We are going to discover and model your expenditure habits, employing the power of R. After reading this chapter, apart from being even more enthusiastic about reading the remaining chapters, you will be able to do the following:

- Summarize your data with functions provided by `dplyr`
- Answer questions regarding your finance habits
- Produce basic and advanced visualizations of your data with the `ggplot2` package

But before actually getting our hands dirty, we need to talk a bit more about the data we are going to handle, and this is what we are going to tackle next.

Acquiring and preparing your banking data

The first step in getting this accomplished is to download our banking data from our bank's website. Obviously, I am not going to describe how to do this for every bank's website, and you should look on your own bank's website, probably within the *account movements* section.

If you don't have a bank account, or your bank doesn't let you download your data, you shouldn't despair, just look at the additional material provided together with the book, and you will find a folder named `data` containing, among other things, an XLS file named `banking`. You can safely use this for your experiments.

Data model

Let's have a closer look at how our data will have to be structured to accomplish the task, that is, let's describe our data model.

This concept is actually employed when dealing with a more structured set of data, such as groups of tables, but can nevertheless be applied to our purposes as well.

Describing a data model means to describe how you are going to organize the data you are going to store or acquire for your data mining activity. In our case, this means how we are going to organize our banking data table.

Despite the original table you will get from your bank's website, you should create a table showing the following columns:

- **Date***:* Showing the date of the given record. It should be formatted in the following way: yyyy-mm-dd, for instance, 2016-06-01. If your date column is formatted differently, please have a look at `Appendix`, *Dealing with Dates, Relative Paths and Functions.*
- **Income**: Storing all positive inflows.
- **Expenditure***:* Storing all negative outflows.

Here is what your data should look like:

Date	Income	Expenditure
2010-06-01	2523	0
2010-06-02	0	-2919
2010-06-03	0	-6341
2010-06-04	5303	0
2010-06-05	4553	0

Be sure to have all your columns named exactly as shown, since the code we are going to execute will rely on this. Now that we have got our data, let's get out some information from it.

Summarizing your data with pivot-like tables

When moving to R, one of the common questions that arises is this, how do I produce a pivot table with R? Purists of the language will probably be horrified at this question, but we do not have to be too fussy: pivot tables are an effective and convenient way to summarize and show data, and are therefore relevant to be able to perform the same summarization in our beloved language.

As you might be guessing, yes, it is actually possible to perform the same kind of summarization, even if it is not called a pivot table. But before getting into detail, let's discuss the concept. What is a pivot table?

We define with this concept a summary of a given detailed dataset, showing descriptive statistics of attributes stored within the dataset, aggregated by keys composed from other attributes of the same dataset.

To be clear, let's imagine having to deal with the following dataset:

cluster_id	segment	amount	accounts
1	retail	€ 477,609	43
2	retail	€ 583,517	82
3	retail	€ 795,772	40
4	bank	€ 912,425	95
5	bank	€ 505,508	77
6	public_entity	€ 765,497	52
7	retail	€ 697,726	84
8	retail	€ 667,229	57
9	retail	€ 282,133	76
10	public_entity	€ 848,601	70

It could be useful to know the total amount and the total number of accounts belonging to any given segment, that is, summarizing the `segment`, the `amount`, and the `account` attributes. In other words, we would like a table like this one:

segment	amount	accounts
retail	€ 3.503.986	382
bank	€ 1.417.933	172
public_entity	€ 1.614.098	122
total	€ 6.536.017	676

We now have a clear idea of what we are looking for. Let's discover how we can get there. The main characters within this section will be the `dplyr` package and the pipe operator. Neither of them are an original feature of R, but were added recently. They both had a major impact within the R community, further boosting the spreading trend of R.

Here is a description of these features:

- The pipe operator, which in R is represented by the `%>%` token, is a logical concept meaning that the result of one previous operation is provided as input to a subsequent operation
- `dplyr` is a set of functions for data wrangling operations such as grouping and summarization

Let's have a closer look at them.

A gentle introduction to the pipe operator

The pipe operator, and the related pipeline concept, were originally developed within the Unix environment as a way to chain together different software, taking the output of one as the input of another. This was quite natural within the Unix philosophy, since one of its principles is this: *Write programs to work together.*

Let's look at some examples to clarify the concept. A possible pipeline could be represented by opening a text file, reading its content, and appending it to another text file. We can easily do this in a Unix environment without leaving the terminal, by typing the following characters:

```
cat written.txt >> blank.txt
```

How does this translate into a programming language?

As we have seen so far, all R entities can be grouped into two main categories:

- Objects
- Functions

The way in which we are going to make those categories interact is to take objects, modify them with functions, create other objects, and maybe merge them, employing other functions. The standard way to do this in R is as follows:

```
manipulated_object <- function(original_object)
more_manipulated_object <- another_function(manipulated_object)
even_more_manipulated_object <- one_more_function(more_manipulated_object)
```

There are two side effects:

1. We are probably only interested in the last object, but nevertheless we are forced to create intermediate objects and take them within our environment or probably throw them out later.
2. Every assignment reserves some space for a new object, and this could cause us to run out of space, especially if we're dealing with a large dataset.

If we look closer at the pseudo-code, we can easily see that the output of the first manipulation becomes the input of the second, and the output of the second becomes the input of the third. It is easily seen that those manipulations are therefore chained into one unique flow. Wouldn't it be great to have some way to efficiently chain them, avoiding wasting the time and space produced by all those useless assignments?

That is where the `%>%` operator comes in. This operator tells the interpreter to take what is on its left and use it as an input of what is on its right. Applying this powerful operator to our previously introduced pseudo-code transforms it as follows:

```
original_object %>% function() %>% another_function() %>%
one_more_function() -> even_more_manipulated_object
```

To make the relationship between the two versions of the code and the effects of the pipeline concept application to the R language more clear, let's try to represent the inputs and the outputs of both versions together:

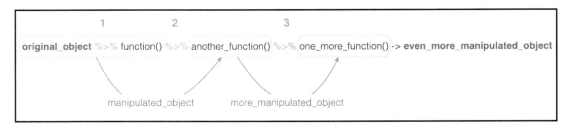

Looking at the diagram, it is easy to understand that the first pipe operator, marked with the number 1, simply takes the `original_object` object and passes it as an argument to the `function` function. What is going to come out from this first piping? We know the answer from the first version of the code: a new object originally named `manipulated_object` is going to be produced. Following on, we see that this object is handled from the second pipe operator, number 2, which takes it and passes it as an input to the `another_function` function, which will produce another manipulated object corresponding to what was originally called `more_manipulated_object`. Finally, the number 3 operator will take the output from `another_function` and pass it to the `one_more_function` function, which will produce the long awaited `even_more_manipulated_object`.

We will try to estimate later how much more efficient this pipeline-style coding is, but it should already be clear how much cleaner and more reasonable it is.

Now that we have the pipe operator in our toolbox, it's time to have a closer look at the `dplyr` package.

An even more gentle introduction to the dplyr package

As suggested by the heading, this section is a really brief introduction to the `dplyr` package. The main purpose of this package is to provide an efficient and consistent way of performing common data wrangling operations.

The main idea here is the one of representing those operations with verbs. `dplyr` has essentially got the following seven main verbs:

- `filter()`: To let you filter your data frame based on some given condition
- `arrange()`: To change the disposition of columns and sort values within columns
- `select()`: To select one or more specific columns within a data frame
- `rename()`: To change the name of a column
- `distinct()`: To produce a list of distinct, unique values within a column or the full data frame
- `mutate()`: To add attributes (columns) to a data frame
- `summarise()`: To aggregate attributes of a data frame around some given key

You are not required to learn all of them now because we are going to introduce and practice them along our journey. At the moment, you just need to put them into your backpack, together with data frames, vectors, and pipe operators.

Finally, the time has come to experiment with the power of R and gain knowledge about your financial habits.

Installing the necessary packages and loading your data into R

As a warm-up, let's install the necessary packages, load them into the environment, and import our banking data into R.

Installing and loading the necessary packages

In this analysis, we are going to use three packages:

- The `rio` package for data import
- The `dplyr` package for data wrangling
- The `ggplot2` package for data visualization

You should know how to install and load these packages, and I, therefore, invite you to try to do it by yourself before looking at the following lines of code. Installing the necessary packages into R requires running the following lines of code:

```
install.packages("rio")
install.packages("dplyr")
install.packages("ggplot2")
```

We are only going to fully load the `dplyr` and `ggplot2` packages, since we are going to use only one function from the `rio` package:

```
library(dplyr)
library(ggplot2)
```

To check whether your packages are properly loaded into your environment, besides looking for your environment browser, you can run the `search()` function, which results in the console printing out the loaded packages:

```
search()

[1] ".GlobalEnv" "package:ggplot2" "package:dplyr"
[4] "package:stats" "package:graphics" "package:grDevices" "package:utils"
[8] "package:datasets" "package:methods" "Autoloads" "package:base"
```

You will notice how crowded your environment is, which, besides the three packages you explicitly loaded, already hosts some other packages autonomously attached by the software itself, such as `base` and `utils`.

Importing your data into R

The R community has developed, and is still developing, different ways to read data into the R environment. Throughout our journey, we are going to use the one provided by `rio` (**R Input Output**). The main purpose of this package is to equip the R language with tools to automatically detect and import different kinds of file.

The package accomplishes this through the `import` function, which takes as an import the full name of the data file you want to import, including the file extensions. The function then automatically performs the operation of detecting the kind of file you are working on and applying appropriate methods and subfunctions to reliably read it into R.

It's no surprise then if we now just run the following line of code to import the data file and assign the resulting data frame to an object named `movements`:

```
movements <- rio::import(file = "data/banking.xls")
```

We are familiar with all the components of this line of code:

- The assignment operator, `<-`, defines a new data frame object named `movements`
- The `rio::` token tells the interpreter to take from the `rio` packages only the function on the right of `:`, without loading all the remaining functions
- `import("data/banking.xls")` runs the `import` function, passing as a value for the `file` argument the relative path of the `banking.xls` file. If you are unsure about how to set and retrieve paths in R, you can find an extensive explanation in `Appendix`, *Dealing with Dates, Relative Paths and Functions*.

Defining the monthly and daily sum of expenses

We have finally managed to import our data into R and we are ready to gain some knowledge of our financial habits. First of all, we are going to compute the daily and monthly sum of our expenses and incomes as a starting point to investigate the presence of patterns within our financial behavior.

We are going to group our dataset with the month and the day of the week as the keys of each transaction. You may have noticed that we do not actually have such information within our dataset, since only `date`, `expenditure`, and `income` are available. The first task we will have to accomplish will therefore be extrapolating the `day` and `month` attributes from the `date` column.

This can be easily done through the `month()` and `wday()` functions available within the `lubridate` package. Once we have installed the `lubridate` package, we are going to actually employ one of the `dplyr` verbs previously introduced— `mutate`.

With this verb, we can easily add an attribute to a data frame, even deriving it from the manipulation of one of more other attributes of the data frame. In our case, we are going to apply `mutate` in order to derive a `day_of_week` and a `month` from the `date` column:

```
movements %>%
  mutate(day_of_week = wday(date_new)) %>%
  mutate(month = month(date_new)) -> movements_clean
```

This is quite a relevant piece of code for our purposes; it applies some of the concepts we have been talking about:

- The pipe operator is employed to pass the output of the previous manipulation to the following functions
- The `mutate()` function is employed to add new columns to the `movements` data frame
- Finally, the assignment operator is employed to define a new object called `movements_clean`

If you want to look at the output of this code, just run the `head()` function on the `movements_clean` object, which will show up the first six lines of this data frame (unless you specify an n argument and set it to the number of rows you would like to see). Your data frame should now look like this:

date	expenditure	income	date_new	day_of_week	month
03/10/16	366.50	0.00	03/10/16	2	10
04/10/16	250.00	0.00	04/10/16	3	10
04/10/16	8.27	0.00	04/10/16	3	10
04/10/16	9.90	0.00	04/10/16	3	10
05/10/16	8.00	0.00	05/10/16	4	1

What is the next step? We are going to add some labels to the numbers to maximize our later data visualization. We are going to follow a straight strategy to perform this task—creating a decoding table, namely the `week_decode` table, and merging it with the `movements` table. Let's create the `week_decode` data frame:

```
week_decode <- data.frame(
  day_of_week = c(1:7),
  name_of_the_day = c("sunday", "monday", "tuesday",
"wednesday","thursday","friday","saturday" ), weekend =
```

```
c("weekend","workday","workday","workday","workday","workday","weekend")
)
```

Nothing special is going on here. We should just take note of the `c(1:7)`, which is creating a sequence from 1 to 7 that is equivalent to this:

```
c(1,2,3,4,5,6,7)
```

One more way, and actually the most flexible and appropriate one, is to employ the `seq()` function. For our purposes, we could have used it as follows:

```
c(seq(from = 1, to= 7, by = 1))
```

Once we are done with this, we can go ahead with our merging activity, applying the `merge.data.frame()` function:

```
movements_clean <- merge.data.frame(movements_clean,week_decode, by =
"day_of_week")
```

This function was explicitly designed to perform merges between two data frames. We can easily apply it to our two data frames because our key column has the same name within both of them. In the opposite case, we should have specified two different arguments, `by.x` for the first data frame and `by.y` for the second one. Alternatively, we could have employed the `inner_join` function directly from the `dplyr` package, which would have required exactly the same arguments.

Our dataset is finally ready, and the moment has come to summarize the data!

To understand how this works, let's imagine doing it manually: how would we do it? We would probably take our records, divide them by attribute, for instance the month of the expenses, and then we would compute the sum of the expenses within each group.

This is exactly how `dplyr` works. We take our data:

```
movements_clean %>%
```

We group it by month:

```
group_by(month) %>%
```

We summarize it:

```
summarise(number_of_movements = n(),
  sum_of_entries = sum(income, na.rm = TRUE),
  sum_of_expenses = sum(expenditure, na.rm = TRUE)) -> monthly_summary
```

Is it that easy? We should notice that there is small trick—our data has to be tidy. It is not a joke; tidy data is data following a precise framework of rules which simplifies data munging and visualization activities. We are going to look at this in more detail in `Chapter` `4`, *Keeping the Home Clean – The Data Mining Architecture*. At the moment, it is enough to keep in mind that not every kind of data is going to work this way and we therefore need to be careful as to what we put into our fabulous `group_by()` function.

Let's have a look at what we have done so far, by calling the `View` function on our `monthly_summary` data frame:

month	number_of_movements	sum_of_entries	sum_of_expenses
10	44	2036.63	12904.03
11	55	205335.55	21264.13
12	71	3755.37	21625.91

This is exactly what we were looking for, a pivot table of our data. Of course, you could start looking at your data and try, for instance, to understand which month was the worst in terms of expenses. I suggest waiting a bit longer, since we are going to easily accomplish the task with our final data visualization.

Let's take what we have learned a bit further, by creating a summary of our expenses by day of the week. How would you do that? Take a few minutes to try to jot it down on your PC before going on. It is actually quite similar to the monthly summary, except for the use of the `name_of_the_day` variable instead of the `month` one:

```
movements_clean %>%
  group_by(name_of_the_day) %>%
  summarise(number_of_movements = n(),
  sum_of_entries = sum(income, na.rm = TRUE),
  sum_of_expenses = sum(expenditure, na.rm = TRUE)) -> daily_summary
```

Once again, let's have a look at the result by calling the `View` function on our freshly produced `daily_summary` data frame:

name_of_the_day	number_of_movements	sum_of_entries	sum_of_expenses
friday	30	1392.33	10001.36
monday	55	0.00	5670.62
saturday	2	1300.00	850.38
sunday	3	0.00	470.61
thursday	22	141686.63	13051.44
tuesday	37	66748.59	2207.12
wednesday	21	0.00	23542.54

What we see is exactly what we are looking for, a summary of our entries and expenses by day of the week. It was pretty easy, wasn't it? We are just at the beginning of the journey, but we already have some powerful tools in our hands, from basic data structures to effective ways of summarizing data. It's now time to add a new piece to our puzzle: data visualization.

Visualizing your data with ggplot2

It is beyond the scope of this book to provide a comprehensive and exhaustive explanation of the data visualization principles and techniques, but in the remaining sections of this chapter, we are going to learn the basic elements of this powerful discipline and how to apply them to our data through the means of the `ggplot2` package.

Basic data visualization principles

As is often the case, when dealing with data visualization we should start from the final objective to work out the best way to accomplish it. The main objective of data visualization is to effectively communicate an insight contained within a given set of data. We can elaborate a bit more on this. The point here is not to show what your data visualization software is able to do or to impress your audience with bells and whistles. This may seem obvious, but we all know that when the *add a neon blinking light to your plot* option appears in front of you, it is really hard to resist it.

It is therefore crucial to possess some strong principles when dealing with data visualization, and to try to adhere to them as best we can. Without aiming to be exhaustive, we can find three principles within every good data visualization:

- Less but better
- Not every chart is good for your message
- Colors are to be chosen carefully

Less but better

This simple, and in some ways counter-intuitive, principle is one of the main tenets of the philosophy of the famous designer Dieter Rams. He is known for his industrial design masterpieces, characterized by an extremely minimal appearance paired with unbeatable functionality. Looking at his watches or electronic shavers, one gets surprised by how simple and pure their shapes are. Using them, you discover how wonderfully they work and how every detail seems to be designed to serve the general purpose of the product.

How is this possible? How is it possible to create a fully functional product by removing features and components rather than adding them? This can be done by following the second part of the principle: *better*.

Dieter Rams' philosophy is to work around the object, working out its purpose, deciding which components are essential and what can be actually removed. The focus is dedicated to the essential components, as they clearly emerge once the additional ones are removed.

How does this translate into data visualization? We can answer the question by looking at the following plots:

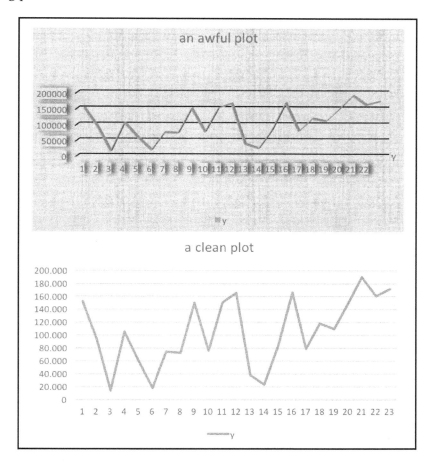

I hope that there is no doubt which is the wrong plot (if any doubt arises, the titles should help). We can focus our attention on why the second plot is awful.

The two plots show exactly the same data, but while the first one lets you immediately focus on what is relevant, the smooth increasing trend, the second one has a prominent background, pointless shadows, and meaningless 3D effects.

Why can't our brains simply focus on what is relevant in the second plot, avoiding looking at the useless details we just listed? Because our brain is crafted to try to acquire a general sense of what it gets in front of it and is not able to process all the information at once. Have a look at the additional reading referenced at the end of the chapter for more on this. Since our brain is not able to immediately focus on the trend, it starts looking around the plot, looking at the background, the shadows, and the 3D effects.

We can bet that if confronted with such a plot, our audience will remember it, but we can also bet that they will probably not remember its main message, which is the trend (no, it is not the papyrus background).

So, less but better—when creating a plot, do not simply add all you can add to it, but focus on what is strictly essential to communicate your message. Is that vertical grid needed on your time chart plot? Probably not, so you can remove it. Have you got any good reason to mark the *y* axis labels in bold? Probably not, and you should probably make them as plain as the *x* axis labels. It may require some practice, but focusing on what is really relevant in your data visualizations will dramatically improve their appearance and effectiveness.

Not every chart is good for your message

As mentioned before, the main objective of a data visualization is to effectively represent and communicate insights gained from a given set of data. This involves, as we have seen, removing pointless features from our plot, but also selecting the appropriate type of chart. Every chart type has its own narrative, and getting to know these narratives is necessary if you want to increase the level of effectiveness of your data visualization.

Scatter plot

A scatter plot is the most basic form of data visualization within two-dimensional space. It consists of single dots, each representing a couple of *x*-*y* coordinates. Even if this is really basic, this kind of representation can be quite powerful, especially to highlight the relationship between two different phenomena. If this is your objective, try to represent one of those phenomena on the *x* axis and the other one on the *y* axis:

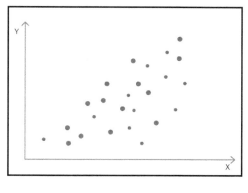

Scatterplot

Line chart

Line charts link together every single data point with a line. This kind of chart can be used to visualize time-related phenomena, where the *x* axis usually represents time:

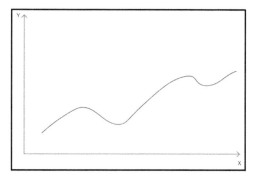

Line chart

We can use them to represent the evolution over time of a given phenomenon, and also to compare two or more phenomena, adding extra lines for each group of data points.

Bar plot

Bar plots are built by adding a bar, or a line, to a basic dot plot, linking every point to its projection on the *x* axis. This kind of chart is really effective when the *x* axis represents different values of a categorical variable, such as the possible answers to a survey, and on the *y* axis, the number of times each answer was given is shown.

Generally speaking, bar plots are the best choice when dealing with comparisons between static representations of different phenomena:

Bar plot

Unless we are dealing with a lot of bars, it is preferable to place them horizontally rather them vertically, since our brains are better able to perform comparisons with horizontal lines.

Other advanced charts

Starting with these ingredients, we can cook nearly every kind of data visualization recipe. A lot of the most advanced visualization techniques are composed of the basic charts we have just discussed:

- Bubble charts are dot plots where the size of the dot is proportional to a third value, so that for each point we have an x, y, and z vector
- Area graphs are line charts where the delimitation from the line is filled to highlight the quantity represented by the y value
- Mosaic plots are plots where tiles are generated and disposed on the canvas, following the order of the variables and their proportions

Colors have to be chosen carefully

Colors play a major role in our lives. They help us distinguish between delicious fruits and uneatable food, they alert us to danger, or just thrill us with a sunset. As human beings, we always pay attention to the colors we see, even at an unconscious level, and we always assign a meaning to them. That is why we cannot ignore which colors we use for our data visualizations. Within this section, we are going to briefly discuss how to use colors to ease the understanding of our data visualizations.

A bit of theory - chromatic circle, hue, and luminosity

Different theories about color have been developed, but there are some shared features:

- The chromatic circle
- Hue
- Luminosity

Chromatic circle: The chromatic circle is a really convenient way to show up the three so-called primary colors: cyan (a kind of blue), magenta (red), and yellow, and how the other colors are related to each other:

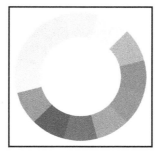

From the circle, we can define two relevant concepts: hue and complementary colors.

Hue: In the theory of color, hues are what are commonly known as colors. For instance, within the previous reproduced chromatic circle, every single component has to be considered as a different hue. We can see that for every given hue there are what we call shades, but how do we obtain them? We simply add black or white to the main hue.

For instance, the following self portrait by Picasso is mainly made from shades of blue:

Credits: https://www.wikiart.org/en/pablo-picasso/self-portrait-1901

Complementary colors: Complementary colors are pairs of colors that highly contrast themselves if placed next to each other. There are different theories on how to define pairs of complementary colors. The traditional pairs are as follows:

- Red - green
- Yellow - purple
- Blue - orange

This is all interesting, isn't it, but how do we leverage these concepts when dealing with our data visualizations? We are going to look now at two simple but powerful rules that make use of what we have just learned. We are going to use here a population of records, each showing three different attributes:

- A numerical x
- A numerical y
- A category, from A to D

Use complementary hues for data pertaining to different families: As shades of the same hue can show and communicate commonality, complementary colors can communicate differences in groups of data. If we are representing data from different categories of a given attribute, we can leverage complementary colors to highlight their differences:

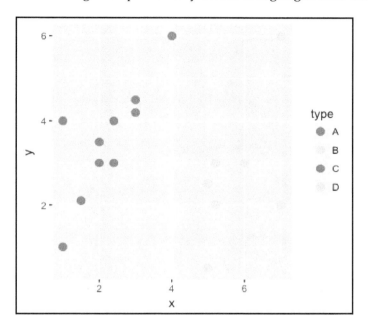

Use the same hue with a different shade for data pertaining to the same family: When dealing with data related to the same group, for instance, all the time series data related to region within a country, a good way to represent their shared pertinence to the group is to color them with the same hue but different shades. This will immediately and effectively communicate their commonality and easily distinguish them from the other groups.

The following figure shows an example of this concept. You will notice that, even without knowing a lot about the data represented, you will be inclined to assume that A-C and B-D are in some way related:

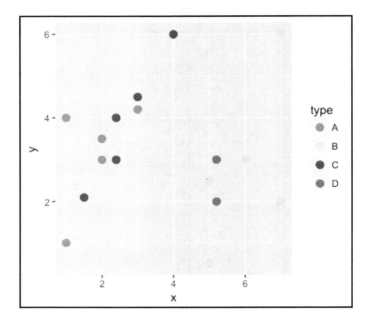

Visualizing your data with ggplot

It is finally time to grab another powerful tool and place it into your backpack: ggplot2. This is one of the most well-known packages within R, and it has rapidly gained the position of the standard package for performing data visualizations with R. Like every good son, it leverages the heritage of its father, the plot() function. ggplot2 is designed to fully take advantage of the powerful graphical environment provided with R. This is put in place within the logical framework of the grammar of graphics developed by Leland Wilkinson.

Within this last section, we are going to do the following:

- Learn a bit, and just a bit, about the grammar of graphics
- Learn how to apply it with the ggplot2 package
- Use the ggplot2 package to visualize the results of our previous summarization activities

One more gentle introduction – the grammar of graphics

The grammar of graphics is a way to declaratively think about graphics, giving us a convenient way to arrange the main components of a plot, like we are used to doing with words to compose a statement.

These main components are as follows:

- **Data**: The actual variables to be plotted
- **Aesthetics:** The scales onto which we will map our data
- **Geometries:** Shapes used to represent our data
- **Facets:** Rows and columns of subplots
- **Statistics:** Statistical models and summaries
- **Coordinates:** The plotting space we are using

A layered grammar of graphics – ggplot2

How do we translate all we have just read into R? Here comes the `ggplot2` package to the rescue, developed by our beloved Hadley Whickam, who was one of the lucky students on the courses taught by the R creators Isaka and Gentleman. `ggplot2` brings the power and logical simplicity of the grammar of graphics into the world of R, through the concept of layered plots. Every `ggplot` graphic is actually composed of at least the following programming components:

- `ggplot(data = data, aes())`: Specifies the data and aesthetic layer
- `geom_whatever()`: Introduces shapes representing the data within the data layer, following the specification given within the `aes()` layer

Those two are the minimum set of layers within the `ggplot` world. We can see that one more layer is implicitly set tighter with this one, which is the coordinates set, since Cartesian coordinates are automatically selected:

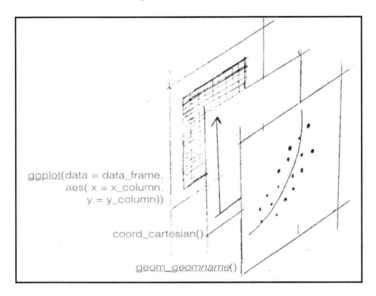

It is crucial to stress from now that every `geom` following the `ggplot()` call will inherit the aesthetics passed within that call if no different aesthetics are specified.

Visualizing your banking movements with ggplot2

It is now time to get our hands dirty with some real data visualization. We are going to show the data we previously summarized and leverage our own data visualization to gain some new knowledge about our financial habits.

Visualizing the number of movements per day of the week

As a warm up, let's visualize the number of movements per day. We are going to do this starting from the `daily_summary` data frame. How do we do that? First of all, let's choose the right type of chart. I can wait for you here while you look at the previous section and try to work out which is the best chart for our purposes.

Since we are going to compare the values of the same attribute (the number of movements) across different values of a categorical variable (day of the week), our best possible choice is going to be a bar plot.

What do we need for a bar plot in `ggplot`?

- A `ggplot()` call, passing the following:
    - The `daily_summary` object as the `data` argument
    - `name_of_the_day` and `number_of_movements` as x and y aesthetics, the values represented in the *x* and the *y* axes
- `geom_bar()` as geometry, specifying that no statistical computation has to be performed to the data specified as aesthetic, through the `stat` argument, set to `identity`

Leveraging the well-known pipe operator, we can write the plot code as follows:

```
daily_summary %>%
  ggplot(aes(x = name_of_the_day,y = number_of_movements)) +
  geom_bar(stat = 'identity')
```

Here it is, our new data visualization:

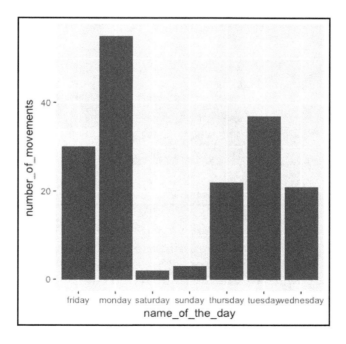

Monday clearly appears to be the day where the greatest number of movements are performed, while we apparently tend to rest during the weekend. We can easily add clarity to this plot by rotating the bars. This will increase the level of readability of the plot since we tend to be more able to compare horizontal lines than the vertical ones. Which layers do you think are impacted by this rotation of the bars? We would probably be tempted to answer *The geom layer.* Well, that would be wrong, since the layer that determines how the bars are oriented on the canvas is the coordinates plot. We can then add a `coord_flip()` call after the code we already showed to rotate our bars:

```
daily_summary %>%
  ggplot(aes(x = name_of_the_day, y = number_of_movements)) +
  geom_bar(stat = 'identity') +
  coord_flip()
```

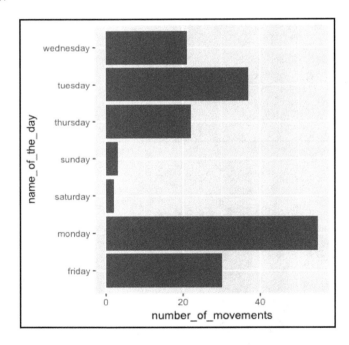

To be fair, knowing how many movements we perform by day of the week is not actually a salient point within our financial habits investigation: what if, on the weekend, we perform fewer movements but more conspicuous ones? We should add to the number information the amount information, which we already summarized within the daily summary data frame.

Let us think about this plot: what would we like to show altogether? Both the number of movements and the amount of those movements for any given day of the week. We will, therefore, have one *x* variable and two *y* variables. Moreover, we will probably need one geometry layer for the number of movements and one for the amount of those movements.

An elegant way to show this information is to draw a line proportional to the number of movements for each day of the week and place, at the top of this line, a point that is proportional to the amount of those movements. We can draw such a plot by employing two new geometries, `geom_linerange` and `geom_point`.

The first one requires us to specify where to start drawing the line, that is, the minimum value of *y* for every *x*, and where to stop the line.

`geom_point` draws a point for every *x*-*y* couple found within the data. One relevant feature of this geometry is the ability to map the point size to the value of another attribute available in the data frame specified within the `ggplot()` call. For instance, we could decide to map the size of the point to the hour of the day in which the transaction was performed, having points greater as the time gets later.

Within our data visualization, we are going to pass the following specification to our geometries:

- The minimum *y* for the line range will be set to zero since we want every line to start from zero
- The maximum *y* will be the number of movements for any *x*
- We are going to make every point size proportional to the mean amount of movements of any given day of the week

Finally, we are going to add labels printing out the mean amount for any given day. This will be done by specifying one more aesthetic within the `ggplot()` call, namely the `label` one, and adding a `geom_text()` layer:

```
daily_summary %>%
  ggplot(aes(x = name_of_the_day, y = number_of_movements, label =
number_of_movements)) +
  geom_linerange(aes(ymin = 0, ymax = number_of_movements)) +
  geom_point(aes(size = (sum_of_entries +
sum_of_expenses)/number_of_movements))+
  geom_text(nudge_y = 1.7)+

coord_flip()
```

This is what we get :

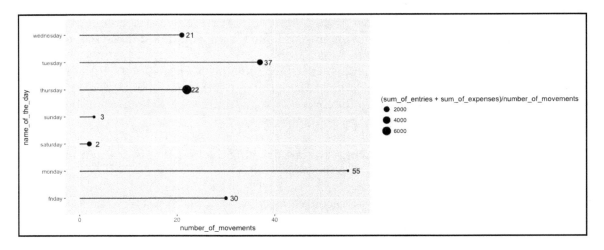

We are going to comment on the result in a moment, but first, let's have a little break and look back at the code we just executed: it's started to become quite a serious piece of code, and we are just warming up!

What this plot clearly shows is that Monday has got the greater absolute number of movements, but those movements tend to have a very small average amount. The movements performed on Thursdays have the greatest value. Are there any recurring expenses we have on a Thursday? This deserves some further analysis, so we'll need to get back to the raw data.

Further references

- On the way our brain visualizes: *Information Visualization by Ware, Colin. (2012) , 3rd Edition*. Morgan Kaufmann
- http://www.datavizcatalogue.com for quite an exhaustive catalogue of data visualization techniques and how to employ them
- *Interaction of Color*, Joseph Alber, one of the greatest books on the theory of colour
- *ggplot2: Elegant Graphics for Data Analysis*, by Hadley Wickham, Springer-Verlag

Summary

Can you feel your backpack becoming heavy? This chapter was a big boost for your R knowledge: nearly 30 pages earlier you were only just aware of how to print "Hello World" with R, and now you have discovered useful insights from your real banking data.

We have learned the following:

- Installing additional packages in the base version of R
- Importing data into your R environment
- Creating pivot tables in R
- Discovering and showing information through data visualization techniques
- Plotting data with `ggplot2`

I am tempted to accelerate further in the next chapter, immediately showing you how to implement data mining algorithms with the powerful weapon we have at our disposal. But, we have to be prudent and firmly cover the foundations to let you soundly build upon them. In the next chapter, we'll learn how to organize and conduct a data mining project through the CRISP-DM methodology.

That said, if you are really reckless, you could always skip to `Chapter 4`, *Keeping the Home Clean – The Data Mining Architecture* .

3

The Data Mining Process - CRISP-DM Methodology

At this point, our backpack is quite full of exciting tools; we have the R language and an R development platform. Moreover, we know how to use them to summarize data in the most effective ways. We have finally gained knowledge on how to effectively represent our data, and we know these tools are powerful. Nevertheless, what if a real data mining problem suddenly shows up? What if we return to the office tomorrow and our boss finally gives the OK: *Yeah, you can try using your magic R on our data, let's start with some data mining on our customers database; show me what you can do.* OK, this is getting a bit too fictional, but you get the point—we need one more tool, something like a structured process to face data mining problems when we encounter them.

When dealing with time and resource constraints, having a well-designed sequence of steps to accomplish our objectives becomes a crucial element to ensure the data mining activities success. You may therefore be wondering whether some kind of golden rule about how to conduct data mining projects was ever set out. It actually was, around 1996, by a pool of leading industries, based on their data mining experiences.

Since then, this methodology has spread to all major industries and is currently considered a best practice within the data mining realm. That is why it is a really good idea to learn it from the very beginning of your data mining journey, letting it shape your data mining behavior based on what the best in the class do.

Before getting into this, there is a final note on this chapter within the general flow of the book. The concepts we are going to look at more theoretically here are going to be more fully examined in future chapters, in particular:

- Business understanding in Chapter 5, *How to Address a Data Mining Problem – Data Cleaning and Validation*
- Data understanding in Chapters 5, *How to Address a Data Mining Problem – Data Cleaning and Validation* and Chapter 6, *Looking into Your Data Eyes – Exploratory Data Analysis*
- Data preparation in Chapter 5, *How to Address a Data Mining Problem – Data Cleaning and Validation* and Chapter 6, *Looking into Your Data Eyes – Exploratory Data Analysis*
- Modeling in Chapters 7, *Our First Guess – a Linear Regression,* to Chapter 12, *Looking for the Culprit – Text Data Mining with R.*
- Deployment in Chapter 13, *Sharing Your Stories with Your Stakeholders through R Markdown*

Moreover, you should understand that we are going employ the tools acquired here to face the same data mining issues throughout the book, so that by the end of it you will have experienced one real-life data mining cycle from the very beginning to the end.

No more additional notes now, since it is time to get into the actual description of what Crisp-DM is!

The Crisp-DM methodology data mining cycle

The CRISP-DM methodology considers the analytical activities as a cyclical set of phases to be repeated until a satisfactory result is obtained. Not surprisingly then, Crisp-DM methodology phases are usually represented as a circle going from business understanding to the final deployment:

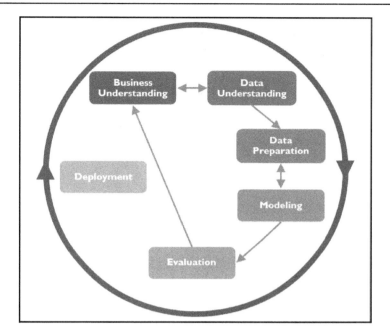

As we can see within the diagram, the cycle is composed of six phases:

- Business understanding
- Data understanding
- Data preparation
- Modeling
- Evaluation
- Deployment

This is the greater abstraction level of the Crisp-DM methodology, meaning one that can apply, with no exception, to all data mining problems. Three more specific layers are then conceived as a conjunction between the general model and the specific data mining project:

- Generic tasks
- Specialized tasks
- Process instances

All of the components of every level are mapped to one component of the layer above, so that when dealing with a specific data mining problem, both bottom-up and top-down approaches are allowed, as we will see in the last paragraph of this chapter.

Business understanding

This is an often underestimated phase, and we should look at it carefully since its role is decisive for all of the remaining phases. Within the business understanding phase, we fundamentally answer the following two questions:

- What are the objectives of the business where the data mining problem is coming from?
- What are the data mining goals for this project?

Giving the wrong answer to either one of these two questions will result in producing results not relevant for the business, or not solving the data mining problem at its core.

The first step in this phase is understanding your client's needs and objectives, since those objectives will become the objectives of the project. Within this phase, we gather information through the means of interviews and technical literature, finally defining a project plan and clearly stating a data mining goal and how we plan to reach it.

The project plan should not be considered an unchangeable one, since the following phases will naturally tend to suggest new or more precise ways to reach the data mining goal, inevitably requiring you to get back to the plan and further develop it.

We also list within the project plan all relevant resources, both in terms of technical resources (hardware, software, and similar) and human resources.

Data understanding

Now that the goals and success criteria of our activity are clear, we can start gathering relevant data for our project. Where should we look for this data? Within the resources, we listed the project plan, of course. The first task of this phase will, therefore, be to actually start acquiring from your resources.

Data collection

A core principle to be respected during these activities is replicability—you should carefully take note of all the steps and criteria employed within the data acquisition phase, so that it can be replicated by a third-party, and also by yourself in future, if needed. The typical output of this phase is a data collection phase, where steps and filtering criteria are listed.

How to perform data collection with R

If your data mining project is going to be performed with R, which we could infer from you reading this book, the data collection phase will essentially be performed by downloading your data from its original source, and importing it within the R environment.

This short description actually hides a great variety of activities, as well as a great variety of tools provided by the R community to perform them. We can briefly try to summarize them, as described in the paragraphs that follow. For a more general overview of how to establish connection to your data sources, you should look at Chapter 4, *Keeping the Home Clean – The Data Mining Architecture*, within the *Data sources* section.

Data import from TXT and CSV files

For this, you can use the old-fashioned read.csv() function, or his new-born nephew import(), which we were introduced to in previous chapters.

Data import from different types of format already structured as tables

We are talking here of file formats such as .STAT and sas7bdat et al.; you should use our best friend import() since its grandparents here, like read.csv and read.txt are not going to be of help. Anyway, if any issue arises, you can always sort to download your data from STAT and SAS into the .csv format, and then import them as a .csv file into R, employing the functions seen before.

Data import from unstructured sources

What if your data came from a web page? No worries, some tools come to the rescue here as well. We are technically talking here about web scraping activities, but since this is outside the scope of this book, which is at an introductory level, I will point you to the useful CRAN task view on web scraping, if you are interested in the topic: https://cran.r-project.org/web/views/WebTechnologies.html.

Data description

This is a formal activity that involves a mere description of the type of file and data structure collected. We should inquire and describe the following attributes of our data:

- File type
- Data attributes
- Requirements satisfaction

Reasoning about file types also involves starting to think about interoperability. Going into more practical detail, within this task you should ask yourself if the data was collected in formats that are able to work together. Let's say, as an example, that we collected some data within the `.STAT` format and some other data within the `.sas7bdat` format; are we able to work with those files without having to change from one programming language to another? Apart from the actual answer to this question (which is yes, since you can read SAS data into STATA and vice versa, or even read them all into R), this exemplifies the kind of operative reasoning needed within this task.

How to perform data description with R

You can easily perform data description tasks within the R environment employing the `describe()` function from the `hmisc` package, or the `str()` function from the R base package. Both of these functions allow you to describe your data through listing their attributes and range of variability.

Moreover, if any need for file type conversion should arise, you can always come back to the already introduced `rio` package, and look for the useful function `convert()`, which takes as an input a string with the full name of the file `file.xlsx` and the desired final name of the converted file, such as `file.sas7bdat`. The function will automatically infer the file format you want to convert to.

Data exploration

Now that you have the data on your PC, how could you resist giving it a glance? That is what this task is all about, getting your hands dirty with data, and acquiring a good descriptive knowledge of your data, so that you can answer a question such as the following:

- Is there any categorical data within my tables?

- What is the maximum number of records I am going to deal with within my analyses?
- What are the min, max, and mean values of my variables?
- Is there any asymmetry within any of my variables?

Tools employed within this step include summary statistics such as mean, median, and quartiles, and exploratory data analysis techniques such as box plots and histograms. Take a look at the paragraph that follows for further details on how to apply these techniques within the R world.

What to use in R to perform this task

Not surprisingly, the base version of R comes packed with all that is needed to perform this task. Let's cover some of the main functions here.

The summary() function

Employing the summary() function is an easy way to take a first immediate look at your data distribution. You just have to pass to the function of the data frame you are working with, to get as a result a print out of the following summary statistics for each of the columns:

- minimum
- first quartile
- median
- mean
- third quartile
- maximum

Let's try, for instance, to apply this function to the Toothgrowth dataset. which is one of the built-in datasets within base R (if you want to discover more of those datasets, just run data() within your R console):

```
summary(ToothGrowth)
      len              supp          dose
 Min.   : 4.20    OJ:30    Min.   :0.500
 1st Qu.:13.07    VC:30    1st Qu.:0.500
 Median :19.25             Median :1.000
 Mean   :18.81             Mean   :1.167
 3rd Qu.:25.27             3rd Qu.:2.000
 Max.   :33.90             Max.   :2.000
```

As you can see, we find here for every and each variable, which are `len`, `supp`, and `dose`, the summary statistics descriptor. One final, relevant note: since the `supp` variable is a categorical one, for this variable we find the two different values the variable assumes, which are `OJ` and `VC`, together with their frequency, which is 30 for both of them. A lot of information for just one function, isn't it?

Box plot

Another way to summarize a lot of information at once about your population attributes is to create a box plot for each of its elements. A box plot is, you will not be surprised to learn, a plot with a box. As is often the case, the point here is what is in the box. Within the box here, we find the fifty percent of our population, and, as usual, also a point highlighting the mean or the median of our distribution. Let's have a look at the following explanatory chart:

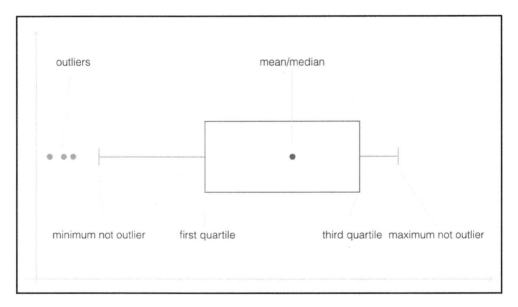

As you can see, the box plot actually conveys a full set of information. We can find, both inside and around the box, the following (from left to right):

- **Outliers**: These can be described as values outside the typical range of the population, and can be found employing different absolute thresholds, such as, for instance, the interquartile range multiplied by a given number. These are relevant values, as we will see later, since they are able to influence statistical models and can sometimes need to be removed.

- **Minimum and maximum**: These mark the lower and upper bounds of the *typical* distribution, in other words, of that part of the distribution not containing the outliers.
- **First and third quartiles**: These show where 25% and 75% of the distribution lies. For instance, saying that the first quartile of a given population of 1,200 records is equal to 36 means that 300 records have a value equal or lower to 36 (1,200 * 0.25). These two indexes are relevant as we consider them to detect the real representative values of a population. These two values are employed to compute the interquartile range (*III quartile - I quartile = interquartile range*), which expresses the typical range of variability within a population, that is, the central range within which lies 50% of the population.
- **Mean, or sometimes the median**: These are both indexes that are able to summarize a population. The second one tends to be more stable and less influenced by outliers. We therefore tend to use median where we have relevant outliers.

Within R, we can easily produce box plots employing the `boxplot()` function. Since we are already used to `ggplot`, it is useful to note that it also has a convenient function for drawing box plots:

```
ggplot(data = ToothGrowth, aes(x = supp, y = len)) + geom_boxplct() +
coord_flip()
```

We ask here to take the `ToothGrowth` dataset and depict one box plot for each value of x, which is the categorical variable we mentioned previously. Each box plot will summarize the distribution of the `len` attribute associate with a given value of x. The actual drawing of the box plot is performed by the `geom_boxplot()` function, which will inherit the x and y coordinates from the `ggplot()`. Finally, we flip the plot, since, as we discovered, human beings are better able to compare lengths when they lie horizontally.

The preceding code will produce the following useful plot:

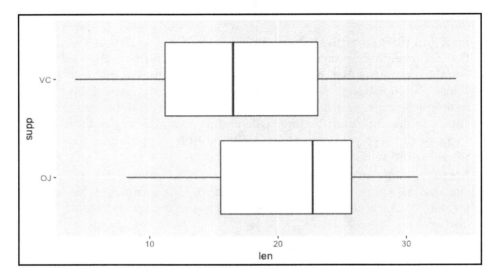

The previous plot highlights one of the relevant aspects of using a box plot—it eases the comparison between distributions. As you can see, it is easy to say from the only box plots that by average the length associated with the *OJ* treatment are greater. You can also observe that this treatment tends to have a more predictable results, since the variability around the mean is lower, as showed by the distance from the minimum and the maximum within the two distributions. We could go on deriving more insights from this plot, but I think this is enough to see how helpful the box plot can be within our data description task.

Histograms

When talking about data exploration with R, we cannot avoid mentioning histograms, which are a very useful way to gain a view on how your population is distributed along the minimum and maximum value. Within histograms, the data is binned in more or less regular intervals, and the plotted bar heights are such that the area of bars is proportional to the number of items within each interval. R comes with a convenient `hist()` function directly within the base version. As mentioned earlier, we are also going to learn how to produce a plot employing the `ggplot2` package. At this stage in our journey, you may already be guessing at least some of the lines of code required, especially the first line, which is the usual `ggplot()` one:

```
ggplot(data = ToothGrowth, aes(x = len)) + geom_histogram()
```

This will produce exactly what we are looking for:

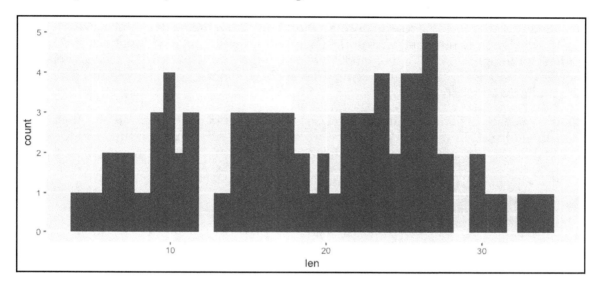

Data preparation

Now that we know a bit more about our data, we can skip to the next step: preparing our data for the modeling activity. This main objective involves a lot of tasks that usually go under the names of data cleaning, data validation, data munging, and data wrangling. The reason behind the need for these activities is quite simple: the modeling techniques we are going to apply to our data will have specific requirements, which could include, for instance, the absence of null values or a specific type of variable as an input (categorical, numerical, and many more). It is, therefore, critical to prepare our data in a way that is suitable for our models. Moreover, we may need to perform basic transformation activities on our raw data, such as merging or appending tables. Finally, we may even need to draw a sample from our data, for instance, to address a matter of resource constraints.

We are going to look closer at how to perform these tasks with R in Chapters 5, *How to Address a Data Mining Problem – Data Cleaning and Validation* and Chapter 6, *Looking into Your Data Eyes – Exploratory Data Analysis*.

Modelling

And finally comes the time to actually start working: within the modeling phase, we try to get knowledge from our data, answering the questions we defined within the business understanding phase. The kind of model we are going to apply here will largely depend on the kind of data we will be dealing with, since every model has got data type and data distribution constraints.

What is relevant to understanding this phase is that it should not be considered a linear and sequential phase, but rather a cyclical one. To understand why, it will be sufficient to consider how it is usually performed, which is through the following three steps:

- Defining a data modeling strategy
- Model assumption evaluation
- Model assessment

Defining a data modeling strategy

In this step, starting from the exploratory analyses we have performed and the objectives we have declared within the business understanding phase, we start to limit the possible applicable models to a limited range, therefore defining our data modeling strategy. This is a set of possible data modeling techniques we are going to apply to our data to in order to reach the results we declared within the business understanding phase. We have to admit that, especially within industries, it is common to be guided by in the choice by the most popular alternatives. For an example, we can look at the logistic regression for the modeling of the customers default events.

This is not per say a real problem, since probably a popular technique is popular because it is showed to be effective; nevertheless we should open up our mind with more organic research, driven by technical literature and discussion with peers.

But research of what? We should focus on some kind of mix of these two components:

- How similar problems were solved in the past
- Any emerging techniques which, given the type of data we have and the question we want to answer, could fit our purposes

How similar problems were solved in the past

Talking about the similar problems of the first components, a problem is similar to our one if:

- It was determined from the same kinds of questions and the same knowledge domain (for instance, some other work on the default forecasting within the banking industry)
- It shares with our problem the same kind of data, for instance, a work on cancer forecasting coming from the medical domain, where we have a yes/no variable to be predicted (having yes or no the cancer instead of a default), and some other variable which could be the cause of this output.

Emerging techniques

Look at recent papers, and look for consultancy; you are lucky because R is usually very up to date.

Classification of modeling problems

When dealing with the choice of the right set of models to experiment with to solve your problem, you should bear in mind the following classification of modeling problems that will help you take your search in the right direction:

- **Clustering**: These are the problems where you need to regroup your data based on common features, that is, measures of similarity. For instance, you may need to cluster your customers to perform further analyses on their shopping behavior.
- **Classification**: Within this kind of problem, you need to define a rule able to assign new elements to one of the categories available within your population, given a set of features. You may, for instance, be wondering about defining the category of products a new customer will most probably like, based on some personal information you have about them.
- **Regression**: You are facing a regression problem when you need to understand how different ingredients contribute to a final outcome. A typical example could be a product you need to advertise, for which you would like to know on which advertising platform you should concentrate the main part of your budget. Imagine having a dataset showing, for a group of products, how much budget was placed for each advertising platform, and the final revenue obtained from that product. Modeling the relationship between the level of investment on each platform and the final revenues would be considered a classic case of regression.

How to perform data modeling with R

We are going to look closer at how to perform those task with R in chapter 7 onward.

Evaluation

The evaluation phase is the one where we look for a validation of the results coming from our modeling activities. This phase can be split into two main questions:

- Is the model performing adequately?
- Is the model answering the questions originally posed?

The first of the two questions involves the identification of a proper set of metrics to establish if the model developed possesses the desired properties.

Following previously-shown model families, we are going to show you here how to overcome the following problems:

- Clustering evaluation
- Classification evaluation
- Regression evaluation
- Anomaly detection evaluation

Clustering evaluation

It is quite easy to understand how to evaluate the effectiveness of a clustering model. Since the objective of a clustering model is to divide a population into a given number of similar elements, evaluation of these kinds of models necessarily goes through the definition of some kind of an ideal clustering, even if defined by human judgment. Evaluating the performance of the model will then be a matter of defining how close to this ideal clustering the real model comes. A typical measure for evaluating the performance of a clustering model is the purity index, which basically assigns each cluster to one of the ideal classes judgmentally defined based on the class to which the majority of the elements of the cluster are assigned. The level of coincidence between the ideal and the actual clustering is then observed.

Classification evaluation

In a way similar to what we have seen for clustering evaluation, when dealing with classification models, we look for closeness to perfection. Every element of the population, and more frequently of a separate validation dataset, is provided with the correct theoretical classification, tagged, and, subsequently, the actual classification is compared with the one provided from the model. The more the model output coincides with the actual classification, the more accurate it is. A useful instrument when dealing with classification evaluation is the so-called confusion matrix, which is a double-entry table useful for understanding the level of performance of the model for a given category of classification.

The confusion matrix shows, on one entry, a true and a false for the model, and on the other entry a true and a false for the actual classification. We therefore have four possible combinations:

- **True positive:** Number of cases for which both the model and the theoretical classification show the given attribute. These are the cases where the model correctly performs.
- **True negative:** Number of cases where the attribute is not shown from both the model and the theoretical classification. Here again, the model is correctly performing.
- **False positive:** The model here shows the presence of the attribute while the theoretical classification doesn't. We count here a first type of error for the models.
- **False negative:** The opposite of the previous one, since the model here doesn't mark the presence of the attribute while the theoretical classification does.

		Model	
		TRUE	FALSE
Theoretical	TRUE	780	154
Classification	FALSE	164	610

Starting from the number shown within the confusion matrix, we can easily compute a comprehensive measure of the model performance: the accuracy.

The accuracy is measured as follows:

$$accuracy = (\Sigma\ True\ positive + \Sigma\ True\ negative)/\Sigma\ Total\ population$$

As can be easily understood, we see here a measure of how many times the model assigns the right classification within a given population.

Regression evaluation

When dealing with regression, the most relevant concept is the one of residuals. *What are residuals?* They are nothing more than the difference between the estimated values and the actual one. Let's imagine we are training a model to predict the level of revenues starting from the investment into advertising activity. We estimated a regression model that associates to one million euros of investment, a revenue of two-and-a-half million. If, within our training dataset, the actual amount of revenue for that given amount is, for instance, one million nine hundred euros, we will have a residual of 600,000 euros. Applying this kind of reasoning through all of the datasets you employed to train your regression model will lead to a whole new data series represented by residuals:

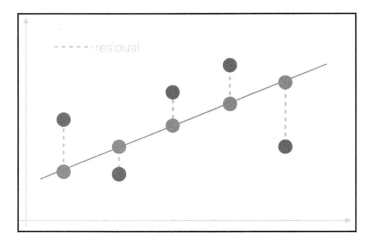

Those residuals are actually really relevant within the regression models for at least two clear reasons:

- They are a direct way to measure the level of accuracy of the model
- Some specific conditions are to be met with their regard in order to confirm that a regression model can be applied to your data

Since the second topic will be better explained in Chapters 7, *Our First Guess – a Linear Regression*, let's focus now on the residuals as a measure of model accuracy.

A very popular method to employ residuals to evaluate the level of accuracy of a model is to use them to compute the **Mean Absolute Error** (**MAE**). This measure is simply the mean of all the residuals into their absolute value:

$$Mean\ Absolute\ Error = (\Sigma\ |residual|)/n$$

This measure will be expressed in the same unit of measurement of the data within the dataset, and will clearly express how, on average, the model misses its predictions.

How to judge the adequacy of a model's performance

From all we have seen previously, we can derive a quite conspicuous set of numbers and metrics, but how do we evaluate if they are good or not? How do we establish whether our business model performs adequately so that we can skip to the next phase? These questions partially involve the answer to one of the two other questions we asked at the beginning of the section: is *the model answering the questions originally posed?*

Establishing the adequacy of a model performance necessarily involves both understanding if the level of quality of the model is acceptable, and if the model is able to answer the questions posed within the business understanding phase. Fortunately, especially within the operational environment, we have some exceptional aid coming from where you would never expect: the profit and losses statement.

When dealing with a model employed within an industrial process, but also a risk management or an accounting process, an easy question which will help you understand if your model fits the role will be: *Is the cost involved into the expectable model error acceptable?* Resorting to anomaly detection techniques, this question will become something like this: *Is the cost of missing the 10% of fraud occurring feasible?* Answering this kind of question, which will presumably involve looking at the historical data series to acquire a measure of how much, historically, fraud has cost the company, will help you to understand if the model developed so far is accurate enough, or if a re-estimation/re-development activity is needed.

Regarding the second question, if the model is able to answer questions posed during the business understanding phase, you will need to understand whether the kinds of answers derivable from your model are what the business was looking for. If, for example, the business was looking for a way to increase cross-selling on their online store based on historical data of customers' orders, and you came up with a recommendation engine able to predict possible future orders of customers based on one or more of their previous orders, you will have probably met the required expectations.

What to use in R to perform this task

We are going to look closer at how to perform those tasks with R in Chapter 8, *A Gentle Introduction to Model Performance Evaluation*.

Deployment

We are now reaching the final phase, and we are going to implement our models into the production system. But, what if one of the previous phases doesn't go well? This is when we understand that the CRISP-DM model is an iterative one. If the previous *evaluation* phase terminates showing that an unsatisfactory level of performance was reached, it would be pointless to develop a deployment plan, since the deployed solution would not meet the business expectations, and this would later produce undesired costs required to fix the problem.

In these circumstances, it would definitely be more appropriate to invest some more time to understand what went wrong, to define which phase of the CRISP-DM process needs to be resorted to. A model performance analysis could, for instance, reveals a poor level of accuracy of the model due to bad data quality of the training dataset employed to estimate model parameters. This would then involve a step back to the data preparation phase, or even to the data acquisition phase.

Once the iteration has produced a satisfactory model, you will be able to enter the deployment phase, which will operationally consist of two main steps:

- Deployment plan development
- Maintenance plan development

Deployment plan development

This is the physical activity of determining which is the best strategy to deploy and industrialize the steps previously developed. Here, we will have to consider the best data architecture to be built to automatically acquire data from previously identified data sources, and process them employing the developed data preparation codes. Finally, we will have to define how to feed the model with the processed data, and how to communicate results to the end user.

All of this will have to be documented and audited, in order to ensure a proper level of quality and ease future activities and costs of maintenance.

It should also be mentioned that, especially within more academic and theoretical environments, the deployment plan development will not involve the development of a proper industrial process like the one described above, which will require us to clearly define and formalize, in a sequential way, all performed steps in order to assure replicability of the process, and quality of the obtained results.

Maintenance plan development

This is quite a crucial phase, since once the model has been in development and its quality has been judged as satisfactory, the job is just half-done. This is because a good level of performance today does not necessarily imply a good level of performance in the days to come, and this can mainly come from two sources:

- Technical changes in the process-generating data employed from the model, with the following need to change the activity of data acquisition and data preparation due, for instance, to changes in the type of file provided or the frequency of value updates.
- Structural changes in the processes producing employed data, which leads to unreliable estimates produced from the model. A typical example is the introduction of a new law which states constraint on the use of cash, which will lead to a structural change in the values of cash withdrawn from ATMs, with a subsequent need to re-estimate our hypothetical fraud-detection model.

How do we overcome these potential problems? With a well-conceived maintenance plan. The plan will state which kind of ongoing analyses will be performed to monitor the level of performance of the model, and, depending on what kind of results appear, the model will be subject to *reestimation* or even *redevelopment* activities.

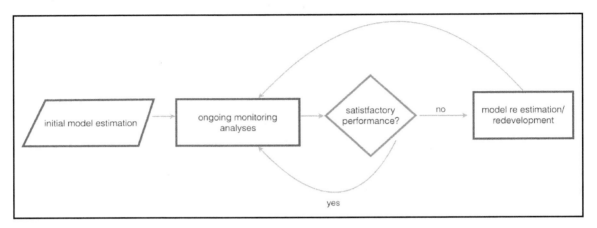

Reproduced previously is a typical flow chart of model maintenance activities:

- The process starts with initial activity of model estimation
- Following the estimation comes the exploitation of predefined ongoing monitoring analyses, which could be, for instance, a systematic evaluation of accuracy metrics
- Here comes a decision point—are the assessed performances satisfactory?
- If yes, the cycle starts again from the ongoing monitoring analyses
- If no, a proper re-estimation or even re-development activity is needed, based on how bad the results were

Once the deployment plan is ready, as well as the model maintenance plan, all that will be left to do is to actually implement them and taste the feel of your data mining success.

Summary

In this chapter, we took some time to better understand how we should structure our data mining activities. Even if it felt like a pause in our exciting riding to R mastery, it was quite a useful one. You are now able to address any kind of data mining task as it shows up. All you have to do is to follow the logical and chronological path you have learned:

- Business understanding (what is the problem, what are the relevant questions?)
- Data understanding (which data is at my disposal to solve the problem?)
- Data preparation (get my data ready to work)
- Data modeling (try to get knowledge from the data to solve the problem)
- Evaluation (see if the problem found a question with your analysis)
- Deployment (place it in production, if needed)

You have a framework and a methodology to help you get started with your project, and this is really powerful. Ready to start riding again? Well, even if you are ready, you will have to wait for a few more pages: in the next chapter, we are going to take a close look at the horse we are going to ride, and discover the basic components of data mining architecture.

4
Keeping the House Clean – The Data Mining Architecture

In the previous chapter, we defined the dynamic part of our data mining activities, understanding how a data mining project should be organized in terms of phases, input, and output. In this chapter, we are going to set our scene, defining the static part of our data mining projects, the data mining architecture.

How do we organize data bases, scripts, and output within our project? This is the question this chapter is going to answer. We are going to look at:

- The general structure of data mining architecture
- How to build such kind of structure with R

This is a really useful chapter, especially if you are approaching the data mining activity for the first time, and no matter the programming language, since it will let you gain a first view on what you will typically find in a data mining environment. No matter whether you are dealing with a single-man project or a whole team initiative, you will more or less always find the elements we are going to introduce here.

It will therefore be useful, every time you approach a new problem, to try to associate the real elements you will find in your environment with the abstracts ones we will discover in the following pages. A useful map to do this job is reproduced within the next paragraph; you can make a copy of it and keep it as a reference point when you start a new data mining journey.

As a final destination of this chapter, we will see how to implement a data mining architecture with our beloved R language.

A general overview

Let's first gain a general view on the main components of a data mining architecture. It is basically composed of all of the basic elements you will need to perform the activities described in the previous chapter. As a minimum set of components, the following are usually considered:

- Data sources
- Data warehouse
- Data mining engine
- User interface

We can find reproduced here a useful logical map of a data mining architecture, where each of the mentioned components is depicted, highlighting through grey arrows the one and two verses connection within the components:

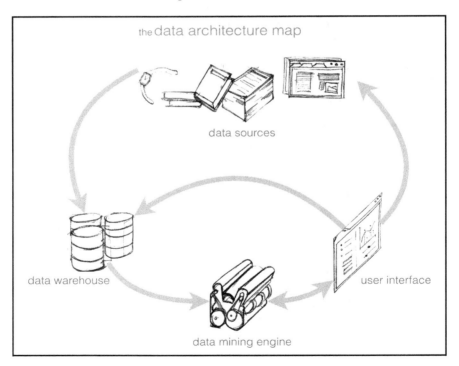

We are going to get into more details in the next paragraph; nevertheless, we can briefly have a look at all these components to get a clear sense of their reciprocal relationships:

- **Data sources**: These are all the possible sources of small bits of information to be analyzed. Data sources feed our data warehouses and are fed by the data produced from our activity toward the user interface.
- **Data warehouse**: This is where the data is stored when acquired from data sources.
- **Data mining engine**: This contains all of the logic and the processes needed to perform the actual data mining activity, taking data from the data warehouse.
- **User interface**: The front office of our machine, which allows the user to interact with the data mining engine, creating data that will be stored within the data warehouse and that could become part of the big ocean of data sources.

Now that we have a clearer picture of how things work, let's have a closer look at every single element.

Data sources

Data sources are everywhere. As the following picture tries to suggest, we can find data within all the realms of reality. This hyperbolic sentence is becoming more true thanks to the well-known trend of the internet of things, and now that every kind of object is getting connected to the internet, we are starting to collect data from tons of new physical sources. This data can come in a form already feasible for being collected and stored within our databases, or in a form that needs to be further modified to become usable for our analyses:

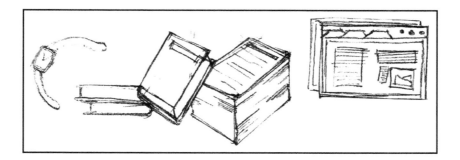

We can, therefore, see that between our data sources and the physical data warehouse where they are going to be stored, a small components lies, which is the set of tools and software needed to make data coming from sources storable.

We should note something here—we are not talking about data cleaning and data validation. Those activities will be performed later on by our data mining engine retrieving the data from our data warehouse. For the sake of exemplification, we can imagine having as a data source a set of physical books (it sounds old-fashioned, doesn't it?). Before actually performing any kind of data mining activity on it, we need to map this analogical data source to some kind of electronic representation of them.

This is where, within this example, the OCR technology comes in to help, giving us the opportunity to extract from the scan of a physical book all the words it contains. You can find some more information about this technology within the information box.

 Optical Character Recognition (OCR) is a group of data analysis techniques employed to derive from physical written documents their electronic transactions. These kinds of techniques apply to both hand-written and printed documents.

This preliminary activity is actually needed before you can feed your databases. Once your books are transformed into digital files, such as, for instance, `.txt` documents, you will be able to store them in a convenient form. It is now clear that the data cleaning activity you will later perform on it, such as, for instance, removing stop words such as `the`, `if`, and `similar`, is logically and chronologically separated from those preliminary ones.

Types of data sources

The example we introduced previously helps us to get a relevant classification within the realm of data sources that includes unstructured and structured data. This classification is a useful one since it allows us to quickly understand the kinds of possible data mining techniques we are going to leverage with the two kinds of data, and therefore define a first level of data modeling strategy (if you are unsure of what we intend to do with the data modeling strategy, you can look back for a moment at the *Modeling* section in Chapter 3, *The Data Mining Process - CRISP-DM Methodology*). In the following paragraph, we are going to have a closer look at the meaning of this classification.

Unstructured data sources

Unstructured data sources are data sources missing a logical data model. Whenever you find a data source where no particular logic and structure is defined to collect, store, and expose it, you are dealing with an unstructured data source. The best example we can provide of an unstructured data is a document full of words.

Within the document, you can actually find a lot of information. Nevertheless, that information is in some way disseminated within the whole document and there is no clear structure defining where each bit of information is stored.

As we will see in `Chapter 12`, *Looking for the Culprit – Text Data Mining with R*, there are some specific data modeling techniques that modelling extract valuable information from this kind of data, and even derive structured data from unstructured data. This kind of analysis is increasingly becoming more of interest, especially for companies, which are now able to analyze comments and feedback related to their products and derive synthetic statistics from them. This is the case with so-called social media listening, where companies catch different kinds of text on social media channels, subsequently analyzing them in order to get valuable information about their competitive position and the one of the competitors.

Structured data sources

Structured data sources are the one with a high degree of organization. These kinds of data sources follow a specific data model, and the engine which makes the storing activity is programmed to respect this model.

An R data frame is a typical example of structured data, where you can find columns and rows, and every column has a specific type of data among all records. A well-known data model behind structured data is the so-called relational model of data. Following this model, each table has to represent an entity within the considered universe of analysis. Each entity will then have a specific attribute within each column, and a related observation within each row. Finally, each entity can be related to the others through key attributes.

We can think of an example of a relational database of a small factory. Within this database, we have a table recording all customers orders and one table recording all shipments. Finally, a table recording the warehouse's movements will be included.

Within this database, we will have:

- The warehouse table linked to the shipment table through the `product_code` attribute
- The shipment table linked to the customer table through the `shipment_code` attribute

It can be easily seen that a relevant advantage of this model is the possibility to easily perform queries within tables, and merges between them. The cost to analyze structured data is far lower than the one to be considered when dealing with unstructured data.

Key issues of data sources

When dealing with data sources and planning their acquisition into your data warehouse, some specific aspects need to be considered:

- **Frequency of feeding**: Is the data updated with a frequency feasible for the scope of your data mining activity?
- **Volume of data**: Can the volume of data be handled by your system, or it is too much? This is often the case for unstructured data, which tends to occupy more space for a given piece of information.
- **Data format**: Is the data format readable by your data warehouse solution, and subsequently, by your data mining engine?

A careful evaluation of these three aspects has to be performed before implementing the data acquisition phase, to avoid relevant problems during the project.

Databases and data warehouses

It is now time to talk about the data warehouse and databases. We will have a look at their theoretical structure and some practical technology available on the market to build these kinds of instruments:

What is a data warehouse, and how is it different from a simple database?

A data warehouse is a software solution aimed at storing usually great amounts of data properly related among them and indexed through a time-related index. We can better understand this by looking at the data warehouse's cousin: the operational database.

These kinds of instruments are usually of small dimensions, and aimed at storing and inquiring data, overwriting old data when new data is available. Data warehouses are therefore usually fed by databases, and stores data from those kinds of sources ensuring a historical depth to them and read-only access from other users and software applications. Moreover, data warehouses are usually employed at a company level, to store, and make available, data from (and to) all company processes, while databases are usually related to one specific process or task.

The third wheel – the data mart

How do you use a data warehouse for your data mining project? Well, you are probably not going to use a data warehouse for your data mining process, while it will be made available of a data mart, which can be considered a partition or a sub-element of a data warehouse. The data marts are set of data that are feed directly from the data warehouse, and related to a specific company area or process. A real-life example is the data mart created to store data related to default events for the purpose of modeling customers probability of default.

This kind of data mart will collect data from different tables within the data warehouse, properly joining them into new tables that will not communicate with the data warehouse one. We can therefore consider the data mart as an extension of the data warehouse.

Data warehouses are usually classified into three main categories:

- One-level architecture where only a simple database is available and the data warehousing activity is performed by the mean of a virtual component
- Two-level architecture composed of a group of operational databases that are related to different activities, and a proper data warehouse is available
- Three-level architecture with one or more operational database, a reconciled database and a proper data warehouse

Let's now have a closer look to those three different alternatives.

One-level database

This is for sure the most simple and, in a way, primitive model. Within one level data warehouses, we actually have just one operational database, where data is written and read, mixing those two kinds of activities. A virtual data warehouse layer is then offered to perform inquiry activities. This is a primitive model for the simple reason that it is not able to warrant the appropriate level of segregation between live data, which is the one currently produced from the process, and historical data. This model could therefore produce inaccurate data and even a data loss episode.

This model would be particularly dangerous for data mining activity, since it would not ensure a clear segregation between the development environment and the production one.

Two-level database

This more sophisticated model encompasses a first level of operational databases, for instance, the one employed within marketing, production, and accounting processes, and a proper data warehouse environment. Within this solution, the databases are to be considered like feeding data sources, where the data is produced, possibly validated, and then made available to the data warehouse.

The data warehouse will then store and freeze data coming from databases, for instance, with a daily frequency.

Every set of data stored within a day will be labeled with a proper attribute showing the date of record. This will later allow us to retrieve records related to a specific time period in a sort of time machine functionality. Going back to our previous probability of default example, this kind of functionality will allow us to retrieve all default events that have occurred within a given time period, constituting the estimation sample for our model.

Two-level architecture is an optimal solution for data mining processes, since they will allow us to provide a safe environment, the previously mentioned data mart, to develop data mining activity, without compromising the quality of data residing within the remaining data warehouses and within the operational databases.

Three-level database

Three-level databases are the most advanced ones. The main difference between them and the two-level ones is the presence of the reconciliation stage, which is performed through **Extraction**, **Transformation**, and **Load** (**ETL**) instruments. To understand the relevance of such kinds of instruments, we can resort to a practical example once again, and to the one we were taking advantage of some lines previously: the probability of the default model.

Imagine we are estimating such kind of model for customers clustered as large corporate, for which public forecasts, outlooks and ratings are made available by financial analyses companies like Moody's, Standard & Poor, and similar.

Since this data could be reasonably related to the probability of default of our customers, we would probably be interested in adding them to our estimation database. This can be easily done through the mean of those ETL instruments. These instruments will ensure, within the reconciliation stage, that data gathered from internal sources, such as personal data and default events data, will be properly matched with the external information we have mentioned.

Moreover, even within internal data fields only, those instruments will ensure the needed level of quality and coherence among different sources, at least within the data warehouse environment.

Technologies

We are now going to look a bit more closely at the actual technology, most of which is open source, and developed to build data warehouse instruments. *What level of knowledge should you have of these technologies?* A proper awareness of their existence and main features should be enough, since, most of the time, you will be taking from them input data for your modeling activity by means of an interface provided by your programming language.

Nevertheless, as is the case with cars, knowing what is under the hood in case of a broken engine or need, for improvement is a very useful thing.

SQL

SQL stands for Structured Query Language, and identifies what has been for many years the standard within the field of data storage. The base for this programming language, employed for storing and querying data, are the so-called relational data bases. The theory behind these data bases was first introduced by IBM engineer Edgar F. Codd, and is based on the following main elements:

- Tables, each of which represent an entity
- Columns, each of which represent an attribute of the entity
- Rows, each one representing a record of the entity
- Key attributes, which permit us to relate two or more tables together, establishing relations between them

Starting from these main elements, SQL language provides a concise and effective way to query and retrieve this data. Moreover, basilar data munging operations, such as table merging and filtering, are possible through SQL language.

As previously mentioned, SQL and relational databases have formed the vast majority of data warehouse systems around the world for many, many years. A really famous example of SQL-based data storing products is the well-known Microsoft Access software. In this software, behind the familiar user interface, hide SQL codes to store, update, and retrieve user's data.

MongoDB

While SQL-based products are still very popular, NoSQL technology has been going for a long time now, showing its relevance and effectiveness. Behind this acronym stands all data storing and managing solutions not based on the relational paradigm and its main elements. Among this is the document-oriented paradigm, where data is represented as documents, which are complex virtual objects identified with some kind of code, and without a fixed scheme.

A popular product developed following this paradigm is **MongoDB**. This product stores data, representing it in the JSON format. Data is therefore organized into documents and collections, that is, a set of documents. A basic example of a document is the following:

```
{
name: "donald" , surname: "duck",
style: "sailor",
friends: ["mickey mouse" , "goofy", "daisy"]
}
```

As you can see, even from this basic example, the MongoDB paradigm will allow you to easily store data even with a rich and complex structure.

Hadoop

Hadoop is a leading technology within the field of data warehouse systems, mainly due to its ability to effectively handle large amounts of data. To maintain this ability, Hadoop fully exploits the concept of parallel computing by means of a central master that divides the all needed data related to a job into smaller chunks to be sent to two or more slaves. Those slaves are to be considered as nodes within a network, each of them working separately and locally. They can actually be physically separated pieces of hardware, but even core within a CPU (which is usually considered pseudo-parallel mode).

At the heart of Hadoop is the **MapReduce** programming model. This model, originally conceptualized by Google, consists of a processing layer, and is responsible for moving the data mining activity close to where data resides. This minimizes the time and cost needed to perform computation, allowing for the possibility to scale the process to hundreds and hundreds of different nodes.

The data mining engine

The data mining engine is the true heart of our data mining architecture. It consists of tools and software employed to gain insights and knowledge from data acquired from data sources, and stored within data warehouses.

What makes a data mining engine?

As you should be able to imagine at this point, a good data mining engine is composed of at least three components:

- An interpreter, able to transmit commands defined within the data mining engine to the computer
- Some kind of gear between the engine and the data warehouse to produce and handle communication in both directions
- A set of instructions, or algorithms, needed to perform data mining activities

We are going to look a bit closer at these three components, remembering that the most important one, the set of instructions, is actually the theme of the whole book, and will therefore be fully developed throughout all the remaining chapters.

The interpreter

We have actually already met this character before in our story; the interpreter is the one that carries out instructions coming from a higher-level programming language, translates them into instructions understandable from the piece of hardware it is running on, and transmits them to it. Obtaining the interpreter for the language you are going to perform data mining with is usually as simple as obtaining the language itself. In the case of our beloved R language, installing the language will automatically install the interpreter as well.

The interface between the engine and the data warehouse

If the interpreter was previously introduced, this interface we are talking about within this section is a new character within our story. The interface we are talking about here is a kind of software that enables your programming language to talk with the data warehouse solution you have been provided with for your data mining project.

To exemplify the concept, let's consider a setup adopting as a data mining engine, a bunch of R scripts, with their related interpreter, while employing an SQL-based database to store data. In this case, what would be the interface between the engine and the data warehouse?

It could be, for instance, the RODBC package, which is a well-established package designed to let R users connect to remote servers, and transfer data from those servers to their R session. By employing this package, it will also be possible to write data to your data warehouse.

This packages works exactly like a gear between the R environment and the SQL database. This means you will write your R code, which will then be translated into a readable language from the database and sent to him.

For sure, this translation also works the other way, meaning that results coming from your instructions, such as new tables of results from a query, will be formatted in a way that's readable from the R environment and conveniently shown to the user.

The data mining algorithms

This last element of the engine is the actual core topic of the book you are reading—the data mining algorithms. To help you gain an organic and systematic view of what we have learned so far, we can consider that these algorithms will be the result of the data modelling phase described in the previous chapter in the context of the CRISP-DM methodology description. This will usually not include code needed to perform basic data validation treatments, such as integrity checking and massive merging among data from different sources, since those kind of activities will be performed within the data warehouse environment. This will be especially true in cases of three-level data warehouses, which have a dedicated reconciliation layer.

Apart from that, the mentioned algorithms will encompass all kinds of activities needed to gain knowledge from available data, and communicate this knowledge. This means that not only the actual estimation of statistical models like the one we are going to look through Chapters 8, *A Gentle Introduction to Model Performance Evaluation* to Chapter 12, *Looking for the Culprit – Text Data Mining with R* will be included within the engine, but also reporting activities like the one treated on Chapter 13, *Sharing Your Stories with Your Stakeholders through R Markdown*.

User interface

Until now, we have been looking at the back office of our data mining architecture, which is the part not directly visible to its end user. Imagine this architecture is provided to be employed by someone not skilled enough to work on the data mining engine itself; we will need some way to let this user interact with the architecture in the right way, and discover the results of its interaction. This is what a user interface is all about.

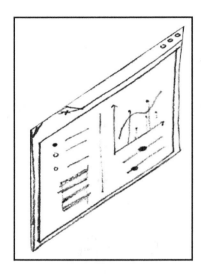

In times when data mining is getting more and more popular every day, a big question is how to make it accessible to a great portion of professionals not classifiable as programmers and statisticians. This is where the user interfaces play a big role.

Even if user interface design is beyond the scope of this book, let's discover some well-established principles of good user interface design, so that you can apply them to evaluate alternative user interfaces and products you could come across on your data mining journey.

Clarity

This principle is the prominent one in UI design theory. If a UI is clear, you can easily understand what it was designed for, what you can do with it, and how to do it. Have you ever been blocked from looking at a web page or piece of software for several minutes, without understanding how it was supposed to work? Maybe it was cozy, full of controls, texts, and colors which did not suggest any path or flow to follow.

What did you to with that web page or software? I can be pretty sure you abandoned it, concluding it could not be a useful resource if you could not even understand how to use it.

This short exemplification clearly explains to you how relevant clarity is in design: we as humans tend to be discouraged by things we do not understand how to use.

Clarity and mystery

This must not be confused with mystery, which is a well-known principle of teaching and design as well. Humans love mystery and incremental learning, situations where we discover step-by-step something new we did not know before. This tends to fascinate us. But to create a sense of mystery, you will have to clearly communicate or suggest a path, and possibly even a final result or objective, clearly focusing the attention of the user to it.

Clarity and simplicity

A great way to obtain clarity is to look for simplicity. We already had a look at this while talking about data visualization in the second chapter. Simplicity implies reasoning on the main purpose of something, and removing everything that is unnecessary for this purpose, as it means removing all unnecessary things. Simplicity is the secret of nature, where every part is necessary and not redundant, and even beauty has its own purpose.

Efficiency

Efficiency is definitely a principle you should consider when evaluating a user interface. You can apply it in answering the following question: *how many steps you need to perform to reach the objective you want to reach with the product?* To make it more real, let's imagine evaluating a data mining tool, and particularly, its data import feature. Evaluating the efficiency of the tool in this regard would involve answering the following question: *how many steps do I need to perform to import a dataset into my data mining environment?*

This would probably involve evaluating if any kind of unnecessary step is placed within the path and, on the opposite side, if any kind of useful mechanism of automatic guessing is applied. To go on with this example, we could cite something at this point that should be well-known to us—the `rio` package. This package, which we have encountered before, has a really efficient (and perhaps clear) user interface; it just asks you to apply a single function, `import()`, to your dataset file, autonomously carrying on all following activities to import it into your data mining environment.

This example also helps us understand the wide meaning of user interface as a term that actually encompasses everything the user comes in to contact with when working with a given product.

Consistency

Have you ever wondered why, from time to time, it seems some kind of design waves start from a website and spread all around? This was the case, for instance, with flat design. After a long period of software design, trying to reproduce our real 3D environment, everything on the web started to appear flat, without shades and potentially pastel colored.

Why did that happen? Why did such so many different brains change their minds so suddenly? Was 3D some kind of fashion which changed at a given time, as all fashions do? There was, for sure, some kind of fashion effect on the spreading of flat design; nevertheless, the consistency principle applied here as well. After starting to see the flat design on some of your products, and particularly your most beloved ones, you started expecting this design on all your other products. Moreover, you, me, and all other users like us started feeling uncomfortable with websites and products with different kinds of design. It is like the feeling you get when having to drive an old car after a long time; yeah, I can make it drive me where I want, but why does it have to be that difficult? In that context you have to, in some way, re-learn a bit about how to drive, since everything you are familiar with is there in the car but in a slightly different position or appearance. This increases your learning costs and diminishes your perceived effectiveness.

This is exactly the same effect that justifies the spreading of flat design: once you got used to it, you started feeling as expensive to adapt to different kinds of designs, and since the majority of the users starte experiencing the same feeling, this pushed all the remaining products to adopt flat design as well. Whether or not this was an overall improvement should be evaluated by resorting to the previously introduced principles of clarity and efficiency.

How do we apply this principle to data mining user interfaces? We can do this reasoning about some bigger and smaller features data mining software users are currently used to. For instance, as two small examples; syntax highlights and auto-completion.

Syntax highlight

This is a very common feature that will help us understand the principle of consistency. It consists of the ability of a data mining tool to understand the syntax of a piece of code, consequently assigning common colors to tokens pertaining to the same logical role into the code. For instance, syntax highlight into R will be highlighted with a same color if and else tokens since they are logically linked within a conditional statement.

Since it is a really useful and common feature, we would feel pleased to find it on a new data mining tool we might come across. The absence of this feature would force us to recall to memory a lot of information we tend to forget due to the help given by the feature, and this would increase our learning costs. This would, therefore, diminish the net value assigned to the tool:

```
#' @importFrom xml2 read_html
#' @importFrom rvest html_nodes
#' @importFrom rvest html_text
#' @importFrom utils download.file
#' @title Downloads and installs the latest version of R for Mac OS X.
#' @description Update your version of R from inside R itself (Mac OS X only).
#' @param admin_password \code{character}. The system-wide password of the user. The parameter will be only employed
to execute commands gaining administrator privileges on the computer and will not be stored anywhere.
#' @author Andrea Cirillo, Robert Myles McDonnell
#' @examples
#' updateR(admin_password = "****")
#' @export
updateR <- function(admin_password = NULL){

  # first test for on OS
  stopifnot(.Platform$OS.type == "unix")
  # test for password
  if(is.null(admin_password)){
    stop("User system password is missing")
  }

  page_source = "https://cran.rstudio.com/bin/macosx/"

  file <- xml2::read_html(page_source) %>%
    rvest::html_nodes("h1+ p a+ a , table:nth-child(8) tr:nth-child(1) td > a") %>%
    rvest::html_text() %>% strsplit("\n", fixed = TRUE) %>%
    .[[2]]

  stopifnot(grepl(".pkg", file) == TRUE)
  url <- paste0(page_source, file)

  # download package, set folder for download
  download.file(url, file)

  #install .pkg file
  pkg <- gsub("\\.pkg" , "", file)
  message(paste0("Installing ", pkg, "...please wait"))
  command <- paste0("echo ", admin_password, " | sudo -S installer -pkg ",
                    "", file, "", " -target /")
  system(command, ignore.stdout = TRUE, ignore.stderr = TRUE)

  arg <- paste0("--check-signature ", file)
  system2("pkgutil", arg)

  x <- system2("R", args = "--version", stdout = TRUE)
  x <- x[1]

  message(paste0("Everything went smoothly, R was updated to ", x))
}
```

Auto-completion

The same applies to code auto-completion. A basic example of this feature is the addition of the closing parenthesis when typing the opening one. A more sophisticated method is the addition of all the basic structures of the function definition, just after typing the `function` token. Again, this feature tends to make us forget basic semantic rules, such as how to define a function, and its absence would increase our learning costs.

If those costs would be higher than the perceived value of the tool, we would discard it, looking for something more familiar that will better meet our needs.

How to build a data mining architecture in R

Until now, we have been treating the data mining architecture topic at a general level, defining its components and their role within the system; but how do we build such kinds of architecture in R? This is what we are going to discover here. At the end of the paragraph, you will then be able not just to understand how a data mining architecture is composed but even how to build one for your own purposes.

To be clear, we have to specify from the beginning here that we are not going to build a firm-wide data mining architecture, but rather a small architecture like the ones needed to develop your first data mining projects with R. Once this is set, we can proceed with looking at each of the aforementioned components and how to implement them with our beloved R language.

Data sources

As seen earlier, this is where everything begins: *the data*. R is well-known for being able to treat different kinds of data coming from a great variety of data sources. This is due to the flexibility we described in the first chapter. The R language is open to be expanded into every direction by means of its packages. When dealing with new data mining projects, you should therefore ask yourself—what kind of data I am going to handle for this project?

Is the data already residing on the web? Is the data still stored on the old and reliable paper? Is it just recorded sounds or images? Resorting to the CRISP-DM methodology, this is part of our business understanding phase. Once we have got this point clear, we can surf one of the most useful pages within the R website—the **CRAN Task View**, at: `cran.r-project.org/web/views`.

Within this page, you can find a list of pages each of which relate to a specific task that can be performed with R. For instance, you will find pages for natural language processing, medical image analysis, and similar great things.

Once you have found the page related to the kind of data you are going to acquire into your data mining architecture, you can surf to it and discover all the available packages developed to perform the given task. Those pages are really useful due to the good maintenance activity performed on them, and their well-articulated content.

What if no page arises for your specific kind of data?

You have at least three more roads to put yourself through, ordered by effort required:

- Look for tasks that are not exactly treating the data you will be facing, but something close to them, and could therefore be useful (at the price of a small amount of customization)
- Look outside the CRAN Task View for packages recently developed or still under development, and therefore not included in CRAN and in the CRAN Task View
- Develop the code required for data acquisition by yourself

Now that we have hopefully discovered how to import our data into R, we can move on to the data warehouse step, and where to store the data once it is acquired.

The data warehouse

We have to be honest—R was not originally designed for handling great amounts of data. It was actually an instrument conceived for being employed within the academic world, where having fifty points of data, especially at that time, was some kind of miraculous event. From this admission comes the observation that R is not naturally provided with the right features for heavy data handling. Nevertheless, we can once again leverage here the great flexibility of our beloved language by means of a package developed to establish a communication between R and some of the most popular data warehouse solutions, such as those previously mentioned, MongoDB and Hadoop. Having these packages at your disposal, such as `mongolite` or `rhdfs`, will give you the possibility to leverage the related Data Warehouse solution within your data mining project. In the hypothesis of being leveraging data already stored within your company, research lab or university, this will also mean to have the possibility to directly access them.

The data mining engine

This component will, for sure, be the one in which R will shine up the most, showing all its great data mining power. Leveraging this language, you will be able to apply the most advanced data mining techniques and models to your data. Getting closer to the topic, while no question arises about the interpreter to be employed, we can invest a few more words regarding the other two components of a data mining engine:

- The interface between the engine and the data warehouse
- The data mining algorithms

The interface between the engine and the data warehouse

We actually already treated this topic within the data warehouse discussion: the interface between the engine and the DW solution will be constituted from packages like the ones introduced previously. To give a more practical view of this point, we can go on with the probability of default example defined earlier. Imagine having a company data warehouse storing all relevant information needed for your modeling activity: default event, anagraphical data, and other attributes. Imagine this data warehouse being developed on a MongoDB instance. You will, in this case, probably need a specific script containing all code used to establish a connection with MongoDB through the `mongolite` package. This package could also include all the data wrangling activity needed to create a complete table to be employed as a proper estimation sample, such as joining and merging procedures. In this way, the script will serve you as an interface between the data warehouse and your data mining engine.

The data mining algorithms

Our last step to building a data mining engine in R is the actual development of the data mining algorithms. Depending on the kind of project you will be working on, and its end user, these algorithms will be applied either just once or will be made available for further use in subsequent analyses. As you may be guessing, we are not going to get into the details here of those algorithms, since they will constitute the main topic of the book.

The user interface

Finally, the user interface. Before bringing this topic into the world of R, we should distinguish between two different data mining projects:

- The ones having a final user, its developer, and are usually developed to be use once just to obtain and share some kind of result
- The ones developed to be recursively employed from some other end user, to obtain new results not defined from the developer, which can be seen as standalone software

Depending on which of the two data mining projects we are facing, the user interface will be a different one:

- In the case of the first kind of project, we will face the user interface of our data mining engine and particularly of the IDE, we will be using to write and execute our scripts, like the ones introduced in the first chapter. In its most basic form, it could even be the safe and sound R interactive console.
- In the case of projects developed to be recursively ployed from some other end user, the Shiny framework appears to be a really convenient choice to develop a proper user interface.

The shiny framework, in its most basic form, consists of a package providing R functions able to initialize HTML and Java-based web pages, taking input from the user further employed to run R code and transmit its output back to the user. The great advantage of this product is that it is completely R-based and does not require the developer to learn any other language to deploy its data mining software to the end user.

We will see more of this in Chapter 13, *Sharing Your Stories with Your Stakeholders through R Markdown*, where we are talking about R markdown documents.

Further references

- **On the RODBC package:** https://support.rstudio.com/hc/en-us/articles/214510788-Setting-up-R-to-connect-to-SQL-Server-
- **On using R with Hadoop:** https://github.com/RevolutionAnalytics/RHadoop/wiki
- **On the mongolite package:** https://datascienceplus.com/using-mongodb-with-r/

Summary

By the end of this chapter, you may feel like the adrenaline accumulated within the first two has got a bit diluted, but you would be wrong. This chapter was all about discovering the basic ingredients of a well-conceived and well-conducted data mining project, namely:

- The data sources (where to find data to answer your questions)
- The data warehouse (where to properly store your data to have it at your disposal when needed)
- The data mining engine (to perform your data modelling activities, and get knowledge from your data)
- The user interface (to interact with your engine)

We are now ready to leave the quiet village where our apprentice took place, where we discovered our weapon, its power and the way to use it. A real and complex problem is waiting for us just on the next page. Good luck, my dear reader.

5
How to Address a Data Mining Problem – Data Cleaning and Validation

This chapter is where our real journey begins (finally!, I can hear you exclaiming). We are now familiar enough with R and the data mining process and architecture to get involved with a real problem.

I say real problem I actually mean real, since we are going to face something that actually happened and that actually puzzled a non-trivial number of people in a real company. Of course, we are going to use randomized dataF here and fictitious names, nevertheless, this will not remove any pathos to the problem. We are shortly going to get immersed into some kind of mystery that actually came up, and we will need to solve it, employing data mining techniques.

I know you may be thinking: *OK, don't make it too serious, is it something which actually already got solved? You would be right, but what if something similar pops up for you some day in the future?* What would you do? The mystery we are going to face will not be presented in the typical way: here is a table, apply models to it, and tell us which fits best. This is not how things usually work in real life. We will just be provided with news about a problem and some unstructured data to look at, asking for an answer.

Are you ready? Do you need to look back at the previous pages? No problem, I will wait for you here.

On a quiet day

It's a nice day today, you get into your 6th-floor office at *Hippalus, Wholesaler Inc*, grab a coffee, and sit down at your desk. Suddenly, an email pops in your inbox: *Urgent - profits drop*. As soon as the meaning of those three words is clear to you, you realize that everybody in the office has received the same email and they are starting to chat about it, there will be a meeting with the head of the office in 15 minutes. When you get into the meeting room, still missing the coffee you left at your desk, a big chart is projected on the wall:

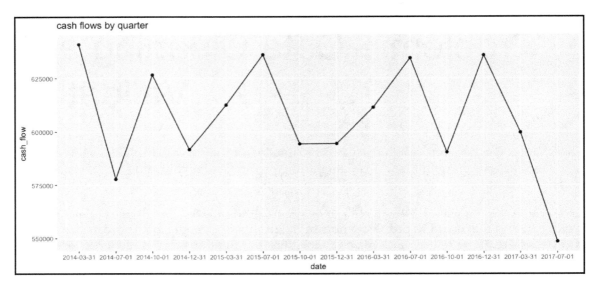

OK, you have just read `Chapter 2`, *A First Primer on Data Mining - Analysing Your Banking Account Data* so you know it is a line chart, and that we are looking at a time series, but no title is included so we can just observe the incredible drop at the end of the series. *Whoa, those are our quarterly cash flows*, says the astonished colleague sitting next to you.

How did we get that low?, replies back the one sitting on your other side. This is when your head of office starts his speech: *Thank you for coming. As you may have noticed, this is a chart showing how we did in the last three years in terms of profits. We have actually had some good times so far, but within this last quarter something went wrong, we have got a 50% drop in our cash flows. The CEO asked us to investigate causes and remedial actions. As you know, we can still not leverage our incoming data mining architecture and therefore we will have to do it the old fashioned way.*

What data do we have to investigate this issue?

Cash flow reports, customer lists, and records about some attributes of those customers.

OK, so we have a list of customers, reports about cash flow incoming, and some tables tracking attributes of those customers. What would you do next?

We are going to proceed by priorities: first of all we need to understand where this drop came from, we are going to perform some EDA on the data to see if there is some market or portfolio originating this big drop.

What is EDA? We will discover it within the next chapter, there's not too long to wait.

Once this is set up, we will apply some data mining techniques to derive an affordable model showing the most relevant causes of this cash shortage. But the first real task is to get the data clean and usable. To do this I need your help, [your name here].

Yeah, he called your name, so you are going to do some data cleaning and validation, lucky you!

This is a crucial task since we are not going to get that much from our data if its quality is low or it is poorly arranged. We have got no more than half a day to do this data cleaning activity. I will send you an email with the data we have. We will meet back here in five hours. Thank you all, and good job.

So, we have five hours to clean this data. You sit back at your desk, grab your coffee, which is now almost cold, and the promised email pops in: *Dirty data.* Not a great subject...

We have exactly the promised data:

- A cash flow report in a `.csv` format, with a side note: *quarterly sales reports by geographic area from 2014 to II Q current year. All data in Euro currency.*
- A customer list in a `.txt` format, and another side note: *list of our customers and some other data. Customers from 2013 on.*
- A table of other records in an `rds` format paired with the following note: *records related to our customers, merged from different databases during the current year. Every data should be recorded once for each customer.*

You can actually find the email attachment in the package associated with this book, named `dirty data.zip`. How would you proceed to clean your data?

Data cleaning

First of all, we need to actually import the data to our R environment (oh yeah, I was taking for granted that we are going to use R for this, hope you do not mind).

We can leverage our old friend the `rio` package, running it on all of the three files we were provided, once we have unzipped them. Take a minute to figure out if you can remember the function needed to perform the task.

Done? OK, find the solution as follows:

```
cash_flow_report  <- import("cash_flow.csv")
customer_list     <- import("customer_list.txt")
stored_data       <- import("stored_data.rds")
```

Tidy data

Before actually looking at our data, we should define how we want it to be arranged in order to allow for future manipulation and analyses. Currently, one of the most adopted frameworks for data arrangement and handling is the so called `tidy data` framework. The concepts behind this framework were originally defined by *Hadley Wickham,* and nowadays come paired with a couple of R packages that help to apply it to your data.

But taking it a step at a time: what is tidy data? In the words of its conceive, tidy data is data arranged in tables where:

- Each variable forms a column
- Each observation forms a row
- Each type of observational unit forms a table

As you may be wondering, these concepts are somehow related with the ones we talked about when dealing with the SQL language. This is clearly declared by Hadley himself, who introduces the tidy data framework as *The relational database theory framed in a way familiar to statistician and focused on single tables rather than groups of tables.*

Look, for instance, at the following table:

city	date	temperature
london	june_2016	15
london	july_2016	18
london	august_2016	19
london	september_2016	18
moscow	june_2016	17
moscow	july_2016	20
moscow	august_2016	19
moscow	september_2016	11
new_york	june_2016	22
new_york	july_2016	26
new_york	august_2016	26
new_york	september_2016	23
rome	june_2016	23
rome	july_2016	27
rome	august_2016	26
rome	september_2016	22

Is it tidy? Let's check one rule at the time. Does it have every column showing only one attribute/variable? Yes it does, since there is no column having more than one variable recorded, as would be the case for an instance with a column showing alternatively temperature and weather.

Does each observation form a row? Once more, we have to answer with a sound yes, since every row shows a distinct date and record.

Finally, does each type of observational unit form a table? To be honest, we do not have enough elements to be sure of this, since only one table is shown and we do not even know which is the topic of analysis. Nevertheless, we can positively confirm that the reproduced table shows an autonomous observational unit, which for the purpose of this example will be considered enough to confirm the third and last rule.

We have therefore just met our first tidy table. Let's get back to our data and face the question I am sure has already popped up in your mind: is our data tidy?

Analysing the structure of our data

When you first get your hands on some data in R, there are a couple of functions that can help you get confident with it. We have already met some of them along the first step of our trip, but it is now time to get a proper introduction.

The str function

Once you understand that the `str` stands for **structure**, you understand that this function helps you get a clear description of attributes and hierarchies within your data. Let's try to run it on the three datasets we are dealing with:

```
str(cash_flow_report)
str(customer_list)
str(stored_data)
```

Can you see the result? For `cash_flow_report` we have:

```
'data.frame': 84 obs. of 3 variables:
 $ x : chr "north_america" "south_america" "asia" "europe" ...
 $ y : chr "2014-03-31" "2014-03-31" "2014-03-31" "2014-03-31" ...
 $ cash_flow: num 100956 111817 132019 91369 109864 ...
```

While `customer_list` gives us:

```
'data.frame':    148555 obs. of  3 variables:
 $ customer_code     : num  1 2 3 4 5 6 7 8 9 10 ...
 $ commercial_portfolio: chr  "less affluent" "less affluent" "less
affluent" "less affluent" ...
 $ business_unit     : chr  "retail_bank" "retail_bank" "retail_bank"
"retail_bank" ...
```

And finally, our `stored_data` results in :

```
'data.frame':       891330 obs. of  9 variables:
 $ attr_3       : num  0 0 0 0 0 0 0 0 0 0 ...
 $ attr_4       : num  0 0 0 0 0 0 0 0 0 0 ...
 $ attr_5       : num  0 0 0 0 0 0 0 0 0 0 ...
 $ attr_6       : num  0 0 0 0 0 0 0 0 0 0 ...
 $ attr_7       : num  0 0 0 0 0 0 0 0 0 0 ...
 $ default_flag : Factor w/ 3 levels "?","0","1": 1 1 1 1 1 1 1 1 1 1 ...
 $ customer_code: num  1 2 3 4 5 6 7 8 9 10 ...
 $ parameter    : chr  "attr_8" "attr_8" "attr_8" "attr_8" ...
 $ value        : num  NA NA -1e+06 -1e+06 NA NA NA -1e+06 NA -1e+06 ...
```

We therefore have for each and every dataset the list of columns, their type (`num` and `Factor` here), and the first ten records. We will evaluate at the end of these paragraphs the level of tidiness of our data, nevertheless you can already think about it: consider the three tidy data rules introduced previously and try to figure out which of the three data frames, if any, respects them.

The describe function

`describe` is the real king of the hill when dealing with data structure description. This function is not one of the built-in functions, but rather it comes from the well crafted `Hmisc` package, created by Professor Frank E Harrell Jr. Running this function on our data will let us not only get a view of its structure, but also discover the range of variability of each and every column.

Just install and load the `Hmisc` package and apply the function over `customer_list` to get an idea of this powerful function:

```
library(Hmisc)
describe(customer_list)

customer_list

 3  Variables      148555  Observations
--------------------------------------------------------------------------
----------------------
customer_code
      n missing  unique    Info    Mean     .05     .10     .25     .50
.75     .90     .95
 148555       0  148555       1   74278    7429   14856   37140   74278
111416  133700  141127

 lowest :      1      2      3      4      5, highest: 148551 148552 148553
```

```
148554 148555
-----------------------------------------------------------------------
----------------------
commercial_portfolio
       n missing  unique
  148555        0       3

 less affluent (145940, 98%), mass affluent (1557, 1%)
 more affluent (1058, 1%)
-----------------------------------------------------------------------
----------------------
business_unit
       n missing  unique
  148555        0       2

 corporate_bank (11288, 8%), retail_bank (137267, 92%)
-----------------------------------------------------------------------
----------------------
```

Looking at the output of the `describe` function, we can easily see the range of variability of our variables, shown in a convenient way based on the data type. While for instance quantile distribution is shown for `customer_code` since it is numeric, the frequency table is printed out for the `business_unit` attribute, which is a categorical one.

Why should we use `str()` if we have `describe()`, you may be wondering?

It is a matter of use cases, sometimes you just want to have a really quick look at your data without getting into greater details. This is when `str()` can be of help, it has a small output and shows information that is easy to get. While, if you are looking for more detailed descriptive statistics of your data, `describe()` should be the solution to go with.

head, tail, and View functions

You now know a lot about your data, but you still think that you are not seeing it face to face. Fortunately, R comes with three functions able to satisfy even this desire: `head`, `tail`, and `View`. The first two of them are conceived to show you within the console the first and the last *n* rows of your data, while the third one produces a spreadsheet-like visualization of all of your data frames, which will open in a separate window. Within `head` and `tail`, the default number of rows to be shown is equal to five, but you can tune this using the *n* argument.

As you may be already guessing, to apply the `head` and `tail` functions you just have to run them on your object, for instance:

```
head(customer_list)
```

This will result in:

```
  customer_code    commercial_portfolio    business_unit
1    1              less affluent           retail_bank
2    2              less affluent           retail_bank
3    3              less affluent           retail_bank
4    4              less affluent           retail_bank
5    5              less affluent           retail_bank
6    6              less affluent           retail_bank
```

Running `View()` on them (be aware of the capital V) will create the following window, or a similar one if not employing RStudio:

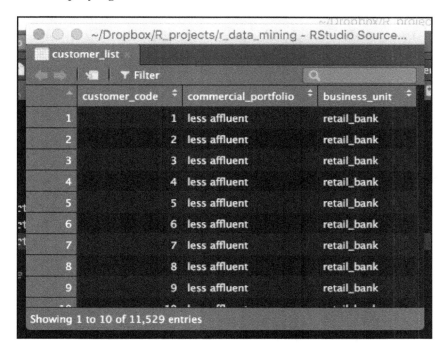

Try to apply those three functions to your data before skipping to the next paragraph. This will let you get a good understanding of what the content of the three tables is, helping you to answer the questions we are soon going to face.

Evaluating your data tidiness

Now that we have acquired a good comprehension of how our data is structured and populated, we can try to address the fundamental question: is our data tidy?

Starting with the first one, go over the three basic questions:

1. Does every column contain an attribute?
2. Does every row contain an observation?
3. Does the table represent just one observational unit?

Answering these questions, we can easily see that the first two tables are structured in an ideal way, since we have one different combination of customer and month within the first table, while the second table shows a different customer for every row, reporting ordered attributes within each column.

What about the third table? I know that since I am questioning about this table separately from the other two you are already guessing it is not a tidy table, but why would you say that? Let's take a closer look at each of the three rules and how they apply to the `stored_data` table.

Every row is a record

What does this rule exactly mean? To get it right we have to start from the context—*what are we recording?* We can resort to the side note comparing the dataset to get a hint: *records related to our customers, merged from different databases during the current year.* Nice, so these are records related to our customers, recorded during the year. Going on reading, we find: *every data should be recorded once for each customer.* This is quite clear, every customer should have every attribute recorded once. Therefore, we can conclude that every record should refer to one customer. Is this the case with the current structure of our data?

We want to see if every record refers to one customer, and therefore we want to see if every customer is shown once or more within our table. We can easily do this thanks to the `unique()` function, which takes a vector as an input and gives as output a vector of the unique values reproduced within the first one. Here is what we are going to do, take our `customer_code` variable and measure its length (observe how many elements are stored within it). Then we are going to obtain a vector showing the unique values within `customer_code` and we are going to measure it. If the two lengths are equal, our rule will be respected, otherwise we will conclude it is broken:

```
stored_data$customer_code %>%
  length()
```

This will result in `891.330` being printed out, which means our table has 891.330 rows (if you are unfamiliar with the `%>%` token, take another look at `Chapter 2`, *A First Primer on Data Mining - Analysing Your Banking Account Data* where we talked about the pipe operator). It is now time to apply the `unique()` function and measure again the resulting vector:

```
stored_data$customer_code %>%
  unique() %>%
  length()
```

This will print out 148.555, one sixth of the original size. How can it be? We will have to find this out, but meanwhile we have our first relevant evidence: our data is not tidy.

Of course we can not stop here, and we need to better understand how our data is not tidy. Let's move to the second rule to try and gain a clearer view on this.

Every column shows an attribute

What's in a name? Yeah, I know this is Shakespeare, nevertheless it is worth mentioning it here: *what is an attribute? How would you define it?* Just to start approximating, we can say that an attribute is something that describes a specific feature of our entity. From this, we can see that every column should show data related to just one feature of our customer, since we have seen previously that every record should be related to one single customer and no repetition should occur.

Since we already know that our customers are shown more than once within the dataset, we can infer that somewhere a column is showing more than one feature. But how can we be sure about it?

Let's have a look back to the structure of our data:

```
'data.frame': 891330 obs. of 9 variables:
$ attr_3 : num 0 0 0 0 0 0 0 0 0 0 ...
$ attr_4 : num 0 0 0 0 0 0 0 0 0 0 ...
$ attr_5 : num 0 0 0 0 0 0 0 0 0 0 ...
$ attr_6 : num 0 0 0 0 0 0 0 0 0 0 ...
$ attr_7 : num 0 0 0 0 0 0 0 0 0 0 ...
$ default_flag : Factor w/ 3 levels "?","0","1": 1 1 1 1 1 1 1 1 1 1 ...
$ customer_code: num 1 2 3 4 5 6 7 8 9 10 ...
$ parameter : chr "attr_8" "attr_8" "attr_8" "attr_8" ...
$ value : num NA NA -1e+06 -1e+06 NA NA NA -1e+06 NA -1e+06 ...
```

We can see that the first five columns are named `attr_3`, `attr_4`, and so on (what attributes are they? I don't know, we will ask someone in the office later), then we find a `default_flag` column and a familiar `customer_code` column. Can you see the next column? It has quite a mysterious name, `parameter`, and it appears to be populated with repetitions of `attr_8`. But we should not let the first rows bias our ideas, are we sure that only `attr_8` is in there? What would you do to gain some more information on this?

We can employ once more the `unique()` function, and this will result in:

```
stored_data$parameter %>% unique()
[1] "attr_8"  "attr_9"  "attr_10" "attr_11" "attr_12" "attr_13"
```

Here we are, a full bouquet of attributes was hiding within that mysterious label. This is relevant, but as far as I can see those are just labels, where are the actual values of our attributes? We could have found something such as eye color, height, and number of sons, but where should we look to find the number of sons for the given customer? Just one column is missing, and we should definitely check it out: the `value` column (I know, it is not very original, I could actually change this in future editions of the book). What do we find in there? Our `str()` function tells us the following:

```
num NA NA -1e+06 -1e+06 NA NA NA -1e+06 NA -1e+06 ...
```

Which is not actually that much, but at least it lets us understand that there are some numbers in there. Things are much clearer now, some attributes are in good order in separate columns, while some others are melted within one column. This is probably due to the fact that this table was obtained by merging together different data sources, as we were made aware of from the side note, as is often the case with industrial data.

Even the second rule is broken, what about the third?

Every table represents an observational unit

To be honest, this represents the less bold of the three rules, and its meaning is never easy to specify. Nevertheless, assuming that the first two broken rules will be fixed, we can imagine that our dataset will show all data pertaining to one observational unit, which is our group of customers, and therefore we can say that this law has been respected.

Tidying our data

While you are smiling to your monitor, happy to have found out that two tables are tidy and one is not, a colleague passes through, asking: *How is it going here? Did you fix this data? Time is running out and the boss wants to close this cleaning phase before twelve.* The colleague definitely got the point: we are now sure that one table is dirty, but our task actually involves cleaning them! Since we are already chatting with our colleague, why not ask for some clarification about the meaning of `attr_1`, `attr_2`, and so on? Our colleague responds: *Those labels? I should have some transcoded tables in an old email, I will have a look and let you know. Nice, this should be fixed hopefully.*

We can get back to our work now and face that hard question: how do we clean our `stored_data` table?

The tidyr package

As is often the case, the one who found the problem also proposed a solution: after defining the problem of untidy data, Hadley Wickham also developed the `tidyr` package, whose explicit purpose is to make your untidy data tidy. This is done by employing a reasoning similar to the one we met with `diplyr`, that is, using verbs. We will have a look at them within the following paragraphs, and once they are clear to us, we will leverage them to untie our dataset. Before we actually get into this, we should introduce a third different way of looking at table structure: long versus wide data.

Long versus wide data

Long/wide dichotomy is actually another way of expressing something we already met when talking about relational databases and tidy data, but it is nevertheless useful to introduce it here since it is the conceptual framework that was employed to develop the `tidyr` verbs we are going to face soon.

The first point that helps to get this concept right is to think of the shape of the table:

- A long table will be much longer than it is wide
- A wide table will be much wider than it is long

The two tables are carrying the same information, but how can it be possible? It is actually because of the way variables are treated within the two kinds of tables. Within a long table, all attributes are shown separately and form a different column, and this produces all the information recorded for a given attribute to be shown along the vertical dimension. Within a wide form, you instead have a combination of different variables in columns, which will increase the number of columns, and therefore make the table wider than it is long. We can visualize this starting from the table we have already met when talking about tidy data, showing temperature and weather for a set of dates and cities. I will avoid you having to skip back to the beginning by reproducing it here:

City	Date	Temperature
london	june_2016	15
london	july_2016	18
london	august_2016	19
london	september_2016	18
moscow	june_2016	17
moscow	july_2016	20
moscow	august_2016	19
moscow	september_2016	11
new_york	june_2016	22
new_york	july_2016	26
new_york	august_2016	26
new_york	september_2016	23
rome	june_2016	23
rome	july_2016	27
rome	august_2016	26
rome	september_2016	22

How could we make it wide? One way could be to arrange the date-temperature information into columns labeled as `may-2016-temperature`, `June-2016-temperature`, and so on. Within each cell corresponding to a given city you would then have to represent the temperature. Here is how it will show up:

city	august_2016	july_2016	june_2016	september_2016
london	19	18	15	18
moscow	19	20	17	11
new_york	26	26	22	23
rome	26	27	23	22

This example helps us understand what `tidyr` is for, arranging long data into wide and wide into long. Before actually looking at the two verbs it provides to accomplish this task, we should mention that, following the previously introduced relational database framework and the tidy data framework, long form is to be considered as the preferred one. But why is it that way? Three classical arguments come to hand here:

- If you have attributes with an extended domain, for instance a lot of dates, showing them along different columns would make the table really wide and therefore difficult to see at a glance.
- The long form makes it clearer as to what the observational units of analysis are.
- If you are going to apply some modelling techniques to your data, you will probably need to have every variable as a separate unit. How could you describe the weather as a function of time employing the wide table reproduced previously? You should restructure it before being able to do it.

Now that you are aware, hopefully, of the positives of working with long data, let's have a look at how to exchange between the two formats by employing the `spread` and `gather` functions. Finally, we will have a look at a third verb provided by `tidyr`, the `separate` one, which helps to create multiple columns from a single one.

The spread function

spread does exactly what it promises—spreads data along columns. It takes tables expressed in the long form and makes them wide. To see how it works, we can once again use the table previously used, showing cities and their temperatures for a bunch of dates. Let's recreate it with some lines of code:

```
city <- c(rep("london",4),rep("moscow",4),rep("new_york",4), rep("rome",4))
date <- c(rep(c("june_2016","july_2016","august_2016","september_2016"),4))
temperature <- c(15,18,19,18,17,20,19,11,22,26,26,23,23,27,26,22) #source :
wunderground.com
temperature_table <- data.frame(city,date,temperature)
```

You should now be familiar with vector and data frame creation. Nevertheless, you can always go back to Chapter 1, *Why to Choose R for Your Data Mining and Where to Start*; if any doubts arise.

What the spread function requires in order to work is the identification of one key column and one value column:

- The key column is the one used to label the multiple columns we are going to create. Within our example, the key column will be the date column, since we want to spread this attribute in a wide form.
- The value column is the one showing the value we are going to employ to populate the newly created columns. As you may be guessing, within our example it will be constituted from the temperature one.

These two are the only two arguments of the spread function that are to be considered mandatory, since no default value is provided for them and therefore running the function without providing them will raise an error. One more argument you should be aware of when dealing with this function is the fill function. Imagine that no temperature was recorded during July 2016 in London. This would not result in a problem while we are in the long form, since it would just translate into one missing row. What about the wide form we are going to create? How should the cell corresponding to the month of July 2016 for the city of London be filled? This is exactly what the fill argument takes care of.

Let's give the function a try, passing *date* and *temperature* as key and value:

```
temperature_table %>%
  spread(key = date, value= temperature)-> wide_temperature
```

Running these two lines of code will results in the following:

	city	august_2016	july_2016	june_2016	september_2016
1	london	19	18	15	18
2	moscow	19	20	17	11
3	new_york	26	26	22	23
4	rome	26	27	23	22

This is what we were looking for: a wide table from the long one we had.

The gather function

Even if we are probably going to look a bit crazy, by employing the `gather` function we are now going to make this wide table long once again. It is somehow useful to imagine an exactly backwise process: *what would you do to get back to the previous situation, the long one?* You would take the labels of the columns from `august_2016` to `september_2016` and store them in a new column, then store all the values of these columns in a new column. You would therefore recreate a `key` column and a `value` column.

In order to perform this task, `gather()` makes a similar reasoning, asking you to specify where to look for labels and values and to set a name for the resulting `key` and `value` columns:

```
wide_temperature %>%
  gather(key = "date", value = "temperature", -city)
```

Which will exactly result in the original long table. Before going on, I would like to point out how we specified to the function where it should have looked for labels and cells. It is by using the `-city` token you can find at the far right within the `gather` call. What is that for? It simply means: *look for labels and cells everywhere except for the city column.* We could have alternatively obtained the same result by explicitly declaring the numerical range of the columns:

```
wide_temperature %>%
gather(key = "date", value = "temperature", 2:5)
```

The separate function

The `separate` function is provided for really dirty data, that is, data having some columns where two or more attributes are merged together. You can get a sense of this by looking at the following table:

Time	Ttemperature
15/05/217 12:25:33	16
15/05/217 13:25:33	16
15/05/217 14:25:33	17
15/05/217 15:25:33	15

As you can see, the time column actually stores two different types of information – the date and hour of recording. How do we tidy that in order to comply with the *every column shows an attribute* rule? As you may be guessing, the `separate` function comes to help here. To apply it to your data you just have to run `separate()` on it, specifying the minimum set of arguments you would expect:

- `column`, which column you would like to split, unquoted
- `into`, the name of the new columns you would like to create from the messy one, in the form of a vector of characters
- `sep`, which is the token the function is going to employ to identify the end of a column and the beginning of another

Going back to our really dirty data, this is how the tidying code will look:

```
really_dirty_data %>%
    separate(time, sep = " ", into = c("date", "hour"))
```

date	hour	temperature
15/05/17	12:25:33	16
16/05/17	13:25:33	16
17/05/17	14:25:33	21
18/05/17	15:25:33	15

Which is now a tidy table, having an attribute per column and a record per row.

Applying tidyr to our dataset

Now that we know what tidy data is, how it looks, and how to obtain it by applying the `tidyr` package, it's time to actually tidy our data, applying all the knowledge we have just gained on the set of data we have.

How would you work on this? The first step is to exactly define what is wrong with our data, and in what way it is untidy, in order to be able to select from the available tidying functions the one that is going to work for us.

As we have seen, the only dirty table we have is the `stored_data` one, but which rule was broken in this table? Our data actually broke two rules, since we found multiple attributes lying within a single column. What does this remind you about? We have an attributes label and its values going a long way down, as was the case with the temperature table where the `city` and `date` attribute were stored in some kind of silos column. What did we call the table? A long table.

And this is exactly what our `stored_data` is, a long table. We can therefore apply here the remediation we already learned for long tables: the `spread()` function. As we already know, the minimum set of arguments required to run the `spread` function are the `key` column and `value` column:

- The `key` column is the one used to label the multiple columns we are going to create
- The `value` column is the one showing the value we are going to employ to populate the newly created columns.

As is often the case, reality is far more complicated than the examples we find in textbooks, and this holds true also within our `stored_data` table: we have here nine columns against the three we met in our temperature table. I would therefore propose to you an exercise to help you fix what we are learning now:

- Go back to the paragraph on the `spread` function, read it again, and try to jot down some code to apply this function to our `stored_data` table. This will help you to fix the use of this function in your mind. Once you have done this, two possible outcomes with related next steps arise:
  - You make the `spread` function work, therefore tidying your data, and you can therefore skip to the next paragraph on *cleaning our data*
  - You try hard but do not manage to tidy your data, and you therefore need to read the following lines.

Since you are reading these lines, things did not go well with the `spread` function, so let's take some time to discuss it: which is the column actually storing the labels of our hidden attributes? As we found out before, it is the parameter one, which is fed with repetitions of `attr_8`, `attr_9`, and similar tokens. We should therefore pass parameter as key column. But what about the `customer_code` column? Is it not fed with repetitions of customer codes? We discovered this before as well.

This is true. Nevertheless, we know for sure that the `spread` function asks for just two arguments: a `key` column and a `value` column. We should therefore focus on this and answer the question, which column holds the label of the attributes that are currently lying within the `value` column? It is the `parameter` column, and we are therefore going to pass it as the key argument. We are going to neglect the `customer_code` attribute, as we did before with the *city* one, and the `spread` function will take care of it.

Let's try to apply all this reasoning through some R code:

```
stored_data %>%
  spread(key = parameter, value = value) %>%
  str()
```

Which will result in the following:

```
'data.frame': 148555 obs. of  13 variables:'data.frame': 148555 obs. of  13
variables:
 $ attr_3        : num  0 0 0 0 0 0 0 0 0 0 ...
 $ attr_4        : num  0 0 0 0 0 0 0 0 0 0 ...
 $ attr_5        : num  0 0 0 0 0 0 0 0 0 0 ...
 $ attr_6        : num  0 0 0 0 0 0 0 0 0 0 ...
 $ attr_7        : num  0 0 0 0 0 0 0 0 0 0 ...
 $ default_flag  : Factor w/ 3 levels "?","0","1": 1 1 1 1 1 1 1 1 1 1 ...
 $ customer_code : num  1 2 3 4 5 6 7 8 9 10 ...
 $ attr_10       : num  NA NA -1e+06 -1e+06 NA NA NA -1e+06 NA -1e+06 ...
 $ attr_11       : num  NA NA -1e+06 0e+00 NA NA NA -1e+06 NA -1e+06 ...
 $ attr_12       : num  NA NA NA NA NA NA NA NA NA NA ...
 $ attr_13       : num  NA NA NA NA NA NA NA NA NA NA ...
 $ attr_8        : num  NA NA -1e+06 -1e+06 NA NA NA -1e+06 NA -1e+06 ...
 $ attr_9        : num  NA NA 1e+06 1e+06 NA NA NA -1e+06 NA 1e+06 ...
```

Which is exactly what we were looking for:

- Every row has a record
- Every column has an attribute

Nice, is our data cleaning work done? To answer this question just look back at the `str()` output and try to figure out what is that question mark just after the `$default_flag` token, or what those NAs stand for. Can you? I'm guessing not, and this is why our data cleaning is not completed yet.

Validating our data

Now that our data is tidy and structured in a convenient way for the purposes of our subsequent analyses, a further question arises, is our data good for the analyses? This question refers to the quality of our data. This is a non-trivial aspect of data mining, and you can easily understand why by reflecting on this popular quote: *Garbage in, garbage out.*

Within our context, this means that if you put as an input poor quality data, you will get unreliable results, meaning results that you should not base your decision on. This main tenet carries on a lot of activities that are regularly performed within companies to ensure that acquired or produced data is free from material quality problems.

But what exactly is a data quality problem?

First of all, we should focus on what data quality is. This property of data is commonly intended both as the fitness for use and the conformance to standards.

Fitness for use

Data that is not intended to be used by anyone is of high quality. This means that no data quality issues arise if no one is going to use the data. This extreme statement lets us get to the point of data fit for use, data has good quality if it is possible to use it for the purposes it was collected for.

You can think for instance of data type mismatching or an excessive number of missing records, and generally speaking, you can think of all those situations where the data provided cannot be employed as it is and needs some kind of cleaning and validation before being used.

As you can see, this attribute is mainly referred to the client who is going to use the data, and is therefore aware of what kind of data is going to fit or unfit his objectives.

Conformance to standards

This attribute lies one step behind the fit for use, since it is intended to refer to the quality criteria against which the data is evaluated to define its level of acceptability. This can be seen as an aspect of the data quality more related to the production environment, when some IT department is requested to run some set of diagnostic checks to establish if the data can be passed on to the final user.

Why did I say that this lies behind the fitness for use criteria? Because since no quality issues arise where no user exists, we will previously define what the user intends by fitness for use, and then we will go back to production, translating this need into standards for evaluating the level of conformance.

Data quality controls

When talking about data quality controls, we actually talk about a wide range of activities, going from diagnostic systems on the raw data to the check on the domain of a single variable during the modelling phase of a data mining project. All of those controls have a common objective: make sure data doesn't produce misleading results based on which bad decisions will be made.

This activity involving checks on the domain of variables is usually also referred to as data validation activity, since it tends to obtain assurance on the validity of the data you use.

Not pretending to be exhaustive, here is a list of common data validation activities:

- Consistency checks
- Data type checks
- Logical checks
- Domain checks
- Uniqueness checks

Consistency checks

These kinds of checks are the ones you could also name common sense checks, since they mainly relate to checks involving normal expectations of your data. Consider for instance a table where a column is expected to show a summary, for example, the mean of some other columns, like for instance the mean of the monthly sales reported within previous columns. A consistency check here would be checking, even for just some records, if this column actually shows that average. Getting back to our `customer_list` table, if we know that the total number of customers of our company is nearly 100, finding 10 customers would surely imply a data quality problem. Even if these kinds of checks can appear to be quite basic and not very sophisticated, you should never forget to perform them, since they are quite effective in letting you catch even big issues on your data.

Data type checks

Here we are with another basic and powerful check, a check on the data type. This kind of check is performed to get assurance that all relevant data type constraints are met. What is a data type constraint? Imagine you are working on an algorithm that sums data related with some of the other attributes of your table. Do you think that having that attribute in a character type could result in a problem for your algorithm? It would indeed, it would actually cause your code to raise an error and all the processes would come to an unpleasant end. You may be thinking that since this problem would be caught by the code itself, it should not be considered that insidious. This is true, but you should always consider placing some kind of check on these constraints within your code and a proper way to handle it (for instance casting data from character to numerical if a character type is found), to avoid causing your code to stop. This will hold especially true in a production environment, where a code stop could imply serious consequences.

Logical checks

Logical checks are in some way related to the consistency checks, and mainly look for respect of some constraints residing within single attributes or the relations among two or more of them. Think for instance of an `age` attribute related to a customer, could we not check that it never reports a value greater than 110? And, talking about age and time, how would you interpret a date of birth greater than today? We should look for those kinds of anomalies as well. Finally, looking for a relationship between attributes, what about the `number_of_sons` column showing zero for a given customer, and the `name_of_sons` column showing one or more names for the same customer? Those are all examples of logical checks that could be performed on your data, if feasible. Once again, we could consider implementing within our code some kind of routine check for those and similar kinds of anomalies.

Domain checks

Domain checks refer to the variability domain of an attribute. For instance, if we are dealing with a Boolean variable, for example alive, we know that it can have only two possible values, true or false. We could therefore check that no third value is shown from our data. One more example could be a discrete variable where only integer values are admitted, such as `number_of_cars`. What about 2.5 cars? Finally, we could look for records out of the allowed domain within attributes related to shares, such as share of equity. Those kinds of attributes could be limited from 0 to 100, and every value going beyond those limits should be treated as a suspect record.

Uniqueness checks

This is the last kind of check we are going to explore. This kind of check has actually a quite limited use key, we have a column that should report some kind of key of our table, that is a value that should be able to unequivocally identify every record within our table. Let's think of the customer code within a customer list, we should be sure that no double customer ID is reported within our table since this would lead to doubts on which records should be considered as reliable for the purposes of retrieving data related to that given customer. As we have already seen, the uniqueness of our data can be checked by comparing the length of our column with the length of the vector composed of just the unique values.

Performing data validation on our data

It is now time to apply some of these checks on our data, getting a sense of how it is possible to do this employing our beloved R language, focusing on the `stored_data` dataset.

Data type checks with str()

We are going to leverage here the *str()* function, which we already met some paragraphs ago. We employed this function to get a closer look at our data frame, and we already noticed that it results in a list of vectors, each of which shows the name of a different column, the type of that column (even if we would better say the type of the vector forming that column), and the first ten records of it. We are now going to try to look more carefully through the output and see if some kind of strange result appears:

```
str(clean_stored_data)
```

This will result in:

```
'data.frame': 27060 obs. of  15 variables:
$ attr_3         : num  0 0 0 0 0 0 0 0 0 0 ...
$ attr_4         : num  1 1 1 1 1 1 1 1 1 1 ...
$ attr_5         : chr  "0" "0" "0" "0" ...
$ attr_6         : num  1 1 1 1 1 1 1 1 1 1 ...
$ attr_7         : num  0 0 0 0 0 0 0 0 0 0 ...
$ default_numeric: chr  "?" "?" "0" "0" ...
$ default_flag   : Factor w/ 3 levels "?","0","1": 1 1 2 2 2 2 2 2 2 2 ...
$ customer_code  : num  6 13 22216 22217 22220 ...
$ geographic_area: chr  "north_america" "asia" "north_america" "europe" ...
$ attr_10        : num  -1.00e+06 -1.00e+06 1.00 9.94e-01 0.00 ...
$ attr_11        : num  0 0.00482 0.01289 0.06422 0.01559 ...
$ attr_12        : num  89 20 150000 685773 11498 ...
$ attr_13        : num  89 20 150000 1243 11498 ...
$ attr_8         : num  0 0.0601 0 0.2066 0.2786 ...
$ attr_9         : num  0.00 1.07 0.00 1.00 -1.00e+06 ...
```

Since we are still waiting for the colleague's email, we are not aware of the meaning and content of each attribute, and we cannot have clear expectations about the type of data within each column. Nevertheless, we can observe that a first group of columns shows zeros or ones, from `attr_3` to `attr_7`, we then have `default_numeric` with a question mark and some zeros, then the default flag with another question mark, zeros and ones, before leaving space for customer ID, geographic area, and a final group of attributes from 8 to 13 which all show numbers. Leaving aside the columns showing question marks, which we are going to handle later, do you think that all the other columns show the type that we could reasonably expect?

If we look back at the first group of attributes, from 3 to 7, we observe that the great part of them has a numerical type, which is reasonable given that they show 0 and 1 as values. The great part, but not all of them. Can you see that `attr_5` column? `str` is saying that it is a character vector, and we can get further assurance on this by running the `mode()` function on it:

```
mode(clean_stored_data$attr_5)

[1] "character"
```

Before moving on and changing its type to numerical, let's be sure about the values it stores, so as not to make a vector numerical that actually stores a mixed type of data. We can do this via the `range` function, which returns the unique values stored in a vector (yes, we could have done this also via the `unique()` function):

```
range(clean_stored_data$attr_5)
[1] "0" "1"
```

We are now sure of what this column stores, and we are ready to change its type from character to numeric. But how do we do it? Let me introduce you to a nice family of R functions, the `as.something` functions. Within R, we have a small group of functions dedicated to data casting, which all work following the same logic: *Take that object, cast it and give it back to me as [type of data]*.

Where you can substitute the type of data with a long list of possible types, for instance:

- Characters, `as.character`
- Numbers, `as.numeric`
- Data frames, `as.data.frame`

Let's see how this works by applying `as.numeric` to our `attr_5` column. We are going to apply it and get a sense of the result by running `mode()` on it once again:

```
clean_stored_data$attr_5 %>%
  as.numeric() %>%
  mode()
```

Which will result in the following output:

```
[1] "numeric"
```

This is exactly what we would have expected. The final step is to actually substitute this numerical version of the vector with the original one residing within `clean_stored_data` `data.frame`. We do this by leveraging the `mutate` function from the `dplyr` package, which can be employed to create new columns or change existing ones within a `data.frame`:

```
clean_stored_data %>%
mutate(attr_5 = as.numeric(attr_5)) %>%
str()
```

Which will now show `attr_5` as being a numeric vector. Just to store this result, let's assign it to a new `clean_casted_stored_data` object:

```
clean_stored_data %>%
mutate(attr_5 = as.numeric(attr_5)) -> clean_casted_stored_data
```

As you probably remember, while talking about data type checks some lines ago, we stated that these kinds of checks should be in some way automatically implemented within the code employed to process your data. But how do we perform those kinds of checks within the flow of our code? As usual, R comes to help us with another family of functions that could be considered close relatives of the `as.something` function: the `is.something` function. I am sure you are starting to understand how this works, you just have to pass your object within the function, and it will result in TRUE if the object is something you are looking for, and FALSE if this is not the case. For instance, run the following code:

```
is.data.frame(clean_stored_data$attr_5)
```

This will give as a result FALSE, since our well known `attr_5` is a vector rather than a `data.frame`. As was the case for the `as.something` family, the `is.something` family is composed of a lot of members, such as:

- `is.numeric`
- `is.character`
- `is.integer`

Once you have placed a data type check in the right point of your code flow, you will be able to provide a different flow for different possible outputs, defining different chunks of code to be executed in case the check has a positive or negative outcome. To do this, you will probably have to employ a conditional statement. Those kinds of statements are outside the scope of this book, but you can find a brief introduction to them in `Appendix`, *Dealing with Dates, Relative Paths and Functions*.

Domain checks

As we previously saw, domain checks are the ones related to the range of variation of our attributes. How could we perform these checks employing the R language? Even if different possible ways are available, we are going to look at one which can be considered as straightforward, a combined use of the `range` and `unique` functions. We are going to use them in order to derive the variation domain of numerical and character variables.

Let's start by looking at the numerical variables, *how can we have a look at their range?* We can employ the well named `range` function, which is going to give us back the minimum and maximum value within a sequence of numbers. For instance, applying it to a simple sequence from 1 to 10 will give us the following:

```
seq(1:10) %>%
range()

[1] 1 10
```

This shows the range of values the vector is composed of, but what if we want to check that the vector is lying between a given range? Among the possible ways to do this, we could perform this task defining the minimum and maximum value we are going to accept, and testing if our vector actually lies within the two values. Taking back our sequence, and supposing we want to check if it lies within 2 and 12, we can easily do this through the following code:

```
domain_test <- seq(1:10) < 12 & seq(1:10) > 2
```

What kind of object will this `domain_test` be? Let's print it out to discover it:

```
[1] FALSE FALSE TRUE TRUE TRUE TRUE TRUE TRUE TRUE TRUE
```

Here we are with a Boolean vector, where each element says if the corresponding value of our sequence meets the requirements we set, `< 12 and >2`.

Within our simple example, it is quite easy to see that all values of our sequence meet our requirements, except for the first two, but what if we have lot of elements and we are not willing, as we should not be, to look through all of them to see if any are FALSE? We can call to our helper `table` function, which will produce a frequency table of our vector, showing all unique values of the vector, TRUE and FALSE, together with their frequency:

```
domain_test %>%
table()
```

Which will result in the following:

```
FALSE   TRUE
2       8
```

Which clearly shows us that two of our records are not respecting our thresholds. Let's apply what we have just learned to our beloved `stored_data` table. Unfortunately, at the moment we do not have enough information to define proper domain variation for our attributes, and we will therefore set some fictitious limits to perform our test.

Looking for instance at `attr_8`, we could be interested in knowing if it always lies within a positive domain, if it is always greater than zero. How do we do that? We are looking here only for a positive limit and will therefore pose only one condition:

```
attr_domain_test <- clean_casted_stored_data$attr_8 > 0
```

To understand what I meant when I talked about looking through a lot of records to spot FALSE tokens, you can try to print attr_domain_test out. I am not going to reproduce here the output you are going to get following my suggestion, mainly to preserve our precious environment. Once you are done with this exciting experience we can move to the next step, involving producing a table from our attr_domain_test object to test in a more convenient way if our limit is met:

```
attr_domain_test %>%
table()
```

Which will print out a more convenient:

```
FALSE  TRUE
20172  6888
```

This shows us that there are 20,172 records that are not meeting our expectations. Since that is the majority of our data, it is actually a great relief to know that we are not looking for this limit to be respected.

One final question about domains check, what if we are dealing with categorical variables? We can check for domain by comparing our vector with one other vector storing values we are considering acceptable, leveraging the %in% operator:

```
c("A", "C","F", "D", "A") %in% c("A", "D", "E")
```

We can read the previous line of code as, is the vector on the left populated by values stored in the vector on the right? And here is the answer to our question:

```
[1]  TRUE FALSE FALSE  TRUE  TRUE
```

Also, in the case of categorical variables, it is possible to employ the table function to count for TRUE and FALSE, in the case of too many elements within the vector being checked.

As a closure of this check, let's take a look once again at our data structure to see if any issues on variable domains arise:

```
str(clean_casted_stored_data)

'data.frame': 27060 obs. of  15 variables:'data.frame': 27060 obs. of  15
variables:
$ attr_3        : num  0 0 0 0 0 0 0 0 0 ...
$ attr_4        : num  1 1 1 1 1 1 1 1 1 ...
$ attr_5        : num  0 0 0 0 0 0 0 0 0 ...
$ attr_6        : num  1 1 1 1 1 1 1 1 1 ...
$ attr_7        : num  0 0 0 0 0 0 0 0 0 ...
```

```
$ default_numeric: chr   "?" "?" "0" "0" ...
$ default_flag    : Factor w/ 3 levels "?","0","1": 1 1 2 2 2 2 2 2 2 ...
$ customer_code   : num  6 13 22216 22217 22220 ...
$ geographic_area: chr  "north_america" "asia" "north_america" "europe" ...
$ attr_10         : num  -1.00e+06 -1.00e+06 1.00 9.94e-01 0.00 ...
$ attr_11         : num  0 0.00482 0.01289 0.06422 0.01559 ...
$ attr_12         : num  89 20 150000 685773 11498 ...
$ attr_13         : num  89 20 150000 1243 11498 ...
$ attr_8          : num  0 0.0601 0 0.2066 0.2786 ...
$ attr_9          : num  0.00 1.07 0.00 1.00 -1.00e+06 ...
```

Can you see that big question mark on the right of $default_numeric and $ default_flag? It really does not look good as the value of two attributes which should by definition be Boolean, TRUE or FALSE, 0 or 1. How are we going to treat it? First of all, let's get a sense of how many of those question marks we have:

```
(clean_casted_stored_data$default_flag) %>%
table()
```

And:

```
(clean_casted_stored_data$default_numeric) %>%
table()
```

Which in both cases will result in:

```
  ?      0        1
 28    4845    22187
```

We can draw at least two conclusions from this table:

- Only a small number of records are affected by the question mark issue (nearly 0.10 %).
- Our table stores more 1s than 0s. This does not appear to be really relevant right now, but we should store it somewhere within our mind, since it will be useful later on.

What do we with those strange records? Since we are still not confident enough with the meaning and content of our data, I propose to you a cautious solution, store them aside within a separate object, and remove them from the clean_casted_stored_data data frame.

How do we do this? We are going to employ one more utility provided by the dplyr package, the filter function. This function, which works exactly how you would expect, lets you filter your data frame stating a rule that has to be respected, and excluding all records not meeting it. Let's try to use it for our purposes:

```
clean_casted_stored_data %>%
  filter(default_flag == 0 | default_flag == 1 )
```

As you can see, we set both conditions in a positive form. Keep within our table all records that are either equal to 0 or equal to 1 (look at the information box for more information about logical operators in R). To check that our filter obtained the desired result, let's look at the number of rows, to see if we can reconcile it with the previously produced table:

```
clean_casted_stored_data %>%
  filter(default_flag == 0 | default_flag == 1 ) %>%
  nrow()
```

Which will show up a reassuring 27032, which is exactly the sum of the number of 0s (4,845) and the number of 1s (22,187) that we previously found. As you may be noticing at the moment, we have not created any of the intended new data frames, neither the clean version of stored_data, nor the backup data frame containing the question marks. Let's fix this with the following lines of code:

```
clean_casted_stored_data %>%
  filter(default_flag == 0 | default_flag == 1 ) ->
clean_casted_stored_data_validated

clean_casted_stored_data %>%
  filter(default_flag != 0 & default_flag != 1 ) -> question_mark_records
```

Two observations here are:

1. The clean_stored_... name is getting too long, but we are going to fix it shortly.
2. To create the question_mark_records, we applied a filter similar to the first one we introduced, but still rather different. This filter says something like, filter all records that are not (!=) equal to 0 and (&) are not equal to 1. As you will be able to verify running now on this new object, the result of this filter is the selection of just those 28 rows we met before within our table() output.

The following logical operators are available in R:

operator	description
<	less than
<=	less than or equal to
>	greater than
>=	greater than or equal to
==	equal to
!=	not equal to
|	or
&	and

The final touch — data merging

While still reasoning about the domain of variation of your attribute 8, you suddenly realize that time is running out, since we are approaching 12 a.m. and you have not shared the clean data with your team. Even if you are tempted to just attach the clean data to a new email and let it go, a final thought comes up, *How are they going to use this data?* As previously stated by your boss, the next step will be to perform some EDA on the data to see if any specific market or portfolio is the main cause of the observed drop.

How are they going to do this? They will probably aggregate customers based on their attributes, such as geographical area, commercial portfolio, and business unit. Those three attributes are at the moment spread across two different datasets, we have the geographical area within the `stored_data` dataset and the other two within the `customer_list` dataset. While no problem will arise when trying to summarize data based on the geographical area, we would face a big issue when trying to do the same on the business unit and commercial portfolio attributes. How can we fix this? Since the problem is that we have two separates tables, there is no better solution than creating one single table.

This is exactly what we are going to do, employing the `left_join()` function provided by `dplyr`. As you may be guessing, this function leverages the SQL-based concept of join, which is the verb describing all operations of merging between tables within the SQL realm. The `left_join` function actually replicates the functioning of a SQL `left_join`, employing the left table as the main one, attaching to this records from the right table, based on a given key. Employing the `left_join` function, you will, therefore, have a table composed of all the records from the left table, enriched with attributes from the right one. The only risk you are taking is of losing some records from the right table. This is actually a reasonable risk, as we will explain shortly.

left_join function

What do you think is needed to perform the kind of merging we were describing earlier? We will need to pass the name of the two data frames we are willing to merge, then a proper key needs to be employed to match records between the two data frames.

What is a key? A key is a bridge between two tables, an attribute, or a combination of attributes, that we found in both of the tables we are merging. Let's have a look at the two tables and see if such an attribute is available:

```
str(clean_casted_stored_data_validated)>
str(clean_casted_stored_data_validated)

'data.frame': 27032 obs. of  15 variables:
$ attr_3          : num 0 0 0 0 0 0 0 0 0 ...
$ attr_4          : num 1 1 1 1 1 1 1 1 1 ...
$ attr_5          : num 0 0 0 0 0 0 0 0 0 ...
$ attr_6          : num 1 1 1 1 1 1 1 1 1 ...
$ attr_7          : num 0 0 0 0 0 0 0 0 0 ...
$ default_numeric: chr  "0" "0" "0" "0" ...
$ default_flag    : Factor w/ 3 levels "?","0","1": 2 2 2 2 2 2 2 2 2 ...
$ customer_code  : num 22216 22217 22220 22221 22222 ...
$ geographic_area: chr  "north_america" "europe" "south_america"
"north_america" ...
$ attr_10         : num 1 0.994 0 1 1 ...
$ attr_11         : num 0.01289 0.06422 0.01559 0.04433 0.00773 ...
$ attr_12         : num 150000 685773 11498 532 500000 ...
$ attr_13         : num 150000 1243 11498 532 500000 ...
$ attr_8          : num 0 0.2066 0.2786 0.0328 0 ...
$ attr_9          : num 0.00 1.00 -1.00e+06 1.00 8.65e-01 ...

str(customer_list)
'data.frame': 27060 obs. of  3 variables:
$ customer_code    : num 1 2 3 4 5 6 7 8 9 10 ...
```

```
$ commercial_portfolio: Factor w/ 3 levels "less affluent",..: 1 1 1 1 1 1
1
1 1 1 ...
$ business_unit        : Factor w/ 2 levels "corporate_bank",..: 2 2 2 2 2 2
2 2 2 ...
```

Can you spot any common attribute? Yeah, the `customer_code` is common. We are nearly done with our merging activity, but let's just take a few more lines to dive into the concept of `left_join`. What are we going to consider here as the left table? As we previously said, on the left we pose the table we want to entirely preserve. What would you preserve? We are interested here in being sure that all our data about losses and sales contained within the `stored_date` table can be grouped by the attributes available within the `customer_list` table. We are therefore more interested in preserving all data within the `stored_data` table. What if some `customer_code` gets lost, that is, if we have customer codes available within the `customer_list` but with no data in the `stored_data` table? Those are customers who either no longer have a relationship with our company, or where a problem of data quality occurred. We can further analyze this, but for the purposes of our analyses this would not be a relevant problem, since it would not impair our objective of grouping data.

It's now time to actually apply the function and take a look at the results:

```
left_join(clean_casted_stored_data_validated,customer_list, by =
"customer_code") %>%
str()

'data.frame': 27032 obs. of  17 variables:
$ attr_3         : num  0 0 0 0 0 0 0 0 0 0 ...
$ attr_4         : num  1 1 1 1 1 1 1 1 1 1 ...
$ attr_5         : num  0 0 0 0 0 0 0 0 0 0 ...
$ attr_6         : num  1 1 1 1 1 1 1 1 1 1 ...
$ attr_7         : num  0 0 0 0 0 0 0 0 0 0 ...
$ default_numeric : chr  "0" "0" "0" "0" ...
$ default_flag    : Factor w/ 3 levels "?","0","1": 2 2 2 2 2 2 2 2 2
...
$ customer_code   : num  22216 22217 22220 22221 22222 ...
$ geographic_area : chr  "north_america" "europe" "south_america"
"north_america" ...
$ attr_10         : num  1 0.994 0 1 1 ...
$ attr_11         : num  0.01289 0.06422 0.01559 0.04433 0.00773 ...
$ attr_12         : num  150000 685773 11498 532 500000 ...
$ attr_13         : num  150000 1243 11498 532 500000 ...
$ attr_8          : num  0 0.2066 0.2786 0.0328 0 ...
$ attr_9          : num  0.00 1.00 -1.00e+06 1.00 8.65e-01 ...
$ commercial_portfolio: Factor w/ 3 levels "less affluent",..: 1 1 1 1 1 1
1
```

```
1 1 1 ...
$ business_unit      : Factor w/ 2 levels "corporate_bank",..: 2 2 2 2 2 2
2 2 2 ...
```

And here we are: our `stored_data` table is now enriched with attributes coming from the `customer_list` table.

moving beyond left_join

Before moving on I would like to make you aware that the full spectrum of join functions is available within `dplyr`, so that all common data merging activities can be replicated within R, like for instance:

- **inner_join(x,y)** which returns all rows in x having matching values in y, and all columns from both x and y. If there are multiple matches between x and y, all combination of the matches are returned.
- **anti_join(x,y)** which returns all rows from x having no matching values in y, keeping just columns from x.
- **full_join(x,y)** which return all rows and all columns from both x and y. in case of no matching values, NAs are returned for the one missing.

Further references

- Hadley Wickham's paper, *Tidy data, Introducing the framework,* http://vita.had.co.nz/papers/tidy-data.pdf.
- Shakespeare's *Romeo and Juliet,* just because it is so well written. I would suggest you read one of the best editions from the Oxford University Press.
- A cheat sheet for the other `dplyr` join functions, which will help you gain a wider view of the possibilities available within `dplyr` for merging tables: http://stat545.com/bit001_dplyr-cheatsheet.html.

Summary

Our journey has begun within this chapter. Leveraging the knowledge gained within previous chapters, we have started facing a challenge that suddenly appeared: discover the origin of a heavy loss our company is suffering.

We received some dirty data to be cleaned, and this was the occasion to learn about data cleaning and tidy data. This was the first set of activities to make our data fit the analyses' needs, and the second a conceptual framework that can be employed to define which structure our data should have to fit those needs. We also learned how to evaluate the respect of the three main rules of tidy data (every row has a record, every column has an attribute, and every table is an entity).

We also learned about data quality and data validation, discovering which metrics define the level of quality of our data and a set of checks that can be employed to assess this quality and spot any needed improvements.

We applied all these concepts to our data, making our data through the gather and spread functions from the tidyr package, and validating its quality using data type and domain checks.

Finally, we learned how to merge two of the tables we were provided with in order to make attributes available from one table to the other. This was obtained by leveraging the left_join function from the dplyr package.

You now possess the necessary theoretical and operational knowledge to perform those data cleaning and validation activities, and we can move on to the next chapter.

Looking into Your Data Eyes – Exploratory Data Analysis

Well *done [your name here]: that data was really messy and you did an excellent job getting it ready for the EDA. Just send it to Francis and take his side: he will show you how those kinds of things are performed. We do not have too much time to invest in your education now, but siding him will be useful for you anyway.*

Once the boss is done complimenting you, you can send the clean data to Francis and reach his desk.

Hi there, so you did the job with this dirty data. Well done! We are now going to perform some Exploratory Data Analysis, to get a closer look at our data, and to understand where this profit drop came from.

So, that is what **EDA** stands for: **Exploratory Data Analysis**. But, let Francis introduce you into this new world: *EDA is a powerful tool in our hands. In the beginning of data analysis, analysts did not give a lot of attention to it since they tended towards the direct application of modeling techniques to their data, just drawing some preliminary descriptive statistics from their data before modeling it.*

But, if I find my notes about the Anscombe quartet, I will show you that those kinds of statistics cannot always be considered as reliable.

Time is short, so let's start munging our data, with some summary EDA.

OK then, it seems Francis is willing to show you how to perform EDA on your data; I will let him be your teacher for this chapter, we will meet again in the summary paragraph. Best of luck with your analyses!

Introducing summary EDA

Have you ever heard about summary EDA? Since you are new to the job, I guess the answer is no. I will tell you something about this while I download the data you sent me, and open it within the RStudio project I prepared for the occasion. I hope you don't mind if I tell you something you already know.

Summary, EDA encompasses all the activities that are based on the computation of one or more indexes useful to describe the data we are dealing with. What differentiates this branch of the EDA from its relatives is the non-graphical nature of this set of measures: here, we are going to compute just a bunch of numbers, while with the graphical EDA we will perform later, plot and visualization will be the core of our techniques.

While we were talking, our data became ready, so we can start working on it. I will start looking at the `cash_flows` report, since it probably has enough info to reveal to us where this drop is coming from.

Describing the population distribution

First of all, let's try to synthetically describe the main features of our cash flow, that is, how much it tends to vary across time, if it is more unbalanced towards high or low values, and what are its typical values. To reach those objectives, we are going to compute the following:

- Quartiles and median
- Mean
- Variance
- Standard deviation
- Skewness

Quartiles and Median

We first need to get a bit more confident with the values of our attribute: what is its lowest value? What is the highest one? Then, we can also have a look at some reference numbers within our population, the so-called **quartiles**.

These quartiles are divided into quarters of the population, so that if you sort the values of your attribute from the lowest to the highest, you find the first quartile after exactly 25% of the records, the median after 50% of the records, and the third quartile after 75% of the records. The zero quartile is the minimum and the fourth the maximum of our population. Let me jot down an explanatory sketch for you:

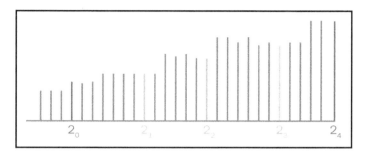

Can you see this? We have all the components of our population sorted by value; you can imagine them as a group of people ordered by their height. Of course, we have some people with the same height, which led to us placing them one next to the other. We have here 20 elements, so after we count five of them, we will have reached 25% of our population. *Which is the height of the fifth man?* That is the first quartile. The same holds true for the median: which is the high of the 10th man? That is the median. Can you spot the third quartile? Mark it on the sketch.

This set of values is useful to quickly describe a population. For instance, if you have the first and the third quartile, and they are really similar to one another, you can conclude that 50% of the population is represented by similar values, and you do not have a lot of dispersion within your data. Let's have a look at the quartiles of our data, employing the fivenum() function, which computes for a given vector the minimum, median, and maximum, together with the quartile:

```
cash_flow_report %>%
select(cash_flow) %>%
unlist() %>%
fivenum()
```

This shows us the following:

```
cash_flow84 cash_flow29 cash_flow44 cash_flow46  cash_flow3
   45089.21    95889.92   102593.81   107281.90   132019.06
```

We can see from this that we are dealing with a quite homogeneous population, since the first quartile is not too far from the third. As I was saying, the distance between the third and first quartile is useful information and is also referred to as the interquartile range:

interquartile range = third quartile - first quartile

Let's compute it for our vector. We can do this at least following two different routes:

- Saving our `fivenum` output into an object and selecting from it the third and first quartile
- Employing the `IQR()` function

To make it quicker, let's employ the built-in `IQR()` function, passing the `cash_flow` vector to it:

```
cash_flow_report %>%
  select(cash_flow) %>%
  unlist() %>%
  IQR()
```

The output for the previous code would be:

```
11234.56
```

Not too many euros, don't you think? If you are trying to compute the interquartile range by writing it down as the difference between the quartiles we found with `fivenum`, you may notice a small difference with the output from `IQR()`. This is due to the algorithm employed from the latter one to compute quantiles to be subtracted, and you should not worry about it.

Mean

The mean is probably the most famous of the summaries that can be drawn from a population. It tries to express a representative value of the entire population, and this is why it is so beloved and hated. We formally compute it, in its simplest possible formulation, by dividing the sum of all the elements of the population by the number of elements themselves minus one, so that we can write it down as:

$$mean = \frac{\sum_{i=1}^{n} x_i}{n-1}$$

Have you noted the minus one? I don't want to be too technical about it, you should just be aware that this is the formula employed when dealing with samples and not the entire population, which is the vast majority of times. As I was saying, it is both beloved and hated. It is beloved and frequently used because of its ease of computation and its level of synthesis. Compared, for instance, with the quartiles we have seen, you do not have to show a series of numbers and describe their meaning and relations, for instance, computing the interquartile range. You just have one number, and you can describe the whole population with it.

Nevertheless, this number tends also to be hated for two main reasons:

- It does not allow the phenomenon going on within subpopulation to emerge
- Tends to be biased from the presence of outliers

The mean and phenomenon going on within sub populations

In relation to the first reason, we can consider studies about customers behavior and, particularly, buying habits. I should have a spreadsheet somewhere on my desktop which looks similar to the following table:

Customer	June	July	August	September
1	200	150	190	195
2	1050	1101	975	1095
3	1300	1130	1340	1315
4	400	410	395	360
5	450	400	378	375
6	1125	1050	1125	1115
7	1090	1070	1110	1190
8	980	990	1200	1001
9	600	540	330	220
10	1130	1290	1170	1310

From this table, you can compute the following averages by month:

	June	July	August	September
average	832.5	813.1	821.3	817.6

These averages would probably lead you to the conclusion that no big change is occurring within your sales figures. But, if we add one more attribute, which is the cluster of the age of the customer, we can gain a better understanding of our numbers:

Customer	Age cluster	June	July	August	September
1	young	200	150	190	195
2	adult	1050	1101	975	1095
3	adult	1300	1130	1340	1315
4	young	400	410	395	360
5	young	450	400	378	375
6	adult	1125	1050	1125	1115
7	elder	1090	1070	1110	1190
8	elder	980	990	1200	1001
9	young	600	540	330	220
10	elder	1130	1290	1170	1310

I am sure you are already spotting some differences between **Age clusters**, but let's try to summarize these differences by computing the total sales by category:

Age cluster	June	July	August	September
young	1650	1500	1293	1150
adult	3475	3281	3440	3525
elder	3200	3350	3480	3501

Can you see it? Behind a substantially stable average, three completely different stories were hiding: the company is losing ground in the young field, is remaining stable within the adult cluster, and is gaining heavily with the elder segment. This is a simple and yet useful example to understand why the average, while being a synthetic way to describe an entire population, can also be unable to properly describe that population. If we had computed, for instance, the interquartile range of this population for the same four months, we would have found the following numbers :

	June	July	August	September
IQR	628,75	650,75	776,5	807,5

This would have shown us, in a clear way, that our population was diverging in some way, and becoming less homogeneous.

The mean being biased by outlier values

What about the second bias? This is far more simply explained: the mean value of a population can be heavily biased from the outliers values, and this can even result in the average value not being representative of the greatest part of the population. You can see this even by looking at just a bunch of numbers:

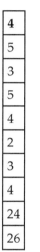

4
5
3
5
4
2
3
4
24
26

Here, we clearly have eight numbers that are enclosed within a small range, 2-5, and then two numbers that can be considered as outliers, 24 and 26. If we compute the average of those numbers, we get a sound 8. *Is this number shown even one time within the population?* No. Nevertheless, if we rely on the average to describe our population, we would conclude that this is a representative value of it.

What if we compute the median of the same population? We get 4, which is far more representative of the values of our population.

This should have made it clear to you why the average, even despite being a powerful summary, should be taken cautiously, and possibly considered together along with other descriptive statistics.

Computing the mean of our population

That said, what is the mean of our cash flows? We compute it easily employing the `mean` function:

```
cash_flow_report %>%
  select(cash_flow) %>%
  unlist() %>%
  mean()
```

This results in `101116.9`. Is this different from the median? We already computed the median, but let's write a small script that directly compares the two quantities:

```
cash_flow_report %>%
  select(cash_flow) %>%
  unlist() %>%
  mean() -> mean

cash_flow_report %>%
  select(cash_flow) %>%
  unlist() %>%
  median() -> median
```

Within this code, we just compute `mean` and `median`, assigning them to two different objects. Computing the difference requires writing an intuitive:

```
mean - median
```

This results in `-1476.926` being printed out. This is not that much of a difference considering the orders of magnitude we are dealing with. Can you guess what the meaning is behind these two numbers being so close? We will get a closer look at this when looking at the `skewness` property.

Variance

The variance of a set of numbers expresses how much variability there is within our data, and, more precisely, how far from the mean your data is on average. It is computed measuring the mean of our set of data, and then all the squared deviations from these from this mean. Once all of these squared deviations are computed, we compute an average of all of them, summing them up and dividing by the number of deviations, that is, the number of elements of the population. Variance is usually written as:

$$variance = \text{Var}(X) = \frac{\sum_{i=1}^{n}(x_i - \overline{x})^2}{n-1}$$

Here, x represents a given value of the population, μ is the population mean, and n is the number of elements of the population.

We can compute the variance in R employing the `var()` function, which just requires you the vector over which we want to measure the variance. Let's compute it on the `cash_flow` attribute:

```
cash_flow_report %>%
 select(cash_flow) %>%
 unlist() %>%
 var()
```

This results in a sound `120722480`.

How would you evaluate this value? Is it high, or low? What is the unit of measurement? It is actually squared euros. I don't know about you, but I am not that confident with squared euros, and this is the main problem with the variance, you do not actually know how to handle it and evaluate it. This is where the standard deviation comes from.

Standard deviation

The standard deviation can be directly obtained by rooting the variance we previously introduced. The meaning of this measure is exactly the same as the previous one, except that it is expressed employing the same unit of measure of the originating variable. This allows you to easily understand how relevant the amount of variation your variable expresses is. We formally derive the standard deviation as follows:

$$standard\ deviation = \sqrt{variance}$$

Employing R, we compute the standard deviation with the `sd()` function:

```
cash_flow_report %>%
 select(cash_flow) %>%
 unlist() %>%
 sd()
```

This results in a more human 10,987.38 euros. Just to put this in the right context, we should recall that the minimum cash flow was 45,089.21, and the maximum was 132,019.06, so we are dealing with a small amount here.

If you think about it, this is coherent with what we found looking at the interquartile range that lets us conclude about the population behind quite homogeneous within the first and third quartile. Reading the story behind the numbers, we can hint that our profits have to have remained quite stable from 2014 onward, and this makes this recent drop even more suspicious.

Skewness

OK, let's move on with our EDA, taking along our first hint about the profits drop. We should now look at our distribution shape, and first of all, whether it is symmetrical or not. Without being too complex, let me just show you the concept with a sketch:

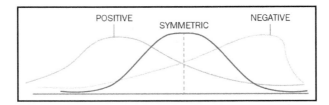

Within all of the three plots, you find, on the *x* axis, the value of a variable, and on the *y* axis, the frequency. It is like a histogram, isn't it?

 eh, ehm, the author here... you should remember histograms since we met them in Chapter 3, *The Data Mining Process - CRISP-DM Methodology*, but you can quickly skip back to refresh this.

Nice, so the blue distribution is symmetrical, that is, it's specular around its mean. The green and red plots are not symmetrical since the first one is biased toward the left, and the third toward the right.

This is the intuition behind the concept of skewness. There are different measures of skewness proposed within literature; let's use the one from Sir Arthur Lyon Bowley since it employs quartile and median, which you should now be familiar with.

Bowley's definition of *skewness* is shown in the following:

$$skewness = \frac{(q_3 - q_2) - (q_2 - q_1)}{q_3 - q_1}$$

Here, q_n is the nth quartile of our vector.

When this number is greater than 0 we are dealing with a positively skewed population, while the opposite is true for a negative value.

Moving a bit closer to the formula, what do you think is in the numerator? As you can see, there we measure the difference between the distance between the third and the second quartile, and the distance between the second and the third quartile.

In a symmetric distribution, those two quantities are equal, while in a skewed the first will be greater than the second, or vice versa based on the distribution being skewed to the left or the right.

You can get it through a numerical example. Consider, for instance, the following vector:

1
1
2
2
2
2.5
3
3
3
4
4

Which is the median, or the second quartile? Right, it is 2.5. The first quartile here is 2 and the third is 3. Let's compute the two distances mentioned in the preceding example:

$$q_2 - q_1 = 2.5 - 2 = 0.5$$

$$q_3 - q_2 = 3 - 2.5 = 0.5$$

As you can see, those two quantities are exactly the same. This is coherent with the population being perfectly symmetrical about the mean, which is exactly *2.5*:

Number	Frequency
1	2
2	3
2.5	1
3	3
4	2

What if we increase the number of **1** ? For instance, substituting it with a **2**? We get this:

1
1
1
2
2
2.5
3
3
3
4
4

The average moves to 2.4 and the two differences now become 1 and 0.5. Let's now compute the Cowley's skewness for both of the examples:

first skewness = (0.5 - 0.5)/(3-2) = 0

>

second skewness = (0.5 - 1)/(3-1.5) = -0.3

Following Cowley's skewness, we see that the first distribution should look symmetric around the mean, while the second should be negatively skewed, that is, it's biased towards higher values. We can check this by computing the number of elements lower and greater than the mean within the first and second population: 5 and 5 for the first (since the median is equal to the mean) and 5 and 6 for the second (since the median here is higher than the mean).

Nice, but what about our cash flow population? Let's compute the Cowley's skewness, employing the quantiles we previously obtained from `fivenum`. We first save the output from this function within a `quartiles` object:

```
cash_flow_report %>%
select(cash_flow) %>%
unlist() %>%
fivenum()-> quartiles
```

Then, we filter out the quartiles we are not interested in, that is, the quartile 0 and 4, which are the first and the fifth element of our resulting vector. We therefore keep only elements from the second to the fourth:

```
q <- quartiles[2:4]
```

Finally, we apply the formula shown in the preceding code:

```
skewness <- ((q[3]- q[2])-(q[2]- q[1]))/(q[3]-q[1])
```

OK, our population seems to be negatively skewed, which means that we are dealing with a historical series biased towards higher values, that is, mainly constituted from higher cash flows. *What do you think this can tell us? Is it another hint about the drop?* For sure, this makes us, even more, suspect our drop, and at least you now know about population skewness!

Measuring the relationship between variables

It is now time to bring our summary EDA to an end, looking for the relationship between variables. Until now, we have just observed how the `cash_flow` variable is distributed, and which are its more representative values, but we have two more attributes within `cash_flow_report`:

- Geographic area, storing the geographic area to which every record is related
- Quarter, related to the time of reporting

How are these attributes related to the cash flows?

Correlation

The best summary statistics to look for when looking for the relationship among variables is a correlation. This measure is able to express the level of dependence between two variables, that is, how much the variation of one of the two is associated with the variation of the other.

To avoid one of the most common misconceptions, I want to immediately warn you against the correlation-causation failure: correlation does not imply causation.

This means that finding evidence of some variable being related to another one would never automatically imply the first being the cause of the second one, or vice versa.

You could, for instance, find a strong correlation between the number of precipitations in a country and the number of people winning the Nobel price in the same country, but this could not lead you to the conclusion that the first one is the cause of the latter, or at least I hope it would not. There should also be a website totally dedicated to the concept. Here it is: http://www.tylervigen.com/spurious-correlations. It is from the great Tyler Vigen.

Give a look, for instance, to this one:

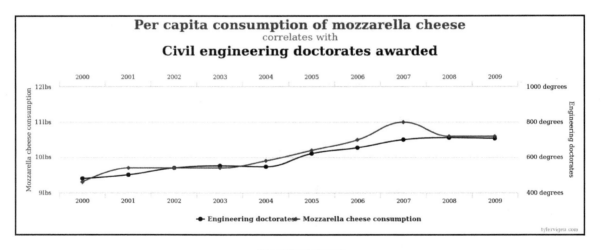

Would you think that any kind of causation is going on here? Hopefully not; nevertheless, a sound 95% correlation coefficient was observed here.

That said, it should also be noted that the opposite holds true: causation implies correlation, since two variables linked from a causation mechanism are going to show a high level of correlation.

But this is not the whole story: we talk about correlation, but there is actually more than one type of correlation, since we have also got linear correlation, and non-linear ones such as quadratic or exponential. There's not enough time to enter into details here, nevertheless, starting from this consideration, we are going to measure our variable relationship with two different coefficients:

- The Pearson coefficient, able to detect only linear correlation
- The distance correlation, able to also detect non-linear correlations

We are going to look at correlation only for time and cash flows, since the geographic area is a categorical variable, and we cannot measure the correlation between continuous and categorical variables. To be more precise, we could do something similar working with dummies, ANOVA analysis, and regressions, but we do not have time for all that fun.

Nevertheless, we will address the relationship between the geographic area and cash flows with some graphical EDA.

The Pearson correlation coefficient

You have probably already heard about the Pearson coefficient, since it is the most popular measure of correlation, and the most widely applied.

This is probably related to its ease of calculation and interpretation. We compute the Pearson correlation coefficient, as follows:

$$\rho_{X,Y} = \frac{\text{cov}(X, Y)}{\sigma_X \sigma_Y}$$

We find, on the numerator, an index named covariance, between X and Y, which we will cover in a second. On the denominator, we see the product of standard deviations of X and Y. The covariance is in some way a raw Pearson correlation value, meaning that within the formula it is the member intended to express the linear relationship between the two variables. We can get this looking at the covariance formula:

$$cov(X, Y) = \frac{\sum_{i=1}^{n}(x_i - \overline{(x)})(y_i - \overline{(y)})}{(n-1)}$$

This is familiar to you, isn't it? We have actually seen this nearly 15 minutes ago, when looking at the variance.

As you see, we are dealing again with a difference from the mean. Nevertheless, something more is introduced here: the product between the differences for variable X and Y. Why do we do that? Because here we are not just interested in getting the single variable variability, but their joint variability, and multiplying their differences to let us reach that point.

Moreover, if you take a second to think about it, each of these elements, that is, the product of their differences, will have a sign based on how the variables are behaving, and this sign will express if they are moving in the same direction or not. For instance, if both of the variables are lower than the mean, this will produce two negative differences, and by that way a positive product, which will indicate that both are going in the same direction. Finally, the sum of these quantities will have a sign by itself, which will summarize what is the overall direction of the relationship.

I see by your face that we need a numerical example. Take the following couple of numbers:

X	Y
2	4
5	3
4	2
6	4
7	3

To compute the covariance for those numbers, we first of all compute the mean for both of the variables:

$$mean\ X = 4.8$$

$$mean\ Y = 3.2$$

We then compute the differences between the mean for each of them:

X	Y	(X-mean(X))	(Y-mean(Y))
2	4	-2,8	0,8
5	3	0,2	-0,2
4	2	-0,8	-1,2
6	4	1,2	0,8
7	3	2,2	-0,2

We can already start thinking about this number: what is the most common occurrence? That a negative difference for X is paired with a positive difference for Y, or vice versa. This expresses an inverse behavior, that is, a specular or symmetric behavior of one variable in relation to the other.

This should by now be confirmed from the products and the final covariance:

X	Y	(X-mean(X))	(Y-mean(Y))	(X-mean(X))*(Y-mean(Y))
2	4	-2,8	0,8	-2,24
5	3	0,2	-0,2	-0,04
4	2	-0,8	-1,2	0,96
6	4	1,2	0,8	0,96
7	3	2,2	-0,2	-0,44

The last column, which shows the majority of times a negative sign, sums up to *0.8*. This is the numerator of our previously introduced covariance formula:

$$\sum_{i=1}^{n}(x_i - \bar{x})(y_i - \bar{y})$$

We now have to divide it by the size of the population minus one. Let's compute the covariance then:

- 0.8/4 = -0.20

As we would have expected, a negative covariance is shown here, which is a result of a negative product of differences, and expresses an inverse relationship between the two variables. But how much is that -0.2? Is it a lot or just a small amount? 0.2 out of ? From these questions, the Pearson coefficient was born. This coefficient solves the problem of covariance interpretation, dividing it by the product of the standard deviations of the two variables. I am not going to show it to you formally, but given the definition of standard deviation, dividing the covariance by this product leads to a ratio that can range from -1 to 1.

The ratio can therefore be easily interpreted as follows:

- ratio > 0 implies direct linear relationship/dependence between variables
- ratio = 0 implies the absence of relationship/dependence between variables
- ratio > 0 implies inverse linear relationship/dependence between variables

How near the ratio will be from the unity will then express the intensity of this direct/inverse relationship. Nice, now let's move on to our real data and compute the correlation coefficient between time and cash flows. We can use the `cor` function. This function can compute different types of correlation, but if you do not specify anything about this, it will compute Pearson:

```
cor (x =cash_flow_report$y, y = cash_flow_report$cash_flow)
Error in cor(x = cash_flow_report$y, y = cash_flow_report$cash_flow) :
  'x' must be numeric
```

Uh, not what we were looking for.

You can take as an example of debugging: *any idea what is going on?* The console is warning us against some problem with the format of our x variable, which is the sequence of date of cash flows reporting.

This means that is is not able to compute the mean and the differences from the means for these dates. We therefore have to transform this variable a bit before passing it to the *cor* function. How would you do this? Yeah... you can check on Google...

Did you find anything? Too much, you say? That is why there is still a meaning into the *training on the job* locution, I guess... Anyway, an elegant way to transform a sequence of dates into a progression of numbers is to compute the difference in days between the oldest date recorded and all the others. This means assigning a value of 0 to the oldest date, for every record where it is shown, and a value equal to the number of days in the middle for any other date.

First, we need to find the oldest date and assign it to a vector:

```
oldest <- min(cash_flow_report$y)
```

Yeah, it is that simple, the min of a sequence of dates is the oldest one. And which is the oldest date?

```
oldest
[1] "2014-03-31"
```

Then, we add a column to our data, named `delays`, where the difference from the given date and the `oldest` object is computed. To do that, we employ the `difftime` function available within base R. This function just requires you to specify the dates for which to compute the difference and the unity of measurement in which you want the result to be expressed:

```
cash_flow_report %>%
mutate(delays = difftime(cash_flow_report$y, oldest, units = "days")) ->
cash_flow_report_mutation
```

Let's have a look at the results employing the `head()` function:

```
x y cash_flow delays
  1 north_america 2014-03-31 100955.81 0 days
  2 south_america 2014-03-31 111817.48 0 days
  3 asia 2014-03-31 132019.06 0 days
  4 europe 2014-03-31 91369.00 0 days
  5 north_africa 2014-03-31 109863.53 0 days
  6 middle_east 2014-03-31 94753.52 0 days
```

Uhm, it seems it actually created the variable computing the difference in days between the `y` variable and the oldest date, which for the first records is the same.

We are now going to actually compute the correlation, adopting one final caution: the `delays` variable is of the `difftime` class, and needs to be transformed into a fully numerical variable before being passed to the `cor` function. We are going to apply the `as.numeric()` function here for that:

```
cor(x = as.numeric(cash_flow_report_mutation$delays),
  y = cash_flow_report_mutation$cash_flow)
```

And here we are: -0.1148544.

This means that a weak inverse relationship is observed between the increase of time and the volume of cash flows. Unfortunately, the number is pretty small and we cannot therefore consider it as a great hint of some kind of general negative trend involving our sales. Nevertheless, we should be aware that we just checked for a linear relationship. Things could change now that we take a look at the distance correlation.

Distance correlation

This is a far more concept than the Pearson coefficient, and we cannot address it in detail here. The main difference between the two concepts are:

- The quantities that are multiplied to investigate the type of relation occurring between data, which were the distance from the mean for Pearson and are the doubly centered distances for the distance correlation
- The kind of relationship spotted from the statistics, which was only the linear one for the Pearson coefficient, while it is any kind of relationship for the distance correlation.

This value is formally defined as follows:

$$dCor(X, Y) = \frac{dCov(X,Y)}{\sqrt{dVar(X)dVar(Y)}}$$

As you see, it is, in a way, similar to the Pearson coefficient, since it is a ratio between a covariance and the square of two variances. Moreover, both of the ratios can range from *-1* to *1*.

Within R, we have the `dcor` function from the `energy` package, which can help us compute these statistics:

```
dcor(cash_flow_report_mutation$delays, cash_flow_report_mutation$cash_flow)
```

This results in 0.14. What does this mean? It means that a small positive correlation is going on within our data, of some functional form different from the linear one. Once again, the value of this coefficient is really near to 0 and cannot therefore be interpreted as strong evidence of a trend of our cash flows over time.

Weaknesses of summary EDA - the Anscombe quartet

In the meantime, I have found my notes about the Anscombe quartet. Look at these four plots:

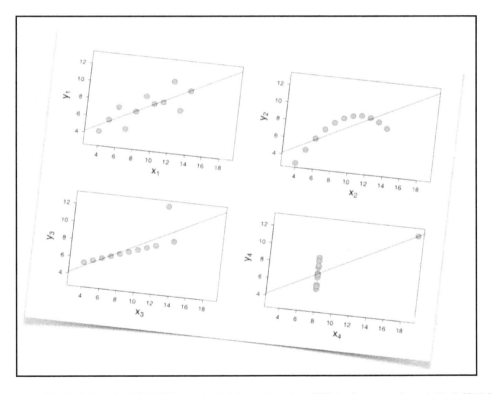

Those are four different plots, aren't they? Nevertheless, as shown by Francis Anscombe in 1973, all of them share the same value for all of the following parameters:

- Mean of x and y
- Variance
- Pearson correlation between x and y

This was quite a shock for some of the first readers of the paper, nevertheless, it served as a really effective way to show how misleading summary statistics can be. Moreover, it was an equally powerful way to show how relevant it was to look at a graphical representation of available data. This was not so common at the time, and it was actually considered as a kind of activity performed by people not enough skilled to compute and understand other kinds of analysis.

OK, following the path opened by Francis with his quartet, let's start performing some graphical exploratory data analysis and see if the reason for the drop finally reveals itself.

Graphical EDA

You can include as **Graphical Exploratory Data Analysis (Graphical EDA)** any kind of technique that implies visualizing your data following some kind of conventional system. This can involve representing it on a Cartesian plot or following polar coordinates; the main point here is that you do not rely on any kind of summary, but just on your eyes to read the story your data has to tell.

Visualizing a variable distribution

One of the first things you can do when performing graphical EDA is to look at the distribution of your data, one variable at a time. To do that, two main types of plot come in to help:

- Histogram
- Boxplot

Histogram

A histogram is a special kind of bar plot, having on the x axis the unique values shown from your variable, or some kind of clusterization of these values, and on the y axis the frequency of these values. Let's plot a histogram for each of our three variables within the cash_flow_report. We are going to use ggplot, which somebody told me you should already be familiar with. Here is some general info about histograms with ggplot:

- You need to pass as aesthetic the variable you want to analyze
- You will have to employ the geom_histogram geom, which is specifically designed for this kind of plot
- When dealing with categorical variables, you will have to specify to ggplot that you want to count them, via the stat = 'count' token

Reporting date histogram

We can generate a histogram for the reporting date attribute with the following two lines:

```
ggplot(data = cash_flow_report,aes(y))+
geom_histogram(stat = 'count')
```

Which produces a quite...ehm...rectangular histogram:

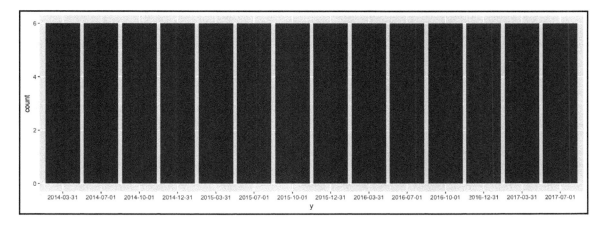

Well, thinking a bit about it, it is actually a reassuring output: it shows us that all dates are recorded an equal number of times, and therefore that there is no missing record. We perform a final check on this looking at the sequence on the *x* axis: *is there any date missing? No, so we can move on to the geographical area.*

Geographical area histogram

Time to look at some spatial data:

```
ggplot(data = cash_flow_report,aes(x))+
geom_histogram(stat = 'count')
```

And here we are, with another rectangular plot:

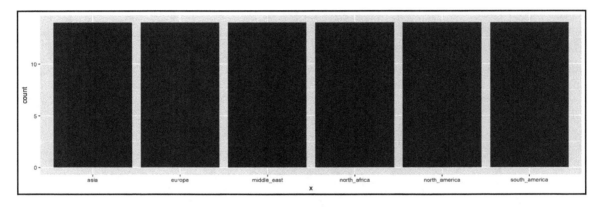

Once again, we don't have to worry about this, it is just reassuring us that every geographical area is recorded an equal number of times.

Cash flow histogram

Finally, let's develop a histogram of our cash flows:

```
ggplot(data = cash_flow_report,aes(cash_flow))+
geom_histogram()
```

And here it is:

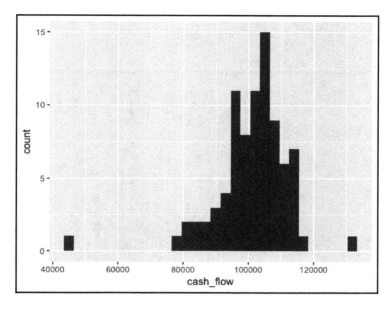

Well, not too bad, we already get quite a relevant confirmation: our population is negatively skewed, that is, it's biased towards higher values. Moreover, we see some kind of extreme values up and down, which could be outliers.

We are going to check for outliers later with boxplots, but let's make our plot a bit more granular, increasing the number of bins, as you can see from the console message `stat_bin()` using `bins = 30`. Pick better value with `binwidth`. ggplot automatically defined bins from our data, collecting together unique values of cash flow to reach a total number of 30 bins. We can change this through two complementary ways:

- Setting the final number of bins that we want, through the `bins` argument.
- Setting the number of unique values to be binned within each bin, through the `binwidth` argument. This is the way suggested by `ggplot` itself.

Let's move on by following the first way, since we already know how many `bins` there are, and we just want to increase the granularity of our plot:

```
ggplot(data = cash_flow_report,aes(cash_flow))+
geom_histogram(bins = 70)
```

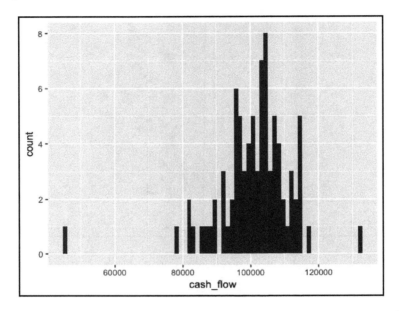

We are definitely gaining focus here: our distribution still tends towards higher values, but it actually seems quite symmetrical around a central value, which is between 100k and 150k euros. This is true for all the population, but not for a lower bin, which is below 60k euros.

It seems to me that we are dealing with an outlier, and it could even be related to our drop, but let's make sure of this by looking at boxplots.

Boxplot

Boxplots are a convenient way to look at distributions. They can visualize in a single plot, such as:

- Minimum and maximum of our population
- First and third quartile
- Median or mean of the population, or both of them
- Outliers, following different possible rules to define them

We are going to look here at a plot from the base R, since for the single variable case, where no grouping variable is available, the base R `boxplot` function results in being far more straightforward than the `ggplot` one:

```
boxplot(x = cash_flow_report$cash_flow, horizontal = TRUE)
```

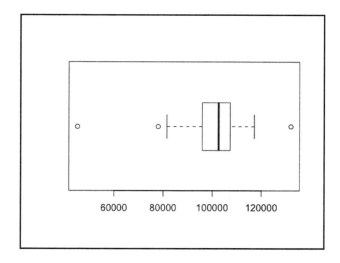

And here it is, our box plot confirming all of our evaluation about the population:

- We have got a shift towards higher values
- We have got three outliers, and one of those is extremely low

The more I look at it, the more I get persuaded that the lower outlier is the missing hint to understanding the origin of the drop. We should definitely have a closer look at it.

Checking for outliers

Within the `boxplot` function, outliers are computed following John Tukey's formula, that is, setting a threshold equal to *1.5 * interquartile* range and marking everything outside the range defined from *1st quartile - 1.5 * interquartile* range and *3rd quartile + 1.5 * interquartile* range as outlier. No, there doesn't seem to be any statistical reason behind that 1.5, nor a cabalistic one.

To get a closer look at the value marked as outlier, we have to resort to the `boxplot.stats` function, which is the one called from the `boxplot` function. This function actually computes stats behind the plot, and outliers are included among them.

Let me try to call it, passing the `cash_flow` attribute as argument:

```
boxplot.stats(x = cash_flow_report$cash_flow)
```

OK then, you find the following as the output:

```
$stats
 [1]  81482.76  95889.92  102593.81  107281.90  117131.77
$n
 [1]  84
$conf
 [1]  100629.9  104557.7
$out
 [1]  132019.06  77958.74  45089.21
```

The `stats` command shows the values of Tukey's upper and lower threshold (first and last term) the first quartile, the median, and the third quartile. The n object just acknowledges the number of records analyzed and the `conf` one report about confidence intervals that do not have any interest for us at the moment.

Finally, the `out` element shows detected outliers, by decreasing value. Can you see it?

```
$out
 [1]  132019.06  77958.74  45089.21
```

`45089.21`, here it is, our first suspect.

But, when was this recorded, and where? We will find this out by storing detected outliers in a vector and filtering out our `cash_flow` report, employing as a filter that `45089.21`:

Store the `outliers`:

```
stats <- boxplot.stats(x = cash_flow_report$cash_flow)
outliers <- stats$out
```

Filter `cash_flow_report` based on the value of `cash_flow` output, looking for records equal to `outliers[3]`, which is our beloved `45089.21`.

```
cash_flow_report %>%
  filter(cash_flow == outliers[3])
```

Look, we did it here, it is our suspect:

```
   x          y                    cash_flow
1  middle_east  2017-07-01         45089.21
```

It is the last recorded cash flow from the Middle East. Is it the last of a decreasing trend affecting this region; is there any general trend over time? We are going to discover this by looking at the cash flows together with the other variables, that is, reporting date and geographic area.

Visualizing relationships between variables

It is now time to visualize how the cash flows evolved over time, and how the different geographic areas performed. The two pieces of information combined will let us understand if that outlier is part of an organic trend, or an isolated point that should be held as responsible for the observed profit drop.

We are going to leverage one main instrument here, that is, the scatterplot.

Scatterplots

Scatterplots are actually the most basic kind of chart you could imagine: on the *x* axis you have one variable, on the *y* you have the other one, and each data is marked with a point, being a couple of *x* and *y*. Even if they are really basic, they tend to be rather powerful for visualizing the existence and intensity of dependence between two variables. This is so true that, as our friend Anscombe used to say:

> *"Before anything else is done, we should scatterplot the y values against the x values and see what sort of relation there is."*

Let's start with a scatterplot showing time against cash flow: we are going to use the `geom_point` geom here, which is shown as follows:

```
cash_flow_report %>%
  ggplot(aes(x = y, y = cash_flow))+
  geom_point()
```

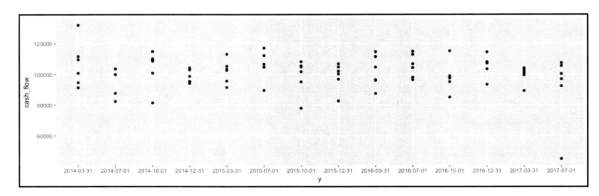

What can you see? I see a quite stationary movement around an average value of 100k euros, which is coherent with what our studies about distribution and standard deviation told us. Moreover, I can see that our famous outlier does not seem to be part of a trend, but seems to have appeared from nowhere. It would actually be interesting to add one or more bits of info to our plot, and here I am talking about the geographic area. Let's try to add it as a grouping variable, which in `ggplot` can be easily done through the `group` aesthetic:

```
cash_flow_report %>%
ggplot(aes(x = y, y = cash_flow, group = x, colour = x))+
  geom_point()
```

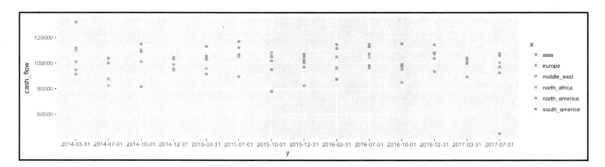

It definitely looks more colored now, nevertheless, I am not sure we have added any meaning to it. The only relevant confirmation we get is that the outlier is still coming from the Middle East. We need to connect points pertaining to the same region and see if any kind of trend appears. To do that, we can create a mixed chart, joining the scatterplot with a line chart:

```
cash_flow_report %>%
ggplot(aes(x = y, y = cash_flow, group = x, colour = x))+
geom_point()+
geom_line()
```

Here we are:

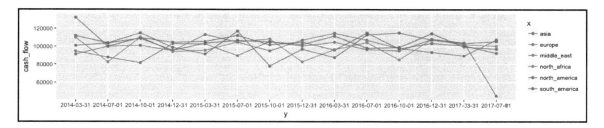

Neat! We now see clearly all we have been talking about, such as low variability, absence of clear trends, and the recent outlier from the Middle East. Our objective is met: we found the origin of the drop. Good job!

We now need to polish this plot up a bit since we are going to use it when sharing our results with the boss. Let's do the following:

- Add a title and a subtitle to the plot
- Add explicative names to the axis label
- Add the source of the plot as a caption
- Fix the coloring by removing the gray space and lightening the weight of the line, since it doesn't keep any message relevant to our point
- Add some explicative text next to the Middle East outlier

Adding title, subtitle, and caption to the plot

We can conveniently do this employing `labs`, which lets us specify a `title`, `subtitle`, and `caption` argument:

```
cash_flow_report %>%
ggplot(aes(x = y, y = cash_flow, group = x, colour = x))+
geom_point()+
```

```
geom_line()+
labs(title = "cash flows over time by region", subtitle="quarterly data
from 2014 to Q2 2017")
```

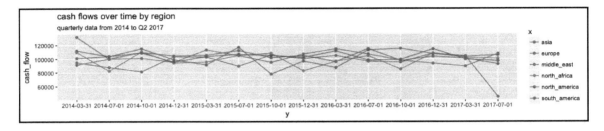

Much, much better. Let's move on to the axis and legend labels.

Setting axis and legend

We are going to give a more explicable name to both the *x* and *y* axis:

- For the first one, we will substitute *y* with a *quarter of reporting*, adding the xlab() function to our plot.
- The *y* axis will need a less invasive refinement, meaning a small change to the wording and the addition of the currency in which data is reported. This will be handled through the ylab() function:

```
cash_flow_report %>%
ggplot(aes(x = y, y = cash_flow, group = x, colour = x))+
geom_point()+
geom_line()+
labs(title = "cash flows over time by region",
subtitle="quarterly data from 2014 to Q2 2017",
caption = "source: cash_flow_report")+
xlab("quarter of reporting")+
ylab("recorded cash flows (euro)")
```

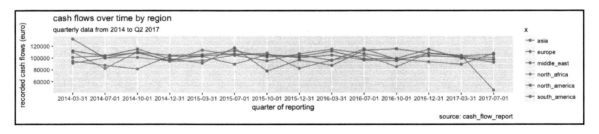

Adding explicative text to the plot

Just to stress the point further, we can now add a text near to the Middle East drop. We can use the `annotate` function here, which can be employed to add both shapes and texts to a `ggplot`. The following arguments will be needed to make our text appear:

- `geom`, which defines the type of annotation. We will set to it **text.**
- `label`, which sets the actual text. We are going to write something like *the Middle East cash flow series shows an unprecedented drop in the Q2 2017.*
- `x` and `y`, which defines the point that will be considered as an anchor point for our text. We will set it near to our outlier, that is on 01/07/2017 at 40k euros.
- `hjust` and `vjust`, to adjust the vertical and horizontal alignment of our text:

```
cash_flow_report %>%
ggplot(aes(x = y, y = cash_flow, group = x, colour = x))-
geom_point()+
geom_line()+
labs(title = "cash flows over time by region",
subtitle="quarterly data from 2014 to Q2 2017",
caption = "source: cash_flow_report")+
xlab("quarter of reporting")+
ylab("recorded cash flows (euro)")+
annotate("text", label = "the middle east cash flow series \n shows
a unprecedent drop on the Q2 2017",
x = "2017-07-01", y= 40000, hjust = 1, vjust =0)
```

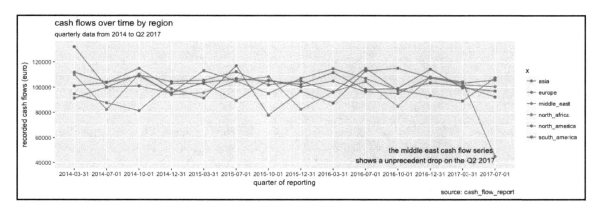

Nearly done; we just need some more touches on color to help make the point at the first glance.

Final touches on colors

To make our point bold and clear, we are going to remove the unessential graphical elements with the `theme_minimal()` function, and differentiate the Middle East series from all the others. While the first is as easy as adding one function to the plot, the second will require us to set a conditional rule for colors and manually set those colors via the `scale_colour_manual`.

Setting a conditional rule for color can be done directly within the first `aes()` included in the `ggplot()` function. We will place a logical check there such as `x == "middle_east"`. This will have, as a consequence, `ggplot` coloring in a different way all the point for which `x` is equal to `middle_east` and all the other points with another color. Since it is a good guy, `ggplot` will also provide a default coloring for the two clusters, but we want to convey the message that `middle_east` is more relevant than all the other regions. That is why we will set, through the `scale_colour_manual`, the two colors:

- A bold red for the `middle_east` series
- A light gray for the others

Finally, we have to remove the legend (which will result in an unpleasant title `x==` `"middle_east"`) and specify within the subtitle that the red series is the one related to the `middle_east`:

```
cash_flow_report %>%
  ggplot(aes(x = y, y = cash_flow, group = x, colour = x == "middle_east"
))+
geom_point()+
geom_line( alpha = .2)+
labs(title = "cash flows over time by region",
subtitle="quarterly data from 2014 to Q2 2017, middle east data in red",
caption = "source: cash_flow_report")+
xlab("quarter of reporting")+
ylab("recorded cash flows (euro)")+
annotate("text", label = "the middle east cash flow series \n shows a
unprecedent drop on the Q2 2017",
x = "2017-07-01", y= 40000, hjust = 1, vjust =0)+
scale_colour_manual(values = c("grey70", "red")) +
theme_minimal()+
theme(legend.position = "none")
```

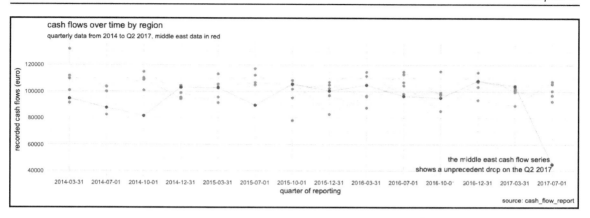

And here we are: we now have a clean plot able to convey our main message quickly and effectively. Next step: *sharing this plot with the boss, and let's see what happens.*

In the meanwhile, thank you for your precious collaboration!

Further references

- The incredibly good website from Tyler Vigen about spurious correlations: http://www.tylervigen.com/spurious-correlations
- Graphs in Statistical Analysis by F. J. Anscombe The American Statistician, Vol. 27, No. 1 (Feb., 1973), pp. 17-21, the paper where the Anscombe quartet was introduced

Summary

The author speaking again: how was your EDA? You found where the drop came from, didn't you? This is great, and we are going to see what the boss thinks about it in a few pages, but let me just summarize here which topic you have been working on with your colleague and what you have learned.

First of all, you were introduced to the concept of EDA and how it can be included within the data analysis process.

You then learned about summary EDA and actually performed it on real data, focusing on quartiles and median, mean, variance, standard deviation, and skewness. For all of them, you first got a sense of what these summary statistics are about and how they work. Finally, you learned what the relevant functions are and how you have to employ them in order to compute each and every one of these statistics.

As a last step within the summary EDA field, you discovered the Anscombe quartet, which is composed of four different datasets sharing a lot of identical summary statistics, even if being very different when actually looking at them through scatterplots. This was shown to you as a way to highlight the limits of summary statistics alone, and to introduce you to the relevance of the graphical EDA.

Moving on to graphical EDA itself, you looked at histograms and boxplots as a way to observe a distribution of univariate values, and particularly as a way to detect outliers. You actually gained a closer look at how the boxplot values are computed and stored.

You finally took a look at multivariate data through scatterplots and linecharts, also looking at advanced ways to customize a plot in order to better convey the desired message and therefore make it ready to be shared with relevant shareholders.

Quite a lot of stuff for a newbie at the Hippalus company! Nevertheless, I have the presentiment that the most thrilling part has still to come: are you ready to discover what caused the Middle East drop?

7
Our First Guess – a Linear Regression

Still smiling from the successful EDA you just obtained, you follow Andy, the colleague who helped you with it, and walk into the office of your boss, Mr. Sheen: *Have you finally discovered where all this mess is coming from?* Not exactly what you would call a warm welcome, I agree.

Nevertheless, your colleague seems to be quite used to these kinds of high-pressure situations and quietly starts to expose all the analyses you have performed, from the summary statistics to the graphical EDA. Your boss is some kind of hybrid profile and Andy knows that: exposing your work with a sufficient level of detail will help your boss understand that, despite the great hurry the work was done in, it was done in the most accurate way possible.

Andy finally comes to the point—the cash flow recorded within the last quarter is coming from the Middle East area.

"The Middle East? We have not been there for a long time. Nevertheless, I personally know Marc, the Chief Operating Officer for that region, we can easily take our analyses further: I will personally call him today."

I would not be that hasty. You just heard the heavy voice of Mr. Clough, internal audit head for the east area. *I personally know Marc Leveque as well. This is such a strange case that we should exclude any hypothesis too early. Immediately contacting Mr. Leveque would place him in a status of alert, and we do not want that. I have got another idea: give me a list of companies related to this drop and I will put some of my guys on them to see if they can highlight anything suspicious. And we have to do it quickly, we need it by tomorrow.*

At the moment, we do not have this kind of data. You know our data mining engine is still not working and we cannot tell you from her who is not paying in the Middle East. Mr. Sheen is not going to let it go too easily.

Mr. Sheen is right, the best we can do by tomorrow is try to understand which companies are historically most prone to default and give you a list of the companies having the same features today in the Middle East.

We can do what Andy is saying, but he was wrong about time: we need two days.

The later we start, the later we fix it. OK, we can arrange for these two days. Thank you for your cooperation as usual. Mr. Sheen, let me know when the results come out. Have a nice day.

Even if the discussion was not pleasant, the final output is clear: we need to find out which kinds of companies are historically most prone to default and develop a list of the companies with the same features today within the Middle East area.

Andy, please take care of this for me, it was your idea. And you can work with Andy on this as well, [your name here]. Nice, you will work with Andy on this. I will leave you alone for this chapter, as I did for the previous one. Let us see in the *Summary* section!

Defining a data modelling strategy

I was perhaps too hasty proposing this solution to Mr Clough—he is a great professional, but I have never heard of one of his requests going unsatisfied. Moreover, his words made me think is not excluding the hypothesis of fraud. And this makes me even more nervous, if that's possible.

Nevertheless, we have to do this as if it is *business as usual*. The point is that we need some kind of data related to default events in the past and the companies that experimented this status. *What? They also gave you a dataset about past default events? And you already cleaned it? That is what I call good news. OK, just send it to me and we can start to work on it immediately.*

clean_casted_stored_data_validated_complete, *uh? You don't fear long names, do you?* Just run glimpse on it and see what is inside:

```
glimpse(clean_casted_stored_data_validated_complete)

Observations: 11,523
 Variables: 16
 $ attr_3 <dbl> 0, 0, 0, 0, 0, 0, 0, 0, 0, 0, 0, 0, 0, 0, 0, 0, 0, 0, 0,
0, 0, 0, 0, 0, 0, 0, 0, 0, 0, 0, 0, 0, 0, 0, 0, 0, 0, 0, 0, ...
 $ attr_4 <dbl> 1, 1, 1, 1, 1, 1, 1, 1, 1, 1, 1, 1, 1, 1, 1, 1, 1, 1, 1,
```

```
1, 1, 1, 1, 1, 1, 1, 1, 1, 1, 1, 1, 1, 1, 1, 1, 1, 1, 1, 1, ...
$ attr_5 <dbl> 0, 0, 0, 0, 0, 0, 0, 0, 0, 0, 0, 0, 0, 0, 0, 0, 0, 0, 0, 0,
0, 0, 0, 0, 0, 0, 0, 0, 0, 0, 0, 0, 0, 0, 0, 0, 0, 0, 0, 0, ...
$ attr_6 <dbl> 1, 1, 1, 1, 1, 1, 1, 1, 1, 1, 1, 1, 1, 1, 1, 1, 1, 1, 1, 1,
1, 1, 1, 1, 1, 1, 1, 1, 1, 1, 1, 1, 1, 1, 1, 1, 1, 1, 1, 1, ...
$ attr_7 <dbl> 0, 0, 0, 0, 0, 0, 0, 0, 0, 0, 0, 0, 0, 0, 0, 0, 0, 0, 0, 0,
0, 0, 0, 0, 0, 0, 0, 0, 0, 0, 0, 0, 0, 0, 0, 0, 0, 0, 0, 0, ...
$ default_numeric <chr> "0", "0", "0", "0", "0", "0", "0", "0", "0", "0",
"0", "0", "0", "0", "0", "0", "0", "0", "0", "0", "0", "0", "0", ...
$ default_flag <fctr> 0, 0, 0, 0, 0, 0, 0, 0, 0, 0, 0, 0, 0, 0, 0, 0, 0, 0,
0, 0, 0, 0, 0, 0, 0, 0, 0, 0, 0, 0, 0, 0, 0, 0, 0, 0, 0, 0, ...
$ customer_code <dbl> 8523, 8524, 8525, 8526, 8527, 8528, 8529, 8530,
8531, 8533, 8534, 8535, 8536, 8537, 8538, 8539, 8540, 8541, 8542, 8544, ...
$ attr_10 <dbl> -1.000000e+06, 7.591818e-01, -1.000000e+06, 6.755027e-01,
1.000000e+00, 1.000000e+00, 9.937470e-01, 1.000000e+00, 3.7204...
$ attr_11 <dbl> 3.267341e-02, 4.683477e-02, 4.092031e-02, 1.482232e-01,
3.383478e-02, 6.593393e-02, 6.422492e-02, 2.287126e-02, 4.475434...
$ attr_12 <dbl> 7598, 565, 50000, 1328460, 389, 25743, 685773, 27054, 48,
648, 1683, 5677342, 322, 775, 150000, 1054413, 116014, 4424, 2...
$ attr_13 <dbl> 7598, 565, 50000, 749792, 389, 25743, 1243, 27054, 48,
648, 1683, 1358, 322, 775, 150000, 16351, 115937, 4424, 273, 827,...
$ attr_8 <dbl> -1.000000e+06, 4.365132e-01, 8.761467e-01, 1.000000e+00,
6.800000e-01, 9.530645e-01, 2.065790e-01, 7.828452e-02, 2.06512...
$ attr_9 <dbl> 10000.83, 10000.84, 10000.70, 10000.78, 10000.28, 10000.15,
10001.00, 10000.00, 10000.00, 10000.00, 10000.89, 10000.99, ...
$ commercial_portfolio <chr> "less affluent", "less affluent", "less
affluent", "less affluent", "less affluent", "less affluent", "less
affluent", "...
$ business_unit <chr> "retail_bank", "retail_bank", "retail_bank",
"retail_bank", "retail_bank", "retail_bank", "retail_bank", "retail_bank",
...
```

glimpse is a function provided by dplyr to quickly inspect the content of a data frame and gain basic information about it, such as the number of variables and the kinds of variables for each column.

Uhm... I can see this table doesn't have exploitative labels for every attribute. Nevertheless, these `attr_...`s remind me of an email I received some time ago about a standard report the IT department was trying to create to merge information related to customers from different legacies. I should still have it here in the mailbox. Here it is:

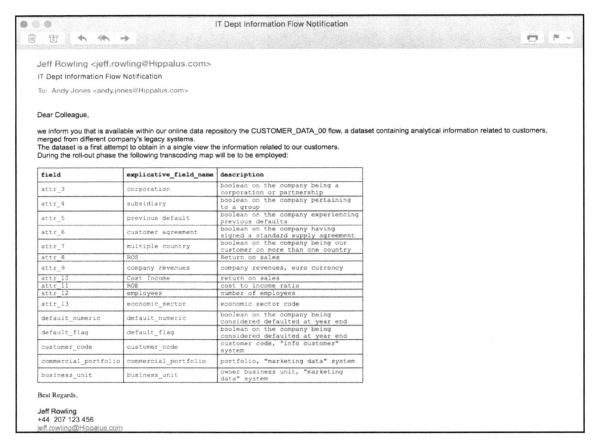

We have here our transcoding map. Let us reassign column names based on this table. First of all we need to check for the actual names and the order of columns. We can use the `colnames()` function for that:

```
colnames(clean_casted_stored_data_validated_complete)

[1]  "attr_3"
[2]  "attr_4"
[3]  "attr_5"
[4]  "attr_6"
```

```
[5]  "attr_7"
[6]  "default_numeric"
[7]  "default_flag"
[8]  "customer_code"
[9]  "geographic_area"
[10] "attr_10"
[11] "attr_11"
[12] "attr_12"
[13] "attr_13"
[14] "attr_8"
[15] "attr_9"
[16] "commercial_portfolio"
[17] "business_unit"
```

We can now change those names, leveraging the same function and an assignment operator:

```
colnames(clean_casted_stored_data_validated_complete) <- c("corporation",
                                "subsidiary" ,
                                "previous_default",
                                "customer_agreement",
                                "multiple_country",
                                "default_numeric",
                                "default_flag" ,
                                "customer_code",
                                "cost_income",
                                "ROE",
                                "employees",
                                "economic_sector",
                                "multiple country",
                                "ROS" ,
                                "commercial_portfolio",
                                "business_unit")
```

While on the first line of code, we are asking to R to show us the column names, on the second block, we are actually telling R what the names are. Calling the same function for the third time will let us appreciate intervened changes.

We now have a dataset containing historical information about our customers, including the relevant information of default status. The next step is defining a data mining plan. *They told me you are familiar with the CRISP-DM methodology. I should have here a typical representation of the CRISP-DM cycle:*

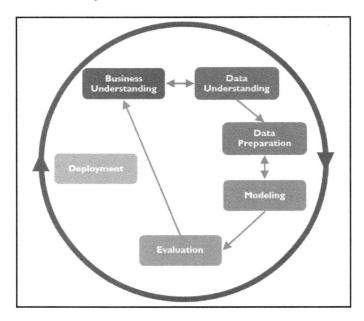

We performed *data understanding* through our **exploratory data analysis** (**EDA**), and we did data preparation when dealing with data cleaning and validation. It is now time to proceed to the modeling phase.

As you know, the first step here is to define a data modeling strategy. Since the problem here is to understand what common features are shared by customers going into default, we are not focused here on the prediction of future defaults, but rather on the analysis of the past.

Data modelling notions

We are therefore considering the default event as the variable to be explained, that is, the response variable. We then have all the other attributes that we hope will explain our response variable, we call them explanatory variables. To go from the explanatory variables to the response variables, we need to establish some kind of rule or relationship. We call this rule a function. However, we need to emphasize that the relationship between them is casual or asymmetric. Calling Y the response variable and $x_1, x_2 ... x_n$ the set of explanatory variables, we use to formalize this concept as:

$$Y = f(x_1, x_2 \cdots x_n)$$

To be true, we usually add an element, which is called the error term and is noted as ϵ. This expresses the impossibility of defining a model able to exactly reproduce the true underlying phenomenon. Sources of this error are:

- The inadequacy of the model
- Error in measures
- Variation of the phenomenon over time

We can therefore write our previous equation as:

$$Y = f(x_1, x_2 \cdots x_n) + \epsilon$$

Starting from this, a whole world opens up to understand how to estimate that small letter f and reduce the even smaller letter ϵ. To let you orientate, we can distinguish between two big modeling strategies:

- Supervised learning
- Unsupervised learning

Supervised learning

When you are dealing with data with both an input and an output, you are dealing with supervised learning. Think of every course you have ever taken: the teacher teaches you the relevant rules with some examples and then you apply the same rules to new examples, which usually are far more difficult than the teacher's one, but this is all another story...

In a more formal way, we talk about supervised learning when our model relies on a set of x, the previously mentioned explanatory variables, and a corresponding set of y. This translates into datasets showing for each record the set of x and the corresponding y.

Starting from cases where the variable to be explained is binary that can be assumed as either one or another value, it is said that for each record a label is attached to it, showing if it has a good output or not. That is why this kind of data is also called labeled.

A great example of labeled data is our customer dataset. For each record we have a label, the `default_flag` column, saying if the given set of explanatory variables resulted in a good result (the customer paying) or a bad result (the customer not paying).

Unsupervised learning

As is always the case with dichotomies, unsupervised learning encompasses all that is not supervised. We are here in the opposite situation—we just have a set of variables with no response. A quite famous example here is when a child is given some wooden toys of different shapes and is asked to separate them into two groups. This child has no rule or expected output, just the request to create two separate groups. He will have to sort out some kind of rule on his own. This will probably involve looking at the color, the shape, or the dimensions.

The modeling strategy

It is now time to actually develop our modeling strategy. We are going to focus here mainly on supervised learning since we are working on labeled data. That said, we should start with some linear regression and gradually add on complexity. Let us write down a list of models and techniques to try with our data:

- Linear regression
- Principal component analysis as a technique of dimensionality reduction
- Decision trees
- Logistic regression
- Linear margin classifiers
- Support vector machine
- Random forest
- Ensemble learning techniques

You should not feel overwhelmed by this list, since we are going to tackle them gradually and I will provide you for each of them the underlying intuition and just the minimum set of required mathematical notation to get it right. We will then apply them to our data via R and visualize the results.

Employing all these different algorithms will allow us to gain a structured and complete view of our data, and finally predict which companies currently have a default status among the customers of Hippalus in the Middle East. I also have cheat sheets for these models; I will share them with you along the way so that you can employ them to quickly recall and apply what we are going to learn.

Applying linear regression to our data

Linear regression is probably the most famous statistical model. It has been around for a long time, since the first concepts behind its development go back to the 1980. This model mainly owes its popularity to the relative ease of application and its great interpretability.

The intuition behind linear regression

When applying linear regression to a set of data, we are making the following assumption—the relationship between one (or more) explanatory variable and the response variable is known and linear. There are two points to consider:

- **Known**: We are assuming the existence of some kind of law ruling the level of y given the level of x. We are also usually implying that the level of x directly causes the level of y. We know from our discussion about linear correlation that this is not necessarily true and that further evidence is needed to assume causality.
- **Linear:** The relation between the explanatory variables and a response is assumed to be representable as a linear combination of the explanatory variables plus an error term.

A real-world example of this kind of relationship is the straight-line motion equation, directly coming from the realm of physics. That equation states the linear and immutable relationship between time and speed, given a certain acceleration. We have, therefore:

$$V_t = at$$

If we try to plot this considering a certain acceleration, let's say $4\ m/s^2$ and three different moments 0,2,3, we will get the linear nature of this relationship:

- For moment 0, we will have a speed equal to 0
- For moment 2, we will have a speed equal to $2*4 = 8$
- For moment 3, we will find a speed of $3*4 = 12$

Let's jot down a plot:

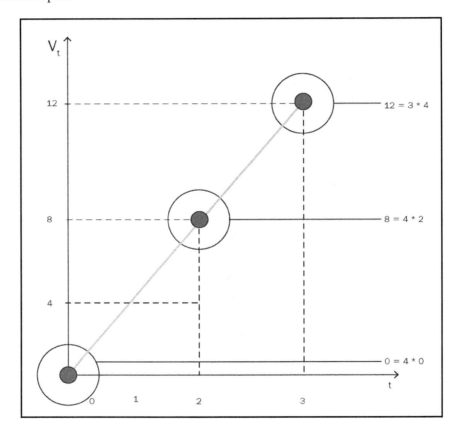

If we look closer at the equation, we see that the most relevant component is the acceleration coefficient. This number is actually the one that defines how inclined the line will be. You can be sure of this by changing 4 to 7 and re-performing the same computation and plotting: doesn't it get steeper?

In a more formal way, that component is called the slope, and its estimation is actually the core point of linear regression models.

The math behind the linear regression

In the example of straight-line motion, the slope was known, which was a hypothesis we made to observe how the speed of our object would have changed over time. When applying this linear relationship model to a set of data, like for instance our data, we do not know this parameter and estimating it is actually the main point when dealing with a linear regression model.

The following equation formally represents a linear regression model:

$$y_i = \beta_0 + \beta_1 * x_i$$

As you can see, it is similar to the speed formula, except for the β_0 term, which is called the intercept. It defines the value of y in the case of x being equal to zero. The β_1 term is the slope we were talking about before.

As we were also saying, the main task when estimating a linear regression model is to define that slope parameter. Which criterion would you follow to estimate this coefficient? You should definitely try to draw your line in a way that goes as close as possible to the points of your population. Let me show you this with a sketch:

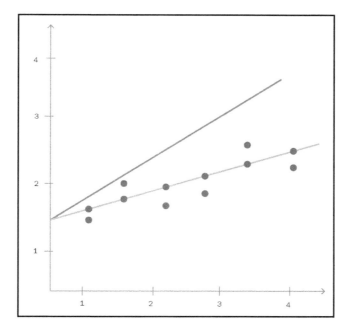

As you can see, we have here two lines that both start from the same point, but the first one, the green one, goes through the points representing the records, while the red one starts very soon going into the sky. What is the difference? I know you are guessing it: *the difference is the slope since they all start from the same point, that is, they have the same intercept.*

And by the way, saying they start from the same point means they both have the same intercept: you can verify this looking at the point where *x* is equal to 0. You see? Both start from *x* equal to 0 and *y* equal to 1.5.

So, we know that the desired line has to go through the observed records. But, how do we measure *how much through it is going?* An intuitive is the residual, the difference between the estimated value and the observed one. If you take the previous example, you can see that, for instance, when *x* is equal to 2, our observed *y* is equal to 2.5, while the estimated y is equal to 2. Within this case, we have a residual of 2.5 - 2.

We therefore want to minimize these residuals. The most common way to minimize these residuals is by employing the *ordinary least squares* technique.

Ordinary least squares technique

I am not going to show you all the calculus behind this; Mr Clough wouldn't appreciate it, but just remember that ordinary least squares first of all defines the **residual sum of squares (RSS)** as the sum of all the residuals to the second power:

$$RSS = \sum_{i=1}^{n} (y_i - \beta_0 + \beta_1 * x_i)^2$$

We minimize the RSS, as it signifies the difference between expected and actual values. Employing the term to the second power allows for avoiding the bias that could be introduced from the residuals having the opposite sign, and therefore compensating their effect.

Employing some calculus, you can conclude that the parameter values that minimize the expression are:

$$\hat{\beta}_0 = \bar{y} - \hat{\beta}_1 \bar{x}$$

$$\hat{\beta}_1 = \frac{\sum_{i=1}^{n} (x_i - \bar{x})(y_i - \bar{y})}{\sum_{i=1}^{n} (x_i - \bar{x})^2}$$

The hat (ˆ) means that this is the estimate value of the parameter whose name is underneath.

Now that you have seen what is behind the scenes, I think you will be pleased to know that R provides a simple `lm()` function that takes care of estimating all of this, just requiring you to specify which variable is to be considered as the response one and which as the explanatory one.

Model requirements – what to look for before applying the model

When applying linear regression to model the relationship between a variable and another, we should always check that the resulting residuals possess the following properties:

- Are uncorrelated
- Are homeostatic

Residuals' uncorrelation

For a linear regression model to be considered valid, residuals resulting from its estimates must be uncorrelated. This means that no clear trend should emerge from the series of residuals. One of the most frequently employed tests to assess this property is the **Durbin-Watson test**. The intuition behind this test is quite simple: it observes if, on average, consequent residuals are near to each other or not. This statistic is defined as:

$$d = \frac{\sum_{t=2}^{T} (e_t - e_{t-1})^2}{\sum_{t=2}^{T} e_t^2}$$

Where e is the difference between the observed y for a given x and the estimated y for the same x. How do you interpret values of this test? First of all, we know that it can vary from zero to four at its maximum. Moreover, it is demonstrated that:

- A value near to two is a sign of absence of correlation within residuals
- A value near to zero is a sign of positive correlation
- A value near to four is a sign of negative correlation

Residuals' homoscedasticity

Homoscedasticity is a strange word, isn't it? It actually stands for a simple concept—homogeneity of the variance. This means that no trend is observed between the y value and the variance of residuals. What is the intuition behind this assumption? You can get it starting from its opposite, the heteroscedasticity. When a population is heteroscedastic, you observe an error that tends to vary as x increases. This is not exactly what you would expect from a good model. On the opposite side, we can consider it acceptable to have an error which, even if not null, tends to remain constant over all the values of x.

A common test to validate this assumption is the so-called **Breusch-Pagan test**. This test is actually a test of hypotheses that assumes as a null hypothesis the error variance being constant, and as an alternative hypothesis, the error variance being not constant.

Without going into great details, you just have to remember that this test will result in a p-value being computed, and if this p-value results in greater than 0.05, you will have the assumption not being satisfied, that is, the null hypothesis being rejected, while the opposite will hold true for values lower than 0.05. If we get the chance, I will explain a bit more about hypotheses later on.

How to apply linear regression in R

OK then, let us move to the practical part: applying the `lm()` function to our data. Let us choose an explanatory variable and see what happens. Just recall the variables we have:

```
colnames(clean_casted_stored_data_validated_complete)
```

```
 [1] "corporation"
 [2] "subsidiary"
 [3] "previous_default"
 [4] "customer_agreement"
 [5] "multiple_country"
 [6] "default_numeric"
 [7] "default_flag"
 [8] "customer_code"
 [9] "cost_income"
[10] "ROE"
[11] "employees"
[12] "economic_sector"
[13] "company_revenues"
[14] "ROS"
[15] "commercial_portfolio"
[16] "business_unit"
```

What would you go for?

Fitting the linear regression model

Let's try with the economic sector. We can legitimately infer that the economic sector should be with a given customer going into default or not.

Let us start by fitting the linear model. As I was saying, this can be easily done in R employing the lm() function:

```
linear_regression_economic_sector <- lm(as.numeric(default_flag) ~
economic_sector, clean_casted_stored_data_validated_complete)
```

As you can see, we define as y the default_flag attribute, and as x the economic_sector. The lm() function takes care of estimating β_0 and β_1.

You can have a look at the estimates by printing out the linear_regression_economic_sector object:

```
linear_regression_economic_sector
```

Which will give you this as an output:

```
Call:
  lm(formula = as.numeric(default_flag) ~ economic_sector, data =
clean_casted_stored_data_validated_complete)

Coefficients:
    (Intercept)    economic_sector
      2.741e+00         -2.083e-09
```

Thinking again about the linear model definition, we can say that our intercept is the β_0 we were discussing before, while the β_1 is represented here from the $-2.083e-09$ related to the economic_sector variable.

Validating model assumption

Now that we have our estimates, it is time to validate the assumptions of absence of correlation and homoscedasticity. As usual, we have a package for that, and it is *car* by Professor John Fox. This package provides a full spectrum of validation tests for linear models. We are going to employ the DurbinWatsonTest() and the ncvTest() functions respectively to validate the auto-correlation and homoscedasticity assumption.

For both of them, all you need to do is call the function passing as an argument the regression model object. Let us start with the Breusch-Pagan test, to test if the variance of our residuals is substantially constant:

```
ncvTest(linear_regression_economic_sector)

Non-constant Variance Score Test
 Variance formula: ~ fitted.values
 Chisquare = 9.532657 Df = 1 p = 0.002018477
```

What do you say? Is it a good output? It is indeed, the p-value, the one you find after p on the second line, is definitely lower than the *0.05* threshold. We can, therefore, refuse the null hypothesis of our residuals not having a constant variance, and conclude that the NCV test has passed.

Now, it's time to move on to the Durbin-Watson test:

```
durbinWatsonTest(linear_regression_economic_sector)

lag Autocorrelation D-W Statistic p-value
 1 0.9958624 0.007780056 0
 Alternative hypothesis: rho != 0
```

The most relevant number here is the D-W one, which is a very low 0.007780056. If you remember, small numbers in the Durbin-Watson test mean the residuals are being positively auto-correlated. This is a bad result. We should, therefore, evaluate alternative formulations for our models. We could, for instance, look at the company_revenues attribute.

As we have just done for the economic sector attribute, just fit the model by employing the lm() function:

```
linear_regression_revenues <- lm(as.numeric(default_flag) ~
company_revenues, clean_casted_stored_data_validated_complete)
```

And then perform our diagnostic tests:

```
ncvTest(linear_regression_revenues)
durbinWatsonTest(linear_regression_revenues)
```

This results in:

```
Non-constant Variance Score Test
 Variance formula: ~ fitted.values
 Chisquare = 19.83106 Df = 1 p = 8.459667e-06
```

And:

```
lag Autocorrelation D-W Statistic p-value
1 0.995317 0.008891022 0
Alternative hypothesis: rho != 0
```

It seems we are having a bad output, aren't we?

To be honest, this was just to show you how those models work and how to estimate them in R. We are now going to make it more serious, considering all the variables we have at our disposal and how they interact with each other. That is to say, we are going to perform multiple linear regression.

Before getting into this, let us invest some time in learning how to visualize results from our estimated model with `ggplot2`. We are going to employ this for other models as well, and this will therefore not be wasted time.

Visualizing fitted values

To get a closer look at our model outputs, we have to take a closer look at the `linear_regression_revenues` object we have just created. What kind of object is it? How would you check this?

We can conveniently employ the `mode()` function for this:

```
mode(linear_regression_revenues)
```

This tells us that `linear_regression_revenues` is a list. And what is this list composed of? Just look at the `str()` output to find out:

```
str(linear_regression_revenues)

List of 12

$ coefficients : Named num [1:2] 2.75 5.84e-08
 ..- attr(*, "names")= chr [1:2] "(Intercept)" "company_revenues"
$ residuals : Named num [1:11523] -0.695 -0.754 -0.754 -0.754 -0.754 ...
 ..- attr(*, "names")= chr [1:11523] "1" "2" "3" "4" ...
$ effects : Named num [1:11523] -294.023 -2.729 -0.743 -0.743 -0.743 ...
 ..- attr(*, "names")= chr [1:11523] "(Intercept)" "company_revenues" "" ""
...
$ rank : int 2
$ fitted.values: Named num [1:11523] 2.7 2.75 2.75 2.75 2.75 ...
 ..- attr(*, "names")= chr [1:11523] "1" "2" "3" "4" ...
$ assign : int [1:2] 0 1
```

```
 $ qr :List of 5
 ..$ qr : num [1:11523, 1:2] -1.07e+02 9.32e-03 9.32e-03 9.32e-03 9.32e-03
...
 .. ..- attr(*, "dimnames")=List of 2
 .. .. ..$ : chr [1:11523] "1" "2" "3" "4" ...
 .. .. ..$ : chr [1:2] "(Intercept)" "company_revenues"
 .. ..- attr(*, "assign")= int [1:2] 0 1
 ..$ qraux: num [1:2] 1.01 1.01
 ..$ pivot: int [1:2] 1 2
 ..$ tol : num 1e-07
 ..$ rank : int 2
 ..- attr(*, "class")= chr "qr"
 $ df.residual : int 11521
 $ xlevels : Named list()
 $ call : language lm(formula = as.numeric(default_flag) ~
company_revenues, data = clean_casted_stored_data_validated_complete)
 $ terms :Classes 'terms', 'formula' language as.numeric(default_flag) ~
company_revenues
 .. ..- attr(*, "variables")= language list(as.numeric(default_flag),
company_revenues)
 .. ..- attr(*, "factors")= int [1:2, 1] 0 1
 .. .. ..- attr(*, "dimnames")=List of 2
 .. .. .. ..$ : chr [1:2] "as.numeric(default_flag)" "company_revenues"
 .. .. .. ..$ : chr "company_revenues"
 .. ..- attr(*, "term.labels")= chr "company_revenues"
 .. ..- attr(*, "order")= int 1
 .. ..- attr(*, "intercept")= int 1
 .. ..- attr(*, "response")= int 1
 .. ..- attr(*, ".Environment")=<environment: R_GlobalEnv>
 .. ..- attr(*, "predvars")= language list(as.numeric(default_flag),
company_revenues)
 .. ..- attr(*, "dataClasses")= Named chr [1:2] "numeric" "numeric"
 .. .. ..- attr(*, "names")= chr [1:2] "as.numeric(default_flag)"
"company_revenues"
 $ model :'data.frame': 11523 obs. of 2 variables:
 ..$ as.numeric(default_flag): num [1:11523] 2 2 2 2 2 2 2 2 2 2 ...
 ..$ company_revenues : num [1:11523] -1.00e+06 4.37e-01 8.76e-01 1.00
6.80e-01 ...
 ..- attr(*, "terms")=Classes 'terms', 'formula' language
as.numeric(default_flag) ~ company_revenues
 .. .. ..- attr(*, "variables")= language list(as.numeric(default_flag),
company_revenues)
 .. .. ..- attr(*, "factors")= int [1:2, 1] 0 1
 .. .. .. ..- attr(*, "dimnames")=List of 2
 .. .. .. .. ..$ : chr [1:2] "as.numeric(default_flag)" "company_revenues"
 .. .. .. .. ..$ : chr "company_revenues"
 .. .. ..- attr(*, "term.labels")= chr "company_revenues"
 .. .. ..- attr(*, "order")= int 1
```

```
.. .. ..- attr(*, "intercept")= int 1
.. .. ..- attr(*, "response")= int 1
.. .. ..- attr(*, ".Environment")=<environment: R_GlobalEnv>
.. .. ..- attr(*, "predvars")= language list(as.numeric(default_flag),
company_revenues)
.. .. ..- attr(*, "dataClasses")= Named chr [1:2] "numeric" "numeric"
.. .. .. ..- attr(*, "names")= chr [1:2] "as.numeric(default_flag)"
"company_revenues"
 - attr(*, "class")= chr "lm"
```

Maybe we should find a way to display this in a more compact way. The str() function itself provides a lot of usual additional arguments to define its output. For instance, you can define how many values are to be shown when providing a preview of vectors (look for instance, at the coefficients element). This can be set via the vec.len argument. For our purposes, we should look at the max.level parameter, which allows for defining how many nested levels we want to show. Setting it at one will allow for only the first levels to be shown:

```
str(linear_regression_revenues, max.level =1)

List of 12
 $ coefficients : Named num [1:2] 2.75 5.84e-08
 ..- attr(*, "names")= chr [1:2] "(Intercept)" "company_revenues"
 $ residuals : Named num [1:11523] -0.695 -0.754 -0.754 -0.754 -0.754 ...
 ..- attr(*, "names")= chr [1:11523] "1" "2" "3" "4" ...
 $ effects : Named num [1:11523] -294.023 -2.729 -0.743 -0.743 -0.743 ...
 ..- attr(*, "names")= chr [1:11523] "(Intercept)" "company_revenues" "" ""
...
 $ rank : int 2
 $ fitted.values: Named num [1:11523] 2.7 2.75 2.75 2.75 2.75 ...
 ..- attr(*, "names")= chr [1:11523] "1" "2" "3" "4" ...
 $ assign : int [1:2] 0 1
 $ qr :List of 5
 ..- attr(*, "class")= chr "qr"
 $ df.residual : int 11521
 $ xlevels : Named list()
 $ call : language lm(formula = as.numeric(default_flag) ~
company_revenues, data = clean..
 $ terms :Classes 'terms', 'formula' language as.numeric(default_flag) ~
company_revenues
 .. ..- attr(*, "variables")= language list(as.numeric(default_flag),
company_revenues)
 .. ..- attr(*, "factors")= int [1:2, 1] 0 1
 .. .. ..- attr(*, "dimnames")=List of 2
 .. ..- attr(*, "term.labels")= chr "company_revenues"
 .. ..- attr(*, "order")= int 1
 .. ..- attr(*, "intercept")= int 1
```

```
.. ..- attr(*, "response")= int 1
.. ..- attr(*, ".Environment")=<environment: R_GlobalEnv>
.. ..- attr(*, "predvars")= language list(as.numeric(default_flag),
company_revenues)
.. ..- attr(*, "dataClasses")= Named chr [1:2] "numeric" "numeric"
.. .. ..- attr(*, "names")= chr [1:2] "as.numeric(default_flag)"
"company_revenues"
 $ model :'data.frame': 11523 obs. of 2 variables:
 ..- attr(*, "terms")=Classes 'terms', 'formula' language
as.numeric(default_flag) ~ company_re..
 .. .. ..- attr(*, "variables")= language list(as.numeric(default_flag),
company_revenues)
 .. .. ..- attr(*, "factors")= int [1:2, 1] 0 1
 .. .. .. ..- attr(*, "dimnames")=List of 2
 .. .. ..- attr(*, "term.labels")= chr "company_revenues"
 .. .. ..- attr(*, "order")= int 1
 .. .. ..- attr(*, "intercept")= int 1
 .. .. ..- attr(*, "response")= int 1
 .. .. ..- attr(*, ".Environment")=<environment: R_GlobalEnv>
 .. .. ..- attr(*, "predvars")= language list(as.numeric(default_flag),
company_revenues)
 .. .. ..- attr(*, "dataClasses")= Named chr [1:2] "numeric" "numeric"
 .. .. .. ..- attr(*, "names")= chr [1:2] "as.numeric(default_flag)"
"company_revenues"
 - attr(*, "class")= chr "lm"
```

If you compare this output with the previous output, you will easily find out that just the first levels are shown. For instance, the `model` object is a data frame of two columns, one for each variable employed (both response and explanatory variables). While in the first output we found the `$model` branch, the `$as.numeric(default_flag)` branch, and `$company_revenues` branch within the second output, with just the first printed out.

Let's take a closer look at the object. We have:

- **Coefficients**, which store the estimate intercept and slope of our fitted model.
- **Residuals**, which store resulting residuals (this is the column used by the `ncvTest` and `durbinWatsonTest` functions).
- **Rank**, which shows the numeric rank of the matrix that can be employed to represent our model. If you do not employ variables obtained as a linear combination of other variables, it will always coincide with the total number of parameters you employ.
- **Fitted_values**, exactly what it seems: our estimated y.

- **odel** model, a data frame storing the data you passed as an input to your lm() function, which in our case are the company_revenues vector and the default_numeric one.

Preparing the data for visualization

What would you employ to visualize results of our estimates? We can take a look at how to visually compare the observed values against the estimated ones and directly observe the residuals. Let's start with observed versus estimated.

What we are going to need here is the column of fitted values and the one of observed values, paired with company revenue values.

We shall, therefore, create a new object storing all of these three values. We are going to structure our data in the long form, following the tidy data framework, so that we can then fully leverage ggplot functionalities.

This will be composed of:

- One attribute *y* that will store together fitted and observed values
- One attribute called type that will store the type of *y* distinguishing between observed and fitted
- One attribute called revenues that repeats the company_revenues both for the observed and the fitted values

Let's create every column separately. We can obtain the *y* column by stacking the default numeric column from the model object within the linear_regression_revenues list together with the fitted.values vector from the linear_regression_revenues object:

```
y = c(linear_regression_revenues$model$`as.numeric(default_numeric)`,
  as.numeric(linear_regression_revenues$fitted.values))
```

As you can see, we are creating here a vector placing as.numeric(default_numeric) before the fitted.values values. We can now create the type column repeating observed and fitted a number of time equal to the length of number of values of as.numeric(default_numeric) and fitted.values. This will be exactly equal to the number of rows of our original clean_casted_stored_data_validated_complete since it is the object from which as.numeric(default_numeric) was taken. We can then employ the nrow() function to retrieve the number of rows within that data.frame, and employ the resulting number to set the number of repetition of the observed and fitted tokens.

Let's do it:

```
type = c(rep("observed",nrow(clean_casted_stored_data_validated_complete)),
    rep("fitted",nrow(clean_casted_stored_data_validated_complete)))
```

As you can see here, we are still stacking two vectors together, both generated by employing the `rep()` function. This function, the name of which stands for *repeat*, produces a vector composed of repetitions of an *x* argument for a number of times set by the *times* argument. Within our `type` object, we create two vectors employing this function, passing once the `observed` token, and once the fitted one. In both cases, we set as the time argument the number of rows of `clean_casted_stored_data_validated_complete`.

Finally, we can move to the `revenues` object. This will simply be composed of the double repetition of the `company_revenues` vector:

```
revenues = c(rep(linear_regression_revenues$model$company_revenues,2
    ))
```

Packing all these three objects together, we have:

```
show_lm <- data.frame(y,type,revenues)
```

Let's inspect this object:

```
show_lm %>% head()

  y         type   revenues
1 0 observed 10000.83
2 0 observed 10000.84
3 0 observed 10000.70
4 0 observed 10000.78
5 0 observed 10000.28
6 0 observed 10000.15
```

Which is exactly what we were thinking about. It's now time to start drawing our data.

Developing the data visualization

As I said, having tidy data gives us the opportunity to leverage all the functionalities of `ggplot`. But, let's start with something basic so that you can see why these functionalities are needed. Just draw a scatterplot, with x the *revenues* vector and y the y vector:

```
show_lm %>%
ggplot(aes(x = revenues, y = y))+
geom_point()
```

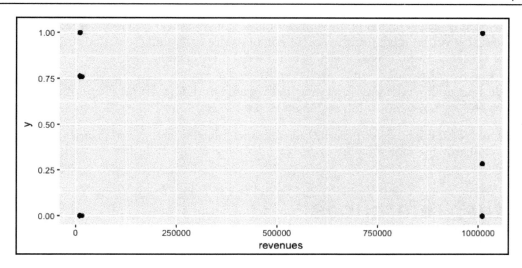

You see? Can you distinguish here which are the fitted and which are the observed values? You could guess it, I know, but we can't rely on guessing. This is why we are going to employ the color aesthetics, setting it to type so that it will distinguish the color of our point based on the value of `type`:

```
show_lm %>%
ggplot(aes(x = revenues, y = y, colour =type))+
geom_point()
```

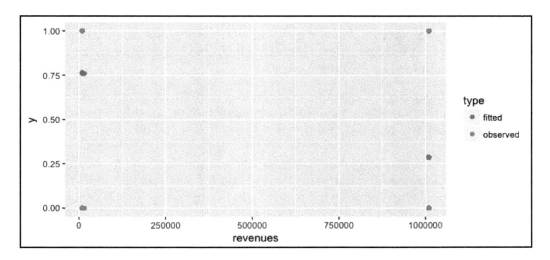

It is now bold and clear what is fitted and what is not. What can you see there? I see that our model seems to not be doing an excellent job, since the fitted data is falling quite far from the observed data. If we look closer at the data, we can also see that `company_revenues` is not that relevant to explain our `default_numeric` variable, since you find both a relevant number of performing and defaults (zero and one) for low revenues and high revenues (left and right of the *x* axis).

We will look at some more structured performance metrics later when performing our multiple linear regression.

Further references

- *Introduction to Statistical Learning*, by Gareth James, Daniela Witten, Trevor Hastie, and Robert Tibshirani. The book treats in a more rigorous and formal way some of the most commonly employed statistical learning models and algorithms. A PDF version is also freely available at: `http://www-bcf.usc.edu/~gareth/ISL/`.

Summary

How was your estimation activity? Andy is showing you both theoretical and practical aspects of what you will come to do, letting you keep them all together.

Within this chapter, you actually learned a lot and you are now able to estimate a simple (one variable) linear regression model and check whether its assumptions are satisfied. This is not to be underestimated for two main reasons:

- Simple linear models are quite often an oversimplification of the real relationship between two variables. Nevertheless, they tend to be considered good enough for the level of accuracy requested within many fields, and this is why they are very popular.
- You will find that a lot of models estimate without checking for assumptions, and you should remember that estimates coming from an invalid model are invalid estimates, at least for descriptive purposes (more on this within `Chapter 8`, A *Gentle Introduction to Model Performance Evaluation*). Knowing which are the assumptions behind this popular model and how to check them will distinguish you from less acknowledged analysts who barely apply statistical formulas.

You also learned how to structure a `lm` output and how to employ it to visualize your model's results with `ggplot`.

It is now time to move one step further and discover multiple linear regression. Our univariate experience did not help us explain the defaults, and Mr Clough is still waiting for a list of companies.

8
A Gentle Introduction to Model Performance Evaluation

I have just received a soft follow-up from our dear Mr. Clough, and I have bought some time. How are things proceeding? Despite his kind words, Mr. Sheen doesn't look too friendly while asking for an update.

We are doing good, Mr. Sheen. We have already fitted some models and discovered some good hints. Nevertheless, I would like to have some sound results before sharing what we have found. Andy definitely looks comfortable in these kinds of situations, and this lets you gain some more time before actually having to show the results of your analyses. To be fair, at the moment you would not have that much to share with Mr. Sheen, and this is probably why Andy was so determined to buy some time.

As we told you before closing the previous chapter, you are now going to learn how to evaluate the performance of your models. This is, together with model estimation and validation, one of the most relevant technical skills in the field of data analysis: model performance evaluation.

But, I don't want to buy time (I would be the third person doing that in a short space of time), so let us let Andy speak. As usual, we will meet again in the summary paragraph.

Defining model performance

OK then, let's ask a question to start talking about performance: when you estimate a model, how do you say if it is a good model? As you have probably already heard, the American statistician George Box used to say: *All models are wrong, but some are useful.*

This is, besides a nice quote, also a great truth: there is no perfect model, all models are some kind of an abstraction from reality, like maps are an abstraction from the real Earth. Nevertheless, if those maps are accurate enough, they are invaluable friends in the hands of travelers. This could seem to you nothing more than a suggestive analogy, but it's actually a useful way to intend models since it captures two of their most relevant aspects:

- Models need to have a good level of abstraction from the real phenomenon they are trying to model
- Models have to be accurate enough to be useful

I don't need to say to you that the main topics here are to define *what a good level of abstraction is* and define *what it means for a model to be accurate enough*. This gives room for two concepts that I am going to discuss with you now:

- The trade-off between fitting and interpretability, which is closely related to the definition of the good level of abstractions
- The concept of materiality when making predictions with models, which helps to define if a model is accurate enough

Fitting versus interpretability

Just a few days ago, I was talking with a friend of mine who works in the data science field as a consultant. My friend is doing well and is working with great companies, and I was wondering what kinds of sophisticated algorithms and methods they were employing to satisfy their needs.

I asked him to tell me what models and algorithms he most frequently employs for his jobs, and I was surprised by his answer. He told me that yes, he sometimes applies fancy models and algorithms, but the most part of his customers' needs are satisfied through regression models and quite basic classification algorithms. Are they working with unsophisticated customers? Not quite, but most of the time their customer wants to be provided with a model that gives them decisional instruments, and those kinds of models are able to play this role.

When we estimated our multiple linear regression model, we saw the meaning of its coefficients: the influence of a variation of a given x over the level of a response variable y. This is a decisional instrument, since it lets the business owner set the desired level of y, and on this basis derive the needed level of x, and even the right combination of x to obtain y.

On the other hand, giving the customer a black box model where they just know the final level of prediction without knowing how different predictors worked together and influenced the output, will actually be a lot less useful. This will hold true even if the **black-box prediction** is more accurate than the basic one.

This exemplifies the trade-off between fitting and interpretability: models such as linear regression may not be the best in terms of fitting over a given dataset, but their estimation always produces an output that can be easily interpreted and can provide precious elements for planning and control activities. Nevertheless, they can't be considered as interpretable since they don't adapt to the shape of underlying trends of the phenomenon they are modelling. That is why they can be considered as an extreme: highly interpretable, poorly flexible.

On the other had, we find models that are highly flexible but poorly flexible. Those are models such as the support vector machine we are going to experiment with later on. Their greater quality is the ability to accurately model what is going on within the data they are provided, but if you ask them to help you in making a decision you would probably remain deluded.

So, what do you think: is it better to work with interpretable but rigid models, or the opposite?

There is no universal answer, and it is actually a matter of what the objectives of your analysis are:

- If your primary need is to obtain a model that **helps you make decisions** besides predicting the possible future outcome of a given phenomenon, you will go for models with a high level of interpretability, even sacrificing the overall accuracy of your predictions. Think for instance, about the expected value of GDP in a country as a function of macroeconomic variables. A policymaker will be interested to understand and weigh the relationship between the macroeconomic variables and the GDP, in order to prioritize their actions on those that result to be more relevant. They will be less interested in exactly predicting the future level of GDP for the next period (this will perhaps be of interest for some other purposes such as the definition of the public budget).

- If your primary need is to obtain an **accurate prediction** of a future event or perfectly model the phenomenon that is going on in your data, you will prefer models with a **high level of flexibility**. A good example of this situation could be a state of emergency where a hurricane is expected to come in the next days and you need to plan for the evacuation of an entire city. You are not actually interested in knowing what are the main variables that influenced the origination of the hurricane or its direction, what you actually care about is the day and possibly the hour when the hurricane will hit your city.

Making predictions with models

We were saying before that a model should be accurate enough. It turns out that this "enough" is strictly related to the context in which the model is going to be applied. Let's look at the example we just made about the hurricane: *What is enough within that context?*

We could probably say that to be accurate enough our models should be able to tell us with a high level of precision how much time is left before the disaster, and by that mean, allow us to evacuate the region.

Moving to a less dangerous example, we can consider an industrial process: what is enough in that context? When talking about factories you are usually talking about money, and this is not an exception—the main driver employed to evaluate the performance of a model would be in this context the overall cost of its errors.

To make it more clear, consider the following problem: optimizing the level of maintenance of a plant. Starting from the available data we estimate a model that relates to the level of qualitatively adequate prices to the level of maintenance. We therefore know that to meet a given level of production we need to ensure a given level of maintenance.

How would you measure the performance of this model? You can get closer to the answer with another question, *What is the pay-off for every wrong prediction made from the model?* We can imagine that missing the right level of maintenance would cause the predefined level of production not to be reached, and by that way a loss in revenues or even getting into the losses zone. In any case, we could first of all measure our model's error in missing pieces, that is pieces that we didn't produce and sell because of the inadequate level of maintenance. Once this is done, we will be able to weigh each missing piece by its price.

Can you see now what is enough in this context? It will probably be the maximum level of missing revenues that the company can suffer without getting into trouble.

One last example, just to let you understand that not all kinds of errors are equal. Imagine we are working on a model to derive from the combined result of some kinds of tests a final verdict on a patient having a cancer or not.

Within this setting, our model can be wrong in two possible ways:

- The patient has cancer and our model says they don't (so they are called **false negative**)
- The patient doesn't have cancer and our model says they have (so they are called **false positive**)

Do you think those two errors should be considered as equal? I don't think so, and it is actually quite obvious they are not:

- A false negative could result in serious dangers for our patient, and even death
- A false positive would probably result in a first set of (useless) cares with subsequent analyses that would hopefully detect our first mistake

Those considerations could to lead us placing more weight on the first kind of error and less on the second. This last example helps you understand another shade of the model performance measure.

You can now understand how true George Box was when he said that all models are wrong but some are useful, all models are an abstraction of reality but some, the ones that effectively balance interpretability and fitting and results in prediction accurate enough, are useful.

This directly leads us into a technical discussion about alternatives available to measure a model's performance: all metrics will have a theoretical minimum and maximum, but in order to determine which intermediate level will have to be considered as an acceptability threshold, you will always have to consider the application's context and objectives.

Before getting into details about measuring performance, and since we will spend some time talking about it, let me give you a general warning about model assumptions and predictions. As we have seen, it is relevant to always check that your model meets the assumptions that were defined for it. When making predictions, you may be considered as free from this worry, since the most relevant point here will be the ability of the model to make correct predictions.

To make it clearer, you can consider the difference between descriptive models and predictive models. In the first kind of model, you are trying to find models that are able to describe the phenomenon you are facing and the influence of different variables on this phenomenon. For the conclusion coming from these models to be valid and reliable, like for instance the beta coefficients of different explanatory variables, you will have to check that the model assumptions are respected. In the predictive setting, you will be far less worried about this stuff, since, as we were saying, the most relevant topic is the ability to predict correctly its future evolution.

Measuring performance in regression models

Let's make it more technical and discuss the most common metrics available when dealing with regression models. First of all, let's recall what a regression is: we are trying to explain here a response variable with a set of explanatory variables. A reasonable model performance metric will therefore be one that summarizes how well our model is able to explain the explanatory variable itself.

It is no surprise that the most popular regression model metrics are both able to explain this:

- Mean squared error
- R-squared

Both of them are based on the concept of error, which we already encountered when dealing with model coefficient estimation. We defined as error for a given record of the estimation dataset the difference between the actual value of the response variable and the value of the response value we estimate with our model:

$$e = y_i - \hat{y}_i$$

We also called this residual, and employed it to test some of the most relevant assumptions regarding linear regression models. Let me show you now how it is also employed to derive useful metrics to assess our model's performance.

Mean squared error

Let me jot down an example to help you visualize residuals:

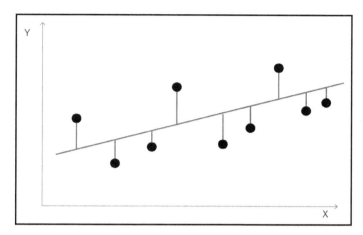

Those bold blue lines are the residuals of our models. *How do we compute an index that is able to summarize how our model performs overall?* We could just sum up all our errors and obtain a comprehensive measure of our errors. But, what about underestimation and overestimation?

Let's take, for instance the following model:

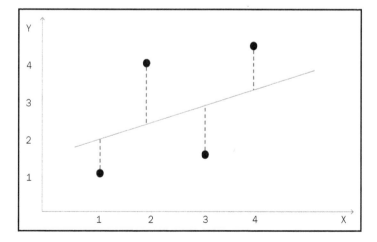

As you can see, on the first and third point the model overestimates the actual value of *y*, while the model underestimates the actual value of *y* for the second and fourth points. The overestimation is roughly of *1* and *1.5*, while the underestimation is of *-1.5* and *-1*.

What if we compute our overall sum of error here?

$$1+1.5-1-1.5 = 0$$

Which would tell us that no error is occurring in our model. We can say for sure that overall our model neither underestimates in a systematical way, but we cannot say for sure that our model perfectly fits the data.

This is why all summaries based on errors tend to take them on their second power, so that an error with the opposite sign doesn't compensate one with the other.

Let's do the same with our simple model:

$$[1]+[1.5]+[-1]^2+[-1.5]^2 = 1+2.25+1+2.25 = 6.5$$

This number looks much more adherent to reality than the previous one, but let's see how it works on the following two models:

First model:

x	y	y_estimated	error
4	8	7,24	0,76
5	10	9,05	0,95
6	12	10,86	1,14
7	14	12,67	1,33
8	16	14,48	1,52
9	18	16,29	1,71

Second model:

x	y	y_estimated	error
4	8	7,80	0,20
5	10	9,75	0,25

6	12	11,70	0,30
7	14	13,65	0,35
8	16	15,60	0,40
9	18	17,55	0,45
10	20	19,50	0,50
11	22	21,45	0,55
12	24	23,40	0,60
13	26	25,35	0,65
14	28	27,30	0,70
15	30	29,25	0,75
16	32	31,20	0,80
17	34	33,15	0,85
18	36	35,10	0,90
19	38	37,05	0,95
20	40	39,00	1,00
21	42	40,95	1,05

To compute the sum of squared errors, we first raise to the second power our errors and then compute the sum:

For the first model:

$error^2$
0,5776
0,9025
1,2996
1,7689
2,3104
2,9241

Which sums to 9,78. And for the second model we have:

error^2
0,04
0,06
0,09
0,12
0,16
0,20
0,25
0,30
0,36
0,42
0,49
0,56
0,64
0,72
0,81
0,90
1,00
1,10

Which sums to 8,24. These are substantially comparable numbers, but would you say they are performing in the same way? We actually see that while the first model almost never scores an error lower than one, the second model reaches one only for two records. We see from this example that the simple sum of all errors, even if taken in their absolute value, cannot be considered as an appropriate metric of performance for our models.

This is where the mean squared error comes from: instead of taking the sum, we take the average of errors in order to understand how much, on average, our model falls far from the observed values of our response variable.

We formally define the mean squared error as:

$$MSE = \frac{1}{n} \sum e^2 = \frac{1}{n} \sum (y_i - \hat{y}_i)^2$$

Let's compute this for our two models:

- **MSE first model**: *1,63*
- **MSE second model**: 0,46

Those two values are way more representative of the **typical** level of error shown from our two models.

We can easily compute the mean squared error of our model in R by taking its residuals, raising them to the second power, and averaging the result.

Take for instance, the `multiple_regression_new` we estimated before. As we saw, the object resulting from the call to `lm()` stores an object called `residuals` containing all residuals produced by our model. You can have a look at them, as follows:

```
multiple_regression$residuals
```

We now take them at their second power, as follows:

```
multiple_regression_new$residuals^2
```

And finally compute the `mean`, obtaining the mean squared error:

```
multiple_regression_new$residuals^2 %>%
mean()-> mean_squared_error
```

Which results in 0.177. Is that a lot or not? If you think about it, you can easily notice that our mean squared error is expressed in terms of our unit of measure raised to the second power. It is therefore not easy to understand the level of this index. To understand why, just think of a model estimating revenues in euro unit: how would you interpret euro^2? That is why it is also useful to consider the square root of our MSE, also called **root mean square deviation**. We can simply calculate this through the `sqrt()` function, which exactly computes the square root of the number passed as an argument:

```
sqrt(mean_squared_error)
```

```
0.4203241
```

What is that? We are dealing with the prediction of default events, ranging from zero to one, and our model is making on average errors of 0.4. It is actually not that small a number one would expect from an accurate number. Yeah, you can take it as the umpteenth evidence of our multiple linear regression not being the best way to model our phenomenon.

But let's move to the R-squared, the other relevant number to look at when dealing with regression models.

R-squared

The R-squared can roughly be considered as a measure of how much the model is able to explain what's going on within the data. More formally, it measures how much of the variability observed within the response variable is explained from the model.

This value is actually closely related to the error measure we were seeing before, since one of its most common definitions is one minus the ratio between the total sum of squared errors and the **total sum of squares (TSS)**:

$$r\ squared = 1 - \frac{TSSE}{TSS}$$

The total sum of squares can be considered as the total variance observed within a set of values of the response variable, and is formally defined as:

$$TSS = \sum_{i=1}^{n} y_i - \bar{y}$$

As you can see, we are talking about the sum of all the differences from the mean raised to the second power. Let's take back the second model we were looking at before and compute this value:

x	y	y_estimated
4	8	7,80
5	10	9,75
6	12	11,70
7	14	13,65

8	16	15,60
9	18	17,55
10	20	19,50
11	22	21,45
12	24	23,40
13	26	25,35
14	28	27,30
15	30	29,25
16	32	31,20
17	34	33,15
18	36	35,10
19	38	37,05
20	40	39,00
21	42	40,95

First of all, we compute the mean of our population, which results in being equal to 25. We then compute for each observation the difference between the y and 25, and then raise it to the second power:

x	y	y-mean(y)	(y-mean(y))^2
4	8	-17,00	289
5	10	-15,00	225
6	12	-13,00	169
7	14	-11,00	121
8	16	-9,00	81
9	18	-7,00	49
10	20	-5,00	25
11	22	-3,00	9
12	24	-1,00	1

13	26	1,00	1
14	28	3,00	9
15	30	5,00	25
16	32	7,00	49
17	34	9,00	81
18	36	11,00	121
19	38	13,00	169
20	40	15,00	225
21	42	17,00	289

Summing up the last column, we obtain the TSS, which is roughly equal to 1,938. To compute the R-squared we just have to obtain the ratio between the total sum of squared errors, also called **residual sum of squares**, and TSS, and compute its complement to unity. The residual sum of squares can be computed as the sum of the column of errors raised to the second we previously computed, and it results equal to *8,24*.

Our R-squared will therefore be equal to *1- 8,24/1938 = 0,99; or 99%*.

R-squared meaning and interpretation

What does this number mean? We have explained the denominator as the total variance observed within the response variable, which can be thought of as all the statuses in which the variable is observed within our dataset. If you think again to the revenues, we can think of it as all the possible levels of revenues observed during our observation period for a given set of companies or a single company. This phenomenon we want to explain, the one for which we want to be able to say:

At a given time, our revenues will be determined for an x% by the last year ROE, for a p% by the market total level of revenues, and for a z% by the number of employees.

We now move to the numerator, where we find the total sum of squared errors. What is this? Look again at our revenues: we fit the model and find *x*, *p*, and *z*. For a given year, we predict a certain level of revenues, let's say *250,000* euros. For that year, we observe a higher *270,000* euros. What does that mean? It means that we are missing something that determines the actual level of revenues. With our data and model, we are able to explain the observed level of revenue just until a certain level, which is the *250,000* euros we estimated. There is then another piece that we are not able to explain, a part of the response variable that remains unexplained.

This is exactly the error determined from our model for that given observation. Summing all these errors and dividing them by the total variability of the response variable means computing the proportion of variance not explained from our model. It turns out that this ratio will always vary from zero to one.

Once you have obtained this number, subtracting it from unity will let you obtain its complement, which is the proportion of variability explained by the model. The R-squared will then represent, as we we said before, the amount of model variance explained from the model.

The closer this number is to one, the better our model will be considered, at least in terms of explanation of the observed data on which it was estimated.

R-squared computation in R

How could we compute this in R?

Well, to be honest, you are probably not going to compute it by yourself for the models you will estimate, since the basic lm() function already computes this summary statistic for you. All you have to remember is how to retrieve it when you need it. Two main possible ways arise, you are able to:

- Retrieve it through the summary function
- Retrieve it as a component of the object resulting from the application of the lm function or the other available regression functions

Let's try both on our multiple_regression_new object:

```
multiple_regression_new %>% summary()
```

Can you spot in the output our R-squared? You should actually find two of them in your output, the multiple R-squared and the adjusted R-squared. We are going to look at the difference between them in a second; for now let's just take note of their value and think about them:

Multiple R-squared: *0.08393, adjusted R-squared: 0.08297*

Once again, we find that our model is able to explain little about the observed default events since our R-squared is just equal to a very low 8%.

Adjusted R-squared

What about the multiple and adjusted R-squared? First of all, you should know that the multiple R-squared is simply the R-squared computed in the presence of more than one explanatory variable. That said, the adjusted R-squared is a kind of rectified version of the multiple R-squared, defined to correct this number from the effect of increasing the number of predictors.

It turns out that a very simple way to increase the R-squared is to increase the number of predictors employed: *The R-squared will never decrease, and most of the time it will increase.*

The adjusted R-squared is therefore defined to consider this effect and remove it from the final value. This means that through the adjusted R-squared you can compare models that have a different number of predictors.

R-squared misconceptions

Now that I have told you what the R-squared means, let me tell you what the R-squared doesn't mean. This summary statistic is one of the most used and abused within the regression realm, and possessing a sound understanding of its meaning will help you avoid common and dangerous pitfalls in your analyses.

The R-squared doesn't measure the goodness of fit

We said that the R-squared measures how much of the variability of the response variable is explained by the model. *Does it measure how well our model describes the shape of our variable?* No, because of at least one main reason, it can produce really high values even in the presence of data that is far away from having a linear trend.

Let's have a look at this sketch:

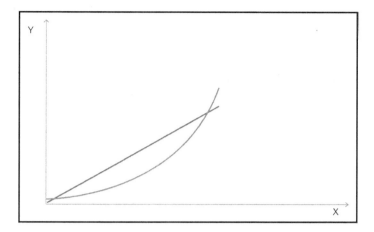

As you can see, we have here a non-linear relationship between *x* and *y*, namely an exponential trend, which is far from the shape assumed from our linear regression model. Nevertheless, if we fit a linear regression model we find here a high R-squared. Why? Because we have a small variance here, and our straight line never falls too far from the observed values.

Doesn't that mean that our model is good at describing our data? Let me extend our observations to answer this question:

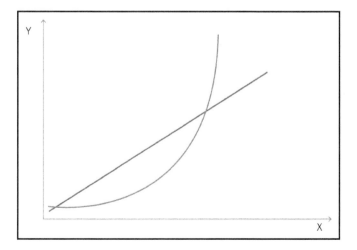

Can you see? If we keep the old model and apply it to the newest observation, we fall way under the real observations. This is because our model doesn't properly fit the real behaviour of the data.

If we then fit a new linear model on the most extended data, we find that our R-squared goes sensibly down. As you might be wondering, it is because the variance within our data is increased, and our model is making more wrong predictions than it was before.

A low R-squared doesn't mean your model is not statistically significant

Moving to the second bold statement we made, let's recall what statistical significance is in this context.

When regressing a linear model on our data, we make the following assumptions:

- There is a causal relationship between x and y
- There is no multicollinearity among explanatory variables
- Residuals originating from our model are not auto-correlated and have a constant variance

It turns out that the level of the R-squared doesn't say anything about our model respecting those three assumptions.

Let me show you with a simple example in R:

```
x <- seq(1,100)
set.seed(29)
y <- 2 + 1.2*x + rnorm(100,0,sd = 100)
regression <- lm(y ~ x)
```

We define here an x vector of 100 numbers ranging from 1 to 100. Then we define y as 2 plus the x multiplied by a 1.2 coefficient, added with a random component drawn from a normal distribution, having a mean of 0 and a standard deviation equal to 100. I don't want to make it too complicated, you just have to observe that we define y in a way that it can be perfectly described as in linear relation with x. This lets us conclude that the assumption of a causal relation between x and y is satisfied.

The random component we add at the end is actually the error that our model will not be able to model. This error, or residual, will not be auto-correlated and is normally distributed since it is drawn on a random basis from a normal distribution. We finally fit a linear regression model to our data.

Let's now validate the hypothesis over our residuals by employing the well-known **Durbin-Watson** test:

```
durbinWatsonTest(regression)

lag Autocorrelation D-W Statistic p-value
 1 -0.1005777 2.182347 0.428

Alternative hypothesis: rho != 0
```

As you remember, a value of around two means that no auto-correlation is observed within the residual. We then have assumptions on residuals validated as well.

Let's finally observe the R-squared value to see if this confirms our opinion about the validity of the model:

```
summary(regression) -> summary_regression
summary_regression$r.squared

[1] 0.05245096
```

Which is equal to a really poor 5%. What does it mean? It actually means what we were trying to show: a low R-squared doesn't mean your model is not statistically significant.

Measuring the performance in classification problems

Until now, we have just looked at regression settings, that is, problems where our main problem is to predict the level or value of a given response variable, starting from a set of explanatory variables. As you know, there are also classification problems, which are problems where you want to assign your observation to one of a given set of categories.

How do we measure the performance of these models? As always, you just have to resonate about the objective of your model to understand how to measure its performance. Our classification model aims to assign each observation to its category. How can you tell if it's doing well? You would probably count how many times it meets its objective, that is, how many correct classifications it performs.

This is actually one of the most common ways to a measure classification models' performance, even with some further development. Let's see it a bit closer.

The confusion matrix

One of the most relevant objects when talking about the performance of classification models is the confusion matrix which, despite its name, is a crucial instrument to get a clear view of how your model is performing. Moreover, it is employed to derive other useful performance metrics.

This matrix is actually a table with two columns and two rows, like the following one:

		predicted	
		TRUE	FALSE
observed	TRUE	54	25
	FALSE	10	30

Let's build up a bit of story here to better understand this matrix. We are trying to predict if a customer will buy a newly introduced car model or not, based on some behavioral and descriptive attributes we have. For instance, we could collect a dataset showing for each customer if he bought that specific model or not, together with a series of attributes such as the annual income and number of sons . Let's say we introduced our model six months ago and now we want to design a new marketing campaign to target the cluster of customers that showed the greatest interest in our new model during these six months.

We then try some kind of model which, based on the values assumed from the mentioned explanatory variables, predicts if the given customer will buy our new model or not. What the confusion matrix does is simply compare the observed type of car bought with the predicted one.

For instance, the observed TRUE-predicted TRUE cell tells us that for 54 cases, both the model and the reality showed the new model being bought by the customer. Similarly, the observed FALSE-predicted X shows the number of cases where both the model and the observed data showed our customer not buying the new car model. In the middle, you find a mixed case, that is, a prediction error, where either the model predicted TRUE and the observed was FALSE or the model predicted FALSE and the observed was TRUE.

It turns our that the confusion matrix is considered as a really relevant object for data mining purposes because it can be employed to compute at least three useful metrics:

- Accuracy
- Sensitivity
- Specificity

Confusion matrix in R

I will tell you about these statistics in a second, but first let me show you a little and basic trick to obtain a confusion matrix in the R language. If you think about it, a confusion matrix is no more than a double entry frequency table, where the conjoint frequencies of two modalities of two different variables are shown.

Those variables are the observed response and the predicted response, while the modalities are usually TRUE and FALSE, but there can also be three or more. Think for instance, about the prediction of a soccer game which could end up with a win, a loss, or a tie.

The R language provides a simple and rather useful way to compute a frequency table like the one we just described. This function is named table and requires the vectors for which you want to observe the frequencies to be specified.

You can pass from one to *n* variables to the table function, but let's start with a simple two-way example to show you how this works.

We start by creating some fake data, with an ID, an observed value, and a predicted value. To produce the observed and predicted column we will randomly sample from a vector containing TRUE and FALSE. This will be done through the sample function:

```
outcome <- c(TRUE,FALSE)
set.seed(4)
data <- data.frame(id=seq(1:100),
 observed = sample(outcome , size= 100, replace = TRUE),
 predicted= sample(outcome, size = 100, replace = TRUE))
```

We are now ready to see how the table function works:

```
table(data$observed,data$predicted)
```

	FALSE	TRUE
FALSE	24	33
TRUE	20	23

This is exactly the confusion matrix we were looking for. Just remember that in the case of two variables, the first one passed to the table function will be represented over the rows while the second over the columns.

We can even save our confusion matrix as a matrix or `data.frame`. It's up to you to choose the type of object to save your matrix in, but you should be aware that those two objects sensibly differ in this case. Let's try to save our matrix in both in order to understand what we are talking about:

```
table(data$observed,data$predicted) %>% as.matrix()
```

Which will produce:

	FALSE	TRUE
FALSE	24	33
TRUE	20	23

```
table(data$observed,data$predicted) %>% as.data.frame
```

Which produces:

```
  Var1 Var2 Freq
1 FALSE FALSE 24
2 TRUE FALSE 20
3 FALSE TRUE 33
4 TRUE TRUE 23
```

As you can see, both show the same data, but arranged in different ways. To be formal here, we have a matrix exposed in the wide form and a data frame exposed in the long form.

You will probably choose the object type based on what you are going to use your confusion matrix for.

We are going to store it in a data frame in order to have it ready for some data mining when talking about confusion matrix statistics:

```
table(data$observed,data$predicted) %>%
  as.data.frame() %>%
  rename(observed = Var1,
  predicted = Var2)-> confusion_matrix
```

And yeah, we also renamed the `Var1` and `Var2` variables, just to make it easier to handle them when computing statistics.

Accuracy

Accuracy is a measure of how many right predictions the model is making overall. You can easily find out that there are two ways in which our model can make right predictions:

- Saying the output will be TRUE when it was actually TRUE, which is called a **true positive**
- Saying the output will be FALSE when it was actually FALSE, which is called a **true negative**

To get a measure of how many good predictions the model is making overall, we sum up all true positives and true negatives, and divide this sum by the total number of predictions made:

$$accuracy = \frac{true\,positive + true\,negative}{total\,number\,of\,prediction}$$

How to compute accuracy in R

Let's see how to compute this from our confusion matrix.

First of all, let's create a new column, assigning to each combination a label describing the cluster of prediction:

```
confusion_matrix %>%
 mutate(label =
c("true_negative","false_negative","false_positive","true_positive"))
```

	observed	predicted	Freq	label
1	FALSE	FALSE	24	true_negative
2	TRUE	FALSE	20	false_negative
3	FALSE	TRUE	33	false_positive
4	TRUE	TRUE	23	true_positive

We have here the true negatives and true positives we were talking about before, but also the false negatives and false positives, which are simply where the model is predicting **FALSE** but reality says **TRUE,** or vice-versa.

Since we are going to compute our accuracy and all the other statistics by summing up and dividing those clusters, let's perform some data mining to arrange them in a way that reduces the number of steps to perform basic mathematical operations on them:

```
confusion_matrix %>%
 mutate(label =
c("true_negative","false_negative","false_positive","true_positive")) %>%
 select(label,Freq) %>%
 spread(key = label, value = Freq)
```

	false_negative	false_positive	true_negative	true_positive
1	20	33	24	23

What we are doing here is isolating the `label` and `Freq` columns and arranging them in a wide structure. We now save this into a `casted_confusion_matrix` object:

```
confusion_matrix %>%
 mutate(label =
c("true_negative","false_negative","false_positive","true_positive")) %>%
 select(label,Freq) %>%
 spread(key = label, value = Freq) -> casted_confusion_matrix
```

You can now easily compute accuracy as follows:

```
casted_confusion_matrix %>%
 mutate(accuracy = (true_negative+true_positive)/ (true_negative+
true_positive+
false_negative +
false_positive))
```

false_negative	false_positive	true_negative	true_positive	accuracy
20	33	24	23	0.47

Is that a lot or not? Given that statistics can reach a maximum value of one in the hypothesis of having all predictions being true positives or true negatives, we can conclude that our model is not performing greatly.

That computed **0.47** is equal to saying that for every prediction, our model has roughly the same probability of making a good or a bad prediction.

Let's move on to the sensitivity statistics.

Sensitivity

Sensitivity is defined as:

$$sensitivity = \frac{true\,positive}{real\,positive} = \frac{true\,positive}{true\,positive + false\,negative}$$

Sensitivity can be considered as a measure of how good the model is at predicting the positive outcome. As you can see, it is obtained by computing the ratio between the number of positives predicted from the model that were actually positive, and the number of positives that the model should have predicted.

How to compute sensitivity in R

We can easily compute this from our confusion matrix:

```
casted_confusion_matrix %>%
  mutate(sensitivity = true_positive/(true_positive + false_negative))
```

false_negative	false_positive	true_negative	true_positive	sensitivity
20	33	24	23	0.5348837

Specificity

Specificity is some kind of complementary measure with respect to sensitivity and is defined as:

$$specificity = \frac{true\,negative}{real\,negative} = \frac{true\,negative}{true\,negative + false\,negative}$$

As you can see, we are looking here to understand how good the model is at predicting negative outcomes.

How to compute specificity in R

Let's compute it with our confusion matrix:

```
casted_confusion_matrix %>%
  mutate(specificity = true_negative/(true_negative + false_positive))
```

false_negative	false_positive	true_negative	true_positive	specificity
20	33	24	23	0.4210526

Now that you understand how to compute all of those metrics the hard way, I can tell you that we will see later on an easier way to compute these, and even more performance metrics running fewer lines of code. This will involve taking a closer look at the *caret* package, which we will do after having applied all of the models listed within our data modeling strategy.

How to choose the right performance statistics

We have seen here just three of the possible performance statistics that can be drawn from a confusion matrix. I will give you the title of a good academic paper exposing a bunch of other relevant measures, in case you want to deepen your understanding of the topic.

Now that you have a clear, or at least a more clear, understanding of how to measure the performance of regression and classification models, we are going to move on to estimating a classification model with our data. But first, let me ask you a question: which is the best performance statistic among those we have seen? Which one should you use on your model?

As is often the case, it depends, is a good first answer to this question. This is because there is not simply a best performance statistic for all models, and the one you are going to employ will depend on the objectives of your data mining activity.

You will probably always take a look at the accuracy of your model, that is, at the overall ability of making right predictions, but then you will probably focus on the kind of prediction that is more relevant to you.

Going back to the example we used with cancer diagnosis, within that context you will be probably be more interested in the sensitivity of your model, that is, in its ability to detect patients actually being affected by this illness.

A final general warning – training versus test datasets

I know I said we were going to move on to new models estimation, but let me clarify a concept before that—the difference between the training and test datasets.

When you estimate a model, you usually have at least two different datases:

- **The training dataset**: This is the one on which you actually estimate the model. To be clear, the one over which you apply the `lm()` function, or whatever algorithm you want to employ.
- **The testing dataset**: This is a separate dataset you use to validate your model's performance. It can also be a new dataset that becomes available after you first estimate your model.

Why are there two different datasets and why do we need a separate dataset to test our model? This is because of the danger of overfitting, that is, fitting a model that is really good for the dataset it was estimated for, but underperforms when it is applied to new data.

To understand it, you can think of your high school or university tests and exams. Your teacher probably used to provide you with a bunch of previous years' exam assignments so you could get confident with exam-style problems and exercises. It sometimes happened that I would get really good at those previous years exams, perfectly understanding the logic and becoming effective and quick at solving them.

However, on the day of the exam I found myself looking desperately at the assignment paper, unable to move on and perform the exercises.

What happened? I didn't actually study and learn the topic, but just how to answer a specific kind of question on that topic. Those two were different things, and my final grade on was there to remind me about that.

The same holds true for overfitting: when you overfit your model it gets very good at predicting your response variable or performing the desired classification given that specific context it found in the data, but it doesn't learn how to effectively predict you response variable in the variety of possible contexts it could encounter.

That is why you need to have a training dataset and a testing dataset; on the first, you train your model, while on the testing dataset you verify if the level of performance stays around the same level observed on the first one.

Let's link this with the regression and classification performance metrics we just discussed. You are for sure interested in discovering which is the R-squared and MSE of your model on the training dataset, but you will probably be even more interested in knowing if your model keeps an adequate predictive power on a new dataset providing fresh data and probably data on which you want to base your predictions.

Think for instance, of a model employed to predict stocks prices for investment purposes; what will your profits be based on, training or test dataset? You will earn based on how well your model performs on the new data.

To be clear, the testing dataset will not always be represented by new data provided after the estimation of the model: it will most often be represented by a different sub-sample from the population in which you are observing the phenomenon you are trying to model, or even from a sub-sample of the training dataset.

Further references

- *Evaluation: From Precision, Recall and F-Factor to ROC, Informedness, Markedness and Correlation*: http://www.flinders.edu.au/science_engineering/fms/School-CSEM/publications/tech_reps-research_artfcts/TRRA_2007.pdf

Summary

This is the author speaking here. Did you solve the mystery of the revenues drop? You did not, I guess. Nevertheless, you made some relevant steps on your journey to learning how to use R for data mining activities.

In this chapter, you learned some conceptual and some practical stuff, and you now possess medium-level skills to define and measure the performance of data mining models.

Andy first explained to you what we do intend for model performance and how this concept is related to the one of model interpretability and the purposes for which the model was estimated.

You then learned what the main model metrics are for both regression and classification problems.

Firstly, you were introduced to the relevant concepts of error, mean squared errors, and R-squared.

About this latter statistics, you also carefully analyzed its meaning and the common misconceptions regarding it. I strongly advise you to carefully hold these misconceptions in your mind, since in your everyday professional practice in the data mining field the R-squared will be often employed. Knowing its exact meaning will help you avoid potentially painful errors.

From an operational point of view, you learned:

- How to compute mean squared error in R through the `residual` object available as a result of every `lm()` and `lm-like` function
- Where to find the R-squared parameter and the adjusted R-squared, computed to make comparable R-squared values computed on models with different numbers of explanatory variables

Regarding classification problems, you learned what a confusion matrix is and how to compute it leveraging the `table()` function. Concepts such as true positive and true negative naturally descend from the discussion around this matrix.

You then looked at some of the performance statistics that can be drawn from the confusion matrix:

- Accuracy, which measures the overall performance of the model, measuring how many times its predictions were right
- Sensitivity, which measures how good the model is at predicting a positive outcome
- Specificity, which measures how good the model is at predicting a negative outcome

9
Don't Give up – Power up Your Regression Including Multiple Variables

The next step of our analysis will be towards multiple regression. This basically involves using more than one explanatory variable at once to predict the output of our response variable. If you are wondering about making a distinct linear regression for each explanatory variable, I definitely have to discourage you. *How would you compute the final expected value? Would you employ a mean? A simple mean or a weighted mean assigning to each variable a different weight? How would you define this weight?*

Those kinds of questions directly lead us to the multivariate linear regression. Couldn't we choose just the most influential variable and fit a simple regression model with that variable? *Of course, we could, but how would you define which is the most influential one? Nevertheless, we shouldn't throw away the idea of selecting the most influential variables, since we are going to employ it when talking about dimensional reduction for multivariate linear regression.*

But let's place things in order:

- First of all, I will show you a bit of mathematical notation about how to pass from univariate to multivariate analysis
- We will then resonate about the assumption of this extended model
- The last formal step will be talking about dimensional reduction, that is, the family of techniques employed to select the most significant variables, or generally speaking, reducing the number of variables employed

Once all of this is done, we will fit the multiple models, validating assumptions and visualizing results, as you are getting used to doing.

No more time wasting now, let's start with the mathematical notation, but I promise it will be short.

Moving from simple to multiple linear regression

How would you expand a simple model into a multiple one? I know you are guessing it, by adding more slopes. This is actually the right answer, even if its implications are not that trivial.

Notation

We formally define a multivariate linear model as:

$$Y_i = \beta_0 + \beta_1 * x_{1i} + \beta_2 * x_{2i} + \cdots + \beta_n * x_n$$

But what is the actual meaning of this formula? We know that the meaning for the univariate was the relationship between an increase of x and an increase of y, but what is the meaning now that we are dealing with multiple variables?

Once we adopt the **ordinary least squares** (**OLS**) again to estimate those coefficients, it turns out that it means how an increase in the given variable influences the level of y, keeping all other variables constant. We therefore, are not dealing with a dynamic model able to express the level of influence of each variable taking into consideration the level of other variables. For the sake of completeness, I have to tell you that it would also be possible to add interactions between explanatory variables, but we are not going to deal with that here.

Assumptions

The assumptions of this extended model are actually quite similar to the ones we got to know for simple linear regression:

- No auto-correlation of residuals
- Homoscedasticity of residuals

We should nevertheless add one more non-trivial one:

- No perfect collinearity among independent variables

Variables' collinearity

What is the collinearity assumption about? It basically states that for beta coefficients to be unbiased estimators the independent variables should not be too correlated with each other. Take for instance these variables:

x1	x2	x3
119	328,5	715,8
134	406	792,8
183	460,5	981,6
126	390	734,2
177	434,5	951,4
107	362,5	688,4
119	325,5	715,8
165	387,5	904
156	371	876,2

If we compute the linear correlation coefficient, we obtain the following:

variable	x1	x2	x3
x1	1.000	0.79	0.996
x2	0.790	1.00	0.800
x3	0.996	0.80	1.000

As you can see, we have all of the three variables correlated with each other. How does this influence our linear model estimation? It turns out that collinearity (between two variables) and multicollinearity (between more than two variables) tends to cause the following undesired side effects:

- Counterintuitive value of beta coefficient (for instance a negative slope for a variable where a positive contribution would be expected).
- Instability of the model to changes within the sample. The presence of multicollinearity tends to cause high instability within our model coefficient estimates.

Taking one step back, we should formally define a way to decide if collinearity is occurring among two variables. We can do this by calculating the so-called tolerance.

Tolerance

Despite its quite sonorous name, tolerance is actually the complement to unity of the model performance parameter R-squared. As you know from our discussions about model performance metrics, the R-squared can range from zero to one, and the closer it is to one, the more useful the model is to explain the variability within our response variable. The complement of this model is, therefore, a number expressing how much variability within the response variable is not explained by the model.

The relevant points which R-squared you have to consider when looking for collinearity. To get it we can look again at the numbers we have previously seen:

x1	x2	x3
119	328,5	715,8
134	406	792,8
183	460,5	981,6
126	390	734,2
177	434,5	951,4
107	362,5	688,4
119	325,5	715,8
165	387,5	904
156	371	876,2

To compute the tolerance associated for instance to x1 and x3, we have to estimate a univariate linear model of x1 on x3, in order to observe the associated R-squared. You can now easily do it by yourself, just run `lm()` on `x1 ~ x3` and call `summary()` on it.

If everything goes right you should obtain something like the following:

Call:

```
lm(formula = x1 ~ x3)
```

Residuals:

```
Min 1Q Median 3Q Max
-3.8230 -1.3607 0.7504 1.3871 3.8275
```

Coefficients:

```
Estimate Std. Error t value Pr(>|t|)
(Intercept) -59.765450 6.517130 -9.171 3.77e-05 ***
x3 0.247804 0.007903 31.355 8.67e-09 ***
---
Signif. codes: 0 '***' 0.001 '**' 0.01 '*' 0.05 '.' 0.1 ' ' 1
Residual standard error: 2.508 on 7 degrees of freedom
Multiple R-squared: 0.9929, Adjusted R-squared: 0.9919
F-statistic: 983.1 on 1 and 7 DF, p-value: 8.671e-09
```

Where you can locate `Multiple R-squared: 0.9929`, showing the R-squared parameter for that model. We can now just compute the tolerance as:

$$tolerance = 1 - R\text{-}squared = 1 - 0.9929 = 0.0071$$

Is it good news? First of all, we should resonate about the meaning of this number. What is it? It expresses how much of the variability of x1 is not explained from x3. In the presence of collinearity, would that be high or low? If we assume a variable being significantly correlated to another one we can conclude that the variation of one of them would significantly influence, and therefore explain, the variation of the other. In this situation, the R-squared would therefore be very high and its complement very low.

That is why it is expected that for a collinear variable the tolerance value should be low. But how low? Looking around, you will find a threshold most of the time set to 0.10 and sometimes 0.2. We can summarise this as follows:

- Tolerance >= 0.1/0.2 we can exclude collinearity occurring
- Tolerance < 0.10 we should conclude collinearity being in place

Variance inflation factors

Directly from tolerance comes variance inflation factors, another metric often employed to measure the likeliness of multicollinearity occurring among your explanatory variables. To actually compute it you do not need any additional procedures since it is defined, as follows:

$$VIF_k = \frac{1}{1-R^2} = \frac{1}{tolerance}$$

As you can see, it is directly derived from the tolerance parameters, and its interpretation follows the definitions:

- A *VIF* lower than 10 can lead us to exclude the hypothesis of multicollinearity
- A *VIF* greater than 10 should invite us to seriously consider that multicollinearity is occurring

Addressing collinearity

What can you do when your variables show collinearity? You have basically three possible courses of action:

- Remove redundant variables
- Increase sample size, in case this collinearity is only observed in a sub-sample of the population and is therefore going to become irrelevant, increasing the sample
- Create new variables combining two or more collinear variables

Most of the time these remedies will do the trick. Nevertheless, you should check that after applying them all the other assumptions are satisfied and the overall performance of your model still holds adequate.

Dimensionality reduction

We are nearly done with the theoretical lesson, let me just tell you about dimensional reduction, since we are going to employ it in a minute to improve our regression model.

Dimensional reduction is a general category including a variety of techniques employed to effectively reduce the number of variables employed to estimate a regression model. Among these techniques, you should be aware of two of them, since they are of quite easy application but rather powerful:

- Stepwise regression
- Principal component regression

Stepwise regression

When facing a wide enough range of explanatory variables, like we are now with our customer data, a reasonable question that should probably pop up is: *Which is the subset of variables that maximizes the model's performance?* Stepwise regression tries to answer that question.

It consists of a set of incremental procedures, from which the step part of the name comes, where a different combination of variables are tried out to find out the most satisfying combination. You can think about every kind of stepwise regression as being composed of the following steps:

1. Estimate all possible linear models with a number of *n-m* variables.
2. Evaluate the best among that set of linear models.
3. Evaluate the overall best performing model among the ones selected within each step.

While the last step will be performed once during the entire procedure, the first two will be performed a number of times equal to the total number of available explanatory variables. To better understand this, we have to talk about two different families of stepwise regression:

- **Backward stepwise regression**, where the starting point is a model including all the *n* explanatory variables and during each step the number of employed variables is reduced by one
- **Forward stepwise regression**, where the final subset of variables is defined starting from no variable and adding one variable from the *n* during each iteration

I am going to give you some more details in a second, but first you should be aware of the existence of one more kind of stepwise regression that is called alternatively *best subset selection, best subset regression,* or *all possible subsets regression*. This technique involves the actual estimation of all possible models based on the set of variables and the final evaluation of the best fitting model. The main downside of this technique is the exponential growth of the number of models to be fitted corresponding to the increase of the number of variables.

Backward stepwise regression

As we were saying, backward stepwise selection starts from a model encompassing all the available explanatory variables. Let me sketch out the whole algorithm for you:

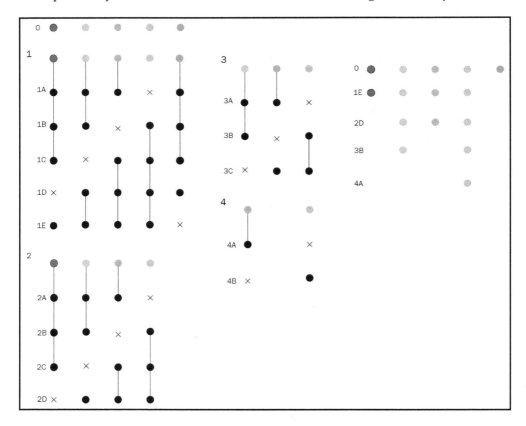

It is clear now, isn't it? No? OK, let's take a closer look at the whole story.

From the full model to the n-1 model

We start with the full model, that is, the model with all variables included:

With the first step we try all possible combinations of 5-1 = 4 variables:

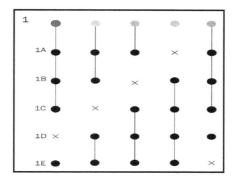

Based on the R-squared of each model from **1A** to **1E**, we choose the best model, which here we are supposing to be the **1E**. In the next step we, therefore, remove the violet variable:

This second step is exactly equal to the first: we try all possible combinations of 4-1 = 3 variables and choose the best one, which is the **2D**:

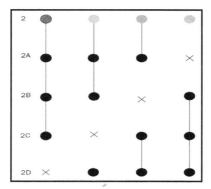

This goes on for two more steps:

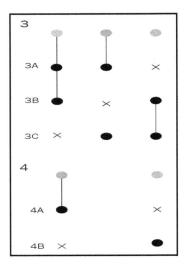

We select here steps **3B** and **4A**. At the end of our iterations we will therefore have five champions; the full model plus one for each iteration step:

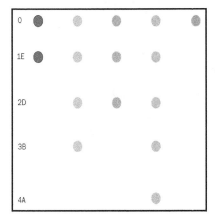

The last logical step will be to select the best models among the *n* models resulting from our iteration. Criteria employed to select the best model among the *n* obtained can be different. One of the most obvious would be the R-squared of each model, but *w* could also employ other criteria such as the AIC, which I will explain to you when we look at classification models (the author here, you can skip to Chapter 10, *A Different Outlook to Problems with Classification Models, The AIC performance metric* section if you are too curious about it).

You should have the whole picture clear now: we start from the full model and, one variable at a time, create a bucket of the best models for the given number of variables. Finally, we select the best of the best, and that becomes our final estimate.

Can you guess what forward stepwise regression looks like?

Forward stepwise regression

Forward stepwise regression can be considered as the opposite of the backward one. In this regression, we start from the null model, that is, from a model having no variable at all, and we go on one step at a time trying possible combinations of *n-m* variables, until we reach *n*.

Rationales that can be applied to select among combinations and final models are exactly the same as for the backward one. Before moving on, I would like to talk briefly about the null model, which is employed as a baseline here. It is actually a constant value that shows for every value of explanatory variables the average level of *y*.

Double direction stepwise regression

Which of the two kinds of regression is better? Do you think that going from the top to the bottom or from the bottom up would give you better results for some specific reason?

It actually turns out that both approaches can be considered as equal. To understand why, you just have to think once more about the best subset selection I was talking about before; subset selection estimates linear models for all possible combinations of explanatory variables. This means that given for instance 10 explanatory variables, it will produce 2^{10} alternative models, 1024 to be correct.

If we now look at both backward and forward stepwise approaches, we can easily see that for a given set of *n* variables we will compute a null or full model, and then at each iteration we will compute *n-m* models, with *m* going from 0 (the full model) to *n-1*.

The total number of fitted models will therefore be:

$$1 + \sum_{m=o}^{n-1} = 1 + \frac{p(p+1)}{2}$$

Which, with our 10 variables example, results in 56, which is approximately 20 times smaller than the best subset number.

We should therefore be aware that even if both backward and forward approaches result in a best model selection, this has to be considered as the best among the ones estimated from the approach rather than the best possible model given that set of explanatory variables.

All that premised, it will not surprise you to discover the existence of some kind of mixed approach, both forward and backward. You can consider this approach as a forward approach where at the end of each iteration, once the best model of that iteration is chosen, the algorithm checks if all variables remain significant. In case of a negative response, the insignificant variables are removed before going on to the next step.

Principal component regression

Principal component regression is an unsupervised technique useful for reducing the number of variables employed within our linear regression model. You may ask what is the difference between this approach and the stepwise regression we have just described. There is a big difference actually.

While the stepwise procedure tries to reduce the dimension of our model by just selecting the best variables based on some performance criteria, the principal component regression meets the same objective by creating new variables as linear combinations of the existing ones. This means that starting from two variables one new variable will be created, reducing in this way the total number of necessary variables.

After performing this first step of variable creation, the model fitting procedure will proceed as usual, estimating the beta coefficient with the ordinary least squares technique.

The main point in this approach, as you are probably guessing, is how to define these new variables. This is where the principal component comes to help, this approach leverages the principal component analysis as a way to estimate the best possible linear combination of the explanatory variables.

A sketch will help you to understand this idea. Let me show you two explanatory variables, one plotted against the other:

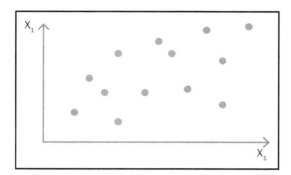

As you can see, there is some kind of relationship among those variables. What principal component analysis does is it formally defines this relationship into a linear combination of the two variables. It is like tracing a line in the previous plot, and tracing it in a way that represents the direction along which the maximum variability is observed:

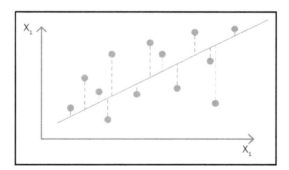

This is usually defined as follows:

$$Z_1 = \varnothing_{i1}(x_i - \hat{x}) + \varnothing_{j1}(x_j - \hat{x})$$

You can see here the first principal component. How is it structured? You have those φ_{i1} and φ_{j1} (read them as f_i) which are the principal components' loading or weights. Each of them is referred to a specific variable and can be read as the weight of the variable into the new Z_1 variable. You then find those terms involving the explanatory variables, which are actually the difference of each variable from its mean.

How many principal components can you have for a given set of variables? The intuition here is that you should find one principal component for each direction along which the variance of variables is distributed. When applying this approach to our data, we will see that the algorithm actually tries a different set of principal components, looking for the combination that maximizes a certain metric.

That said, it is not reasonable to have more principal components than the total number of available explanatory variables, since it would lead you to the opposite result of the one you were looking for: reducing the dimension of your linear model.

Fitting a multiple linear model with R

It is now time to apply all that we have seen until now to our data. First of all, we are going to fit our model, applying the previously introduced `lm()` function. This will not require too much time, and will directly lead us to model assumptions validation, both on multicollinearity and residual behavior. We will finally, for the best possible model, apply both stepwise regression and principal component regression.

Model fitting

Let us define the dataset we are going to employ for our modeling activity. We will employ `clean_casted_stored_data_validated_complete`, removing the `default_flag` and the `customer_code` first because it is actually meaningless as an explanatory variable:

```
clean_casted_stored_data_validated_complete %>%
(-default_flag) %>%
(-customer_code) -> training_data
```

And we are ready now to fit our model:

```
multiple_regression <- lm(as.numeric(default_numeric)~., data=
training_data)
```

You should have already noticed the small point after the ~ token. It actually means that all the available explanatory variables will be fitted against the `as.numeric(default_numeric)` response variable. Before looking at model assumptions validation, we could go for a walk through the `summary` output:

```
summary(multiple_regression)
```

```
Call:
lm(formula = as.numeric(default_numeric) ~ ., data = data)

Residuals:
    Min      1Q   Median      3Q     Max
-0.8993 -0.2275  0.2322  0.2335  1.0183

Coefficients: (2 not defined because of singularities)
                                Estimate Std. Error t value Pr(>|t|)
(Intercept)                     7.441e-01  1.394e-02  53.379  < 2e-16 ***
corporation                    -6.676e-01  4.001e-02 -16.686  < 2e-16 ***
subsidiary                            NA         NA      NA       NA
previous_default                9.266e-02  2.194e-02   4.223 2.43e-05 ***
customer_agreement                    NA         NA      NA       NA
multiple_country               -1.073e-02  2.538e-02  -0.423 0.672559
cost_income                     1.131e-08  1.049e-08   1.079 0.280782
ROE                             9.515e-08  4.754e-08   2.002 0.045356 *
employees                       2.944e-09  1.083e-09   2.718 0.006587 **
economic_sector                -4.616e-09  1.211e-09  -3.811 0.000139 ***
ROS                             3.398e-08  9.596e-09   3.541 0.000401 ***
company_revenues               -4.298e-07  1.948e-08 -22.059  < 2e-16 ***
commercial_portfoliomass affluent 1.357e-01  8.632e-02   1.572 0.115904
commercial_portfoliomore affluent -3.085e-01  1.363e-01  -2.264 0.023599 *
business_unitretail_bank        2.747e-02  1.358e-02   2.023 0.043112 *
---
Signif. codes:  0 '***' 0.001 '**' 0.01 '*' 0.05 '.' 0.1 ' ' 1

Residual standard error: 0.4206 on 11510 degrees of freedom
Multiple R-squared:  0.08393,   Adjusted R-squared:  0.08297
F-statistic: 87.87 on 12 and 11510 DF,  p-value: < 2.2e-16
```

This is actually a rich output that tells us a lot about the model. At first you find the formula you have passed to the `lm()` function. Then you see the actual values of your model coefficients. Starting from the top, you find the intercept, the β_0 term we were talking about some minutes ago, for each of the terms of your model, the value of the related β, the standard error of the parameter estimate related to the variable, a t value, and a probability of finding that t value in the hypothesis of no relationship existing between the explanatory variable and the response variable (the so called p-value). I am starting to think that we should take some time to talk about p-values and hypothesis testing (*ehm ehm ... the author speaking here, you are going to talk about model hypothesis testing in* `Chapter 10`, *A Different Outlook to Problems with Classification Models*), but for now we can just consider those little stars on the far right of the parameters as an extreme way of evaluating the level of significance of the relationship between a given x and the y.

You find a proper legend for those symbols at the bottom of the output:

*Signif. codes: 0 '***' 0.001 '**' 0.01 '*' 0.05 '.' 0.1 ' ' 1*

The maximum level of significance is represented by those three stars with a corresponding probability of causally encountering the observed behavior of the variable y given the level of x equal to, or really close to, zero.

What can you see there? We have some variables such as the corporation or the previous default being extremely significant, while the other has an extremely low level of significance. We are going to deal with this when performing stepwise regression, which will ensure that only the most significant variables will be kept in our model.

Before going into model assumption validation, I think we should take a closer look at the warning message at the beginning of our output:

```
Coefficients: (2 not defined because of singularities)
```

What do you think this singularities term means? Let's try to guess which variables the warning message is referring to. You can easily get it by looking at the NAs you find in the list of coefficients:

```
subsidiary              NA      NA      NA      NA
customer_agreement      NA      NA      NA      NA
```

Shouldn't we take a closer look at those variables?

Let's inspect them by passing them to `unique()` to get an idea of which values they are composed of:

```
clean_casted_stored_data_validated_complete$customer_agreement %>% unique()
[1] 1

clean_casted_stored_data_validated_complete$subsidiary %>% unique()
[1] 1
```

Oh, it seems that we couldn't have obtained that much from those three attributes, since they are both composed of just one value. We'd better remove them from our dataset before moving on:

```
clean_casted_stored_data_validated_complete %>%
(-default_flag) %>%
(-customer_code) %>%
(-c(customer_agreement, subsidiary))-> training_data
```

Let us estimate our model again, employing the new dataset deputed of the two useless attributes:

```
multiple_regression_new <- lm(as.numeric(default_numeric)~., data=
training_data)
```

We are now ready to skip to assumptions validation. Oh yes, you have also got those last three lines at the end of the output:

```
Residual standard error: 0.4206 on 11510 degrees of freedom
 Multiple R-squared: 0.08393, Adjusted R-squared: 0.08297
 F-statistic: 87.87 on 12 and 11510 DF, p-value: < 2.2e-16
```

I told you we were going to talk about model performance shortly, didn't I? We will go through all those R-squared and standard errors in a moment, just after verifying if the assumptions are met. Why?

Because we do not need to worry about our model's performance if our model cannot be held as statistically valid.

Variable assumptions validation

Let's start with multicollinearity. We have a package that comes to hand here, as is often the case with the R language. It is once again the `car` package. We are going to employ the `vif` function, which does what you would expect, it computes the **variance inflation factor** (**VIF**) for each of your attributes. Well, it actually does something similar to what you would expect, since it computes both the variance inflation factor and the **generalized variance inflation factors** (**GVIF**), which is a version of the `vif` function directly developed by Professor Fox and Professor Monette. You want to know a bit more about those two parameters, don't you?

Well, let me teach you a great lesson for an R practitioner: look into the function documentation first. It will always, or at least often, surprise you how much useful information you will find directly within a package's documentation. It is not uncommon to find on the internet great discussions about some particular function that at the end got solved simply by resorting to the package's official documentation.

So, let's start with the documentation:

```
?vif
```

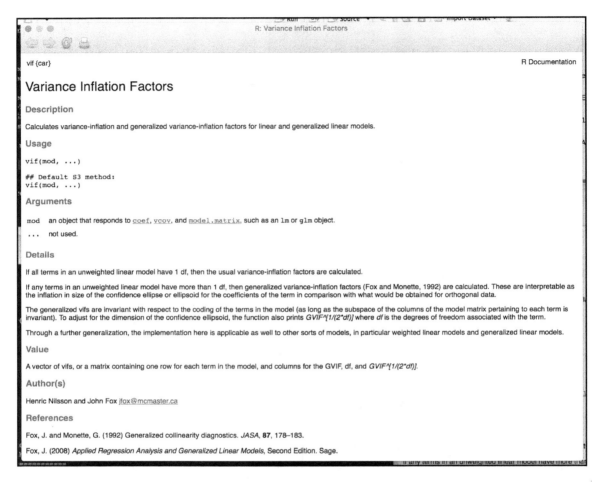

As you can see, we are taught here that if every variable has no more than one degree of freedom, our well-known variance inflation factor's parameter is computed. In case at least one of the parameters has more than one degree of freedom, the generalized form will be computed. What is the difference? To make it simple, you can consider the generalized form as a way of computing the VIF in presence of categorical variables, that is, variables having at least two alternative categories. This is what you can read when looking at the two words degree of freedoms.

It turns out that to apply our VIF thresholds here we have to look at the squared formulation, the one that is indicated within the documentation as $GVIF^{[1/(2*df)]}$. Let's finally apply the `vif` function to our data and analyze the output:

```
vif(multiple_regression_new)
```

```
                        GVIF Df GVIF^(1/(2*Df))
corporation          1.012760  1        1.006360
previous_default     4.340502  1        2.083387
multiple_country     4.820292  1        2.195516
cost_income          1.408289  1        1.186713
ROE                  1.216828  1        1.103099
employees           11.010206  1        3.318163
economic_sector     10.885298  1        3.299287
ROS                  1.137610  1        1.066588
company_revenues     1.128123  1        1.062131
commercial_portfolio 1.225630  2        1.052179
business_unit        1.196208  1        1.093713
```

As you could be guessing, we are looking here at GVIFs rather than VIFs, since our `training_data` shows at least one variable having more than one degree of freedom, especially the `commercial_portfolio` one (can you spot that small 2 surrounded by 1s in the `Df` column?). Let's look at the third column, $GVIF^{[1/(2*df)]}$, to see if any variable shows a value higher than the threshold of 10 we came to know when we first talked about VIFs.

I don't know about you, but I can't find any number greater than 3.3 in the output, and we can therefore conclude that no multicollinearity is going on within our data. Let's move to residual assumptions then, hoping they will get confirmed as well.

Residual assumptions validation

We can easily check assumptions on residuals by employing the two functions we got to know previously when dealing with simple linear regression:

- Durbin-Watson test, to check for the absence of auto-correlation within our residuals
- Breusch-Pagan test, to check for the absence of a trend between the value of y and the variance of residuals

We employ here once again the *car* package and the `durbinWatsonTest()` function, together with the `ncvTest()` function:

```
durbinWatsonTest(multiple_regression_new)
```

Which prints out:

```
lag Autocorrelation D-W Statistic p-value
 1 0.9444973 0.1107351 0
Alternative hypothesis: rho != 0
```

And:

```
ncvTest(multiple_regression_new)
```

Which produces:

```
Non-constant Variance Score Test
 Variance formula: ~ fitted.values
 Chisquare = 1.866399 Df = 1 p = 0.1718881
```

You already know what it means: the auto-correlation stays there while the non-constant variance score test is higher than the 0.05 threshold we discussed before, which means no relation was found between the level of the fitted y and the level of residuals.

One thing we can do to try improving our model is to apply the dimensional reduction techniques we have seen before.

Dimensionality reduction

Let's apply what we saw when talking about dimensional reduction, going through two alternative routes, principal component regression and stepwise regression.

Principal component regression

How do we perform principal component regression in R? We don't have a lot of pain to suffer here, thanks to a simple function from the `pls` package by Bjørn-Helge Mevik and Ron Wehrens. This package provides facilities both for the application of principal component regression and partial least squares in R. We are not going to apply the second to our data, but you should be aware of its existence as an alternative to the ordinary least squares technique we applied for coefficient estimation.

The simple function I was mentioning is the `pcr()` one. It is really similar to the `lm()` function we have already employed, and just requires you to pass the response variable and explanatory variables you are going to employ in your principal component regression model:

```
pcr_regression <- pcr(as.numeric(default_numeric)~., data = training_data)
```

Let's have a look inside by calling `summary`:

```
summary(pcr_regression)
```

```
Data:    X dimension: 11523 12
         Y dimension: 11523 1
Fit method: svdpc
Number of components considered: 12
TRAINING: % variance explained
                          1 comps  2 comps  3 comps  4 comps  5 comps  6 comps  7 comps  8 comps  9 comps  10 comps  11 comps  12 comps
X                         97.4851  99.8305  99.9251  99.9800  99.997   100.000  100.00   100.000  100.000  100.000   100.000   100.000
as.numeric(default_numeric)  0.2268   0.2733   0.6273   0.7504   5.615    5.647    6.07     6.081    6.119    8.325     8.355     8.393
```

What can you see here?

We have got some descriptive information about the data, particularly that our **X** matrix is composed of 12 columns, that is variables, and 11,523 rows, and our **Y** vector is composed of one column and the same number of rows. You then find information about the algorithm employed, which is the singular value decomposition (I will point you to some good references if you want to get some more information on this), and finally a really interesting table on the % of variance explained from different sets of components.

How do you read it?

You can see that by employing just the first principal component, the first column on the left of the table, you have the 97.50 of variance of X explained, while only the 0.22 of variance of Y is explained. Moving on with the number of components, you can see that when employing six principal components we have explained all the variance of X, yet the variance of Y remains mainly unexplained. This is actually true until the end, when the threshold of twelve components is reached.

As I was saying, it doesn't make any sense to go further, since our starting set has twelve variables and we actually want to reduce the dimensions of our model.

We can conclude that no great improvement was obtained through this technique. Nevertheless, we still have one more way to visualize its results, which is to plot the R-squared level associated with each set of components tried. We can conveniently do this through the `R2()` function, provided directly within the `pls()` package. A full set of functionalities like those that are actually provided within the package, and we are going to have closer look at them when talking about performance metrics. For now, let us just plot our R-squared:

```
plot(R2(pcr_regression))
```

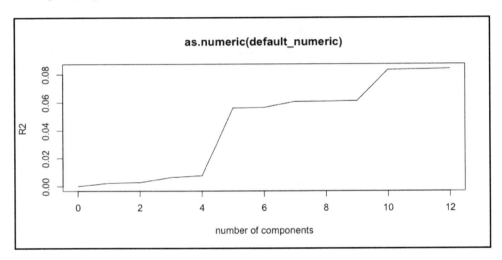

As you can see, we get here a substantial improvement of our R-squared as the number of components improves. You can notice that this metric holds stable from one to four components, then substantially improves around five components, and then has another relevant piece of improvement around 10 components. What is the final level? You can find the number by employing, once again, the `R2()` function:

```
R2(pcr_regression)
```

This shows us the following:

(Intercept)	1 comps	2 comps	3 comps	4 comps	5 comps	6 comps	7 comps	8 comps	9 comps	10 comps	11 comps	12 comps
0.000000	0.002268	0.002733	0.006273	0.007504	0.056145	0.056466	0.060697	0.060813	0.061188	0.383253	0.083551	0.083926

As you can see, we finally come to a 0.08 R-squared, which up to one is not an impressive value. Nevertheless, keep it in mind to compare it with the result we will get from the stepwise regression.

Stepwise regression

We can quickly apply the stepwise regression to our model by employing a convenient function named `stepAIC` from the `MASS` package by Brian Ripley and Bill Venables.

Let me give you a small lesson here, since I know you are an R enthusiast. This package was developed as a support to the relevant book *Modern Applied Statistics with S* authored by the same Brian Ripley and Bill Venables. So it can be considered as a father of R, since the latter was developed as an implementation of the first. R actually also has a brother, which is S-PLUS, a commercial edition of S. These two authors I mentioned, Brian and Bill, are actually two relevant contributors to the development of R, and the second is still an active member of its community.

That said, let's actually apply the function to our model:

```
stepwise_regression <- stepAIC(multiple_regression_new, direction = "both",
trace = TRUE)
```

When running this function, your console should actually get flooded by a relevant quantity of text, this is because the `trace` argument is set to `TRUE`. This argument lets you specify if you are interested in seeing what the algorithm evaluates and produces at each of its iterations. One argument that can be considered even more relevant is the `direction` argument.

It is the argument that specifies which kind of stepwise algorithm will be employed. It can reasonably assume the following values:

- Forward
- Backward
- Both

We are employing here the mixed algorithm, in order to maximize the chance of getting the best possible model selected.

Leveraging the abundant tracing of the function, let's investigate how it works to produce the final estimate stored within the `stepwise_regression` object. Let's start from the first step:

```
Start:  AIC=-19948.64
as.numeric(default_numeric) ~ corporation + previous_default +
    multiple_country + cost_income + ROE + employees + economic_sector +
    ROS + company_revenues + commercial_portfolio + business_unit

                       Df Sum of Sq    RSS    AIC
- multiple_country      1     0.032 2035.8 -19950
- cost_income           1     0.206 2036.0 -19950
<none>                              2035.8 -19949
- ROE                   1     0.709 2036.5 -19947
- business_unit         1     0.724 2036.5 -19946
- commercial_portfolio  2     1.459 2037.2 -19944
- employees             1     1.306 2037.1 -19943
- ROS                   1     2.217 2038.0 -19938
- economic_sector       1     2.568 2038.4 -19936
- previous_default      1     3.154 2039.0 -19933
- corporation           1    49.248 2085.0 -19675
- company_revenues      1    86.062 2121.9 -19474
```

You can see it is beginning from the `Start` on the upper left. As you can see, the algorithm is starting from the null model, which is marked by `<none>` in the third place. This constitutes a baseline for subsequent steps. The algorithm already computes the AIC performance metrics for this null model. Don't worry about it now, I am planning to talk about it later when dealing with classification models (author here, you can skip to `Chapter 10`, *A Different Outlook to Problems with Classification Models*, if you want to know more about it right now). Just consider it as a performance metric, the lower it is, the better it is.

Let's move to the next step:

```
Step:  AIC=-19950.46
as.numeric(default_numeric) ~ corporation + previous_default +
    cost_income + ROE + employees + economic_sector + ROS + company_revenues +
    commercial_portfolio + business_unit

                      Df Sum of Sq   RSS     AIC
- cost_income          1     0.289 2036.1 -19951
<none>                             2035.8 -19950
+ multiple_country     1     0.032 2035.8 -19949
- ROE                  1     0.711 2036.5 -19948
- business_unit        1     0.719 2036.5 -19948
- commercial_portfolio 2     1.466 2037.3 -19946
- employees            1     1.316 2037.1 -19945
- ROS                  1     2.225 2038.0 -19940
- economic_sector      1     2.582 2038.4 -19938
- previous_default     1     9.478 2045.3 -19899
- corporation          1    49.242 2085.1 -19677
- company_revenues     1    86.037 2121.9 -19476
```

This step adds the `multiple_country` variable, as you can infer from the + token. Again, we have the `AIC` computed. The iteration goes on as we described earlier, and the algorithm finally chooses the best model among the estimated ones. We can take a closer look at this final model by looking at the `anova` object stored within the `stepwise_regression` object:

```
stepwise_regression$anova

Stepwise Model Path
 Analysis of Deviance Table
Initial Model:
 as.numeric(default_numeric) ~ corporation + previous_default +
 multiple_country + cost_income + ROE + employees + economic_sector +
 ROS + company_revenues + commercial_portfolio + business_unit
Final Model:
 as.numeric(default_numeric) ~ corporation + previous_default +
 ROE + employees + economic_sector + ROS + company_revenues +
 commercial_portfolio + business_unit
Step Df Deviance Resid. Df Resid. Dev AIC
1 11510 2035.796 -19948.64
2 - multiple_country 1 0.0315951 11511 2035.827 -19950.46
3 - cost_income 1 0.2893156 11512 2036.117 -19950.82
```

We see here the initial model, employing all the eleven available variables, and the final model, which shows only nine variables. This means that our iteration process resulted in two variables being removed from the set of explanatory variables. Looking at the bottom of the output will let us discover that the removed variables were `multiple_country` and `cost_income`.

How does this model compare with the original one and the one coming from the *principal component regression*? Let us focus on the R-squared parameter to get a synthetic summary of the output:

model	R-squared
multiple_regression_new	0.08297
pcr_regression	0.083926
stepwise_regression	0.08299

For `pcr_regression`, as I showed the highest R-squared, pertaining to the 12 components model.

To be honest, we didn't get that great an improvement by applying the principal component regression, and in the end it seems that our linear model is not able to effectively describe the underlying phenomenon of a customer unable to pay their bills, even if powered up with some techniques. This is shown by at least three elements:

- The really low R-squared
- The presence of auto-correlation among residuals
- The presence of non costancy variance of our residuals

There is one further sign that helps us understand that the linear model is not the most useful one, let's try to predict the value of y given the following vector of explanatory values, that we are going to call `new_data`:

corporation	0
previous_default	0
multiple_country	0
default_numeric	0
cost_income	-1,00E+06
ROE	0.009629198

employees	827
economic_sector	710
ROS	0.1813667
company_revenues	10000910
commercial_portfolio	less affluent
business_unit	retail_bank

It's actually really easy to predict some values of *y* once having estimated a linear model in R. You just need to employ the `predict.lm` function, passing the `lm` object you have obtained from the `lm()` function, paired with a set of new data, under the argument `newdata`:

```
predict.lm(multiple_regression_new, newdata = new_data)
```

This will result in a bold **-3.538197** being printed out. How would you interpret it? We know that our explanatory variable is the vent of default, having zero for no default and one for default, how would you interpret a negative number or a number greater than one?

There is no obvious answer to this question, since no standard interpretation can be defined for those kinds of predictions. That is why our model is not a good tool to describe and investigate our phenomenon.

Linear models are not the best possible alternative when modeling a binary phenomenon.

Isn't that a sad ending? It partially is, or at least it means we didn't find the answer we were looking for, that is, we are not able to explain which of the customers are more unlikely to pay their bills. We therefore have to move to another family of models. Before actually doing so, I will show you something more structured about model metrics and how to compute them in R. Finally, good news. I have found one of the cheat sheets I was mentioning before, the one regarding linear models. You will find there the underlying intuitions, the assumptions, and how to implement and validate them in R. Enjoy.

Linear model cheat sheet

Following is the cheat sheet for Linear Regression:

Linear Regression cheatsheet

intuition and maths

linear regression model is based on the idea that the relationship between one response variable Y and a set of explanatory variables X can be expressed in a linear form as the following:

$$y_i = \beta_0 + \beta_1 * x_i$$

having the beta coefficients measuring the level of changed on y determined from a change of x

---

kind of data

as X:
- categorical variables
- continuous variables

as Y:
- continuous variables
- categorical variables (but may generate out of domain estimates) estimates

---

how to fit in R

lm(y ~ .) fits y against all variables
stepAIC() fits linear regression with stepwise procedure
pcr() fits principal component regression

---

assumptions

1. absence of multicollinearity among explanatory variables
2. absence of autocorrelation in model residuals
3. absence of correlation between residual variance and fitted values

---

how to test them in R

1. vif(): <=10 passed, >10 ko
2. DurbinWatsonTest(lm_object): 0 positive correlation (ko), 2 absence of positive correlation (passed) 4 negative correlation (ko)
3. ncvTest(): p-value <0.05 ok, p-value >= 0.05 ko

Further references

- Kahn Academy course about exponentials and logarithm, to let you refresh concepts and properties: `https://www.khanacademy.org/math/algebra2/exponential-and-logarithmic-functions`
- American Mathematical Society explanation of singular value decomposition: `http://www.ams.org/samplings/feature-column/fcarc-svd`

Summary

This is the author speaking here. What a great chapter! Yeah, I know I should not say that since I am the author of the book, nevertheless, I think the one you just completed was a relevant step towards your discovery of R for data mining. You are now able to:

- Fit a linear model in R, both having a single explanatory variable and multiple explanatory variables (univariate and multivariate) through the `lm()` function and assess its estimates through the `summary()` function
- Evaluate whether the linear regression model assumptions are met, through the `durbinWatsonTest()` and `NCVtest()` functions
- Perform principal component regression on your data through the `pcr()` function
- Perform stepwise regression through the `stepAIC()` function and evaluate its output
- Compare and interpret the output and performance of different regression models and evaluate whether your model is a reasonable way to describe the observed phenomenon

It's now time to take a closer look at what a model performance, introducing or examining in greater depth concepts such as R-squared, squared error, and the confusion matrix.

10
A Different Outlook to Problems with Classification Models

Now that you have the instruments to interpret the results of data mining models, it is time to move on to executing the data modeling strategy you defined with Andy. Here, you will look at classification models, first of all understanding why they were developed and in what kinds of problems they can be useful.

You will then look at three of the most common models employed within this field, which are logistic regression, support vector machines, and random forest, carefully evaluating what the assumptions are to be satisfied in order for the model to be useful.

One note of warning before leaving you again with Andy—some of the models we are going to see here as classification models are actually sometimes employed, with slight modifications, as regression models. You should therefore not be too rigid in classifying those models into your memory. The same holds for these models being supervised, since unsupervised versions of the same models are also available. For instance, we will see here support vector machines as a supervised method for classification, but you will often find that they are employed as an unsupervised technique.

Rather than scaring or confusing you, this should just stimulate you in developing critical thinking and carefully evaluating possible alternatives when dealing with your real data mining problems.

But, let Andy speak, and I hope you will have better luck with classification models than you had with your linear regressions.

What is classification and why do we need it?

We don't have much time left, and we still need to try at least four models to get the best one and produce the list of customers potentially involved in our profit drop. We are now going to try classification models.

We have already talked about these models in brief, but let me tell you something more structured about them before actually applying them to our data.

Classification models are the ones employed to predict a categorical output. We have already seen that regression models are a good tool when dealing with quantitative output, that is numerical response variables. A typical example is the revenues we were thinking about before. But, what if you don't have a numerical response variable, but categorical variables?

Linear regression limitations for categorical variables

Let's try to face a problem involving categorical variables with the only model you know—linear regression.

Let's imagine, for instance that you are dealing with a dataset showing; for a group of people, some explanatory variables sided with the obtained level of education articulated as high school, university, and doctor of philosophy:

Degree	Family income	Parents' highest degree
High school	93922	University
High school	63019	High school
University	51787	University
University	31954	High school
University	42681	High school
High school	50378	Doctor of philosophy
Doctor of philosophy	66107	University

How would you apply linear regression to this model? You would probably move the degree of education to a numerical scale. This is reasonable, but how to do that? You would probably resort to a scale from 1 to 3, having 1 as high school and 3 as doctor of philosophy:

n	degree	family_income	parents_highest_degree
1	High school	93922	University
1	High school	63019	High school
2	University	51787	University
2	University	31954	High school
2	University	42681	High school
1	High school	50378	Doctor of philosophy
3	Doctor of philosophy	66107	University

Now, let's try to create a similar dataset in R and fit our regression model to this data:

```
education <- data.frame(n = c(1,1,2,2,2,1,3),
  degree = c("high school","high school", "university",
  "university", "university","high school","doctor of philosophy"),
  family_income = c(93922,63019,51787,31954,42681,50378,66107),
  parents_highest_degree = c("university","high school", "university" ,
"high school" , "high school" , "doctor of philosophy", "university"))

lm_model <- lm(n~ family_income + parents_highest_degree, data = education)
```

This actually results in a linear regression model. Even if you call summary() on it, you find out that it shows not astonishing performances, with an adjusted R-squared (you do remember why we should look at the adjusted one, don't you?) roughly equal to 30%.

But this is not the only problem with this model.

Imagine now that a new record is made available, regarding a student with a family income of 140,000 and university as the highest degree among the student's parents. If you try to predict the expected degree of education for that student, you will get a surprising -0.2029431. We can easily do this in R using the predict function:

```
predict(lm_model,newdata = data.frame(family_income = 140000,
parents_highest_degree = "university"))
```

1
-0.2029431

What degree of education is that? This is the first kind of problem when trying to employ linear regression with categorical problems. But we also have another problem that our first set of data didn't show. Let's look at this dataset:

preferred_movie_type	annual_income	occupation
Action	66322	Doctor
Action	43873	Student
Thriller	2000	Student
Comedy	20360	Musician
Thriller	0	Housewife

Let's say we want to predict the preferred movie type based on the annual income and main occupation, employing our beloved linear regression. How would you proceed? How would you assign a numerical value to `preferred_movie_type`? Every possible choice would involve a high level of arbitrary decisions. There is no clear ranking within movie types, and introducing them just for the need of fitting our model would imply heavily manipulating our data and its original structure, with serious implications on the level of significance of our model's results.

You now have at least two reasons for which it is not advisable to employ linear regression for classification problems, and why we need specific models to perform classification tasks. One really small note before moving on—this holds true also for non-linear regression models, which I am not going to show you, but basically involve a non-linear regression between the response variable and explanatory variables.

Common classification algorithms and models

You now know why we need classification models, but what models do we have at our disposal? Different models and algorithms were proposed along time to perform classification tasks.

If we want to list some of the most popular, we should at least mention:

- Logistic regression
- Support vector machines
- Random forest
- K-nearest neighbour

Each of those four models, plus their variants, share the ability to produce a prediction of what the category pertaining to any given record within a training or testing dataset will be. Nevertheless, all of them differ in some detail, which makes some of them more appropriate for a given type of data and some others more appropriate for other kinds of data. We are going to deepen our knowledge of, and apply to our data, only the first three on the list, but let me briefly summarize in a comparative table the main tenets and features, to help you in case in the future you are confronted with the challenge of choosing the right classification algorithms and models for your problem:

Model/algorithm	Output	Type of categorical response variable	Number/type of explanatory variable	Interpretability	Variants
Logistic regression	Probability of record i pertaining to a category	Boolean (0,1)	No constraint both on the number and type of explanatory variable	Estimated coefficients define the relevance of each explanatory variable to define the final cluster of the record	Variants are available to overcome the constraint on the response variable being Boolean
Support vector machines	Predicted category for each record i	Multimodal (1,...n)	No constraint both on the number and type of explanatory variable	Estimated coefficients define the relevance of each explanatory variable to define the final cluster of the record	Variants are available to overcome the constraint on the number of explanatory variables
Random forest	Predicted category for each record i	Multimodal (1,...n)	No constraint both on the number and type of explanatory variable	Measures of the relative importance of the explanatory variables that are available	Variants are available to change the criteria employed to decide on the path to take through the final estimate
K-nearest neighbour	Predicted category for each record i	Multimodal (1,...n)	No constraint both on the number and type of explanatory variable	Black box	Variants are available to modify the criteria employed to assign records to categories

Let's move on to the logistic regression now, hoping it will help us produce the final list of customers to be sent to the Internal Audit department.

Logistic regression

Logistic regression was developed during the 19th century to study the growth of population and some specific types of chemical reactions, and the first person to formally define it was the Belgian statistician Pierre François Verhulst, who published in 1837 four pages about it within his mentor's publication, *Correspondance Mathématique et Physique.*

Starting from this first publication, a lot of others followed, paired with extensive use of the model in real-life domains far from the original one, such as fraud detection and the estimation of the probability of default.

The intuition behind logistic regression

The intuition behind logistic regression starts exactly where linear regression stops—solving the problem of estimated values outside the natural domain of our response variable. It start from the typical problem of having a response variable that can pertain to two alternative categories, either zero or one, and the need for some record to one of those categories based on a set of explanatory variables.

The logistic function estimates a response variable enclosed within an upper and lower bound

Looking again at the history of this function, it is defined in the tentative of describing the way of growth of a given population—fitting a linear regression to any set of data would have invariantly produced a straight line having the sky as the limit, which would have to be judged as unreasonable. This is why, when studying different possible functional forms, the logistic function was finally derived from Verhulst as a function able to describe a phenomenon starting from a lower limit and characterized from a trait of sustained growth followed from a more stable period, in which the response variable will at its most touch an inviolable upper limit. The easily recognizable shape of a `logistic` function is the following:

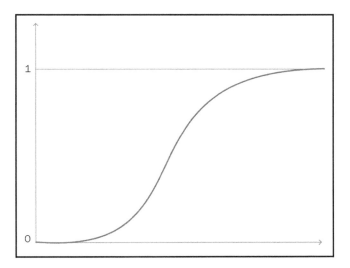

As you can see, this is exactly what we are looking for —a response variable ranging between two bounds, no matter the value of the explanatory variable(s).

The logistic function estimates the probability of an observation pertaining to one of the two available categories

The second intuition behind the logistic regression is that its output is a probability. As written in the table I showed you before, the logistic regression doesn't assign a category among the two available, but only expresses the probability of a given record pertaining to one of the two categories. For instance, and this is not a causal example, estimating a logistic regression on a population having a zero to one response variable will result, for each record, in a number enclosed within zero and one, representing the probability of that particular record pertaining to the one category.

What if we are rather interested in the probability of the record pertaining to the zero category? There's nothing more easy than that, since knowing that zero and one are mutually exclusive events/categories (think, for instance to dead and alive), we can compute the probability of zero as 100%, the probability of one. I will give you references to some good introductory material on probability theory in case you need a refresh on this.

Here we are—a logistic regression model that is able to take a set of explanatory variables and estimate how likely each given record is to pertain to one category rather than the other.

The math behind logistic regression

We just said that our `logistic` function is able to always return a number enclosed within zero and one, but how does this function obtain that desirable result? First of all, let's start with the logistic function formula:

$$f(x) = \frac{e^x}{1+e^x}$$

As you can see, we have a ratio between a strange term e^x and one plus the same strange term e^x. What is that strange term? It turns out that it is the natural number e, which is approximately equal to 2.7183, raised to the power of x. The e^x term is therefore named the exponential function, since it's the function obtained raising e to an exponent equal to x. What is the shape of this function? Let me jot down its typical shape:

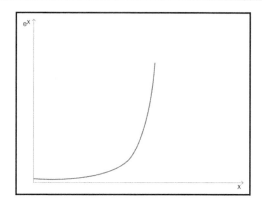

As you can see, the bigger the x gets, the bigger the e^x becomes. Furthermore, as you can guess from the plot, this function never breaches the abscissa, that is, it never returns a negative value. This is a crucial point in understanding the logistic function. The term added to one on the denominator, never becomes negative, and at its minimum, becomes equal to zero.

What about its maximum? If you imagine adding higher x values to the plot, you can continue the line and guess that the curve tends to the sky, that is, it always tends higher values.

Putting all of this together, we can describe the behavior of our denominator, as follows:

- It gets closer to one as x gets smaller (and e^x gets closer to zero)
- It gets bigger and bigger as x gets bigger

The final step to understanding our logistic function is to match this behavior to the behavior of the overall ratio:

- As x increases, the denominator gets bigger and the ratio gets closer to one, since the numerator and the denominator tend to always be a little bit more equal, except for the one which, as x becomes bigger, tends to become less relevant. At its most, the denominator will be exactly equal to one, and therefore our function will touch its maximum at one.
- As x decreases, the denominator will decrease, touching its minimum at one ($1 + e^x$ = $1 + 0 = 1$), and the same will with the numerator. At its minimum, we will find the ratio between zero and one, which will obviously be equal to zero. Nevertheless, the ratio will never breach zero since both the numerator and the denominator will always remain positive.

I think you have now got it—no matter what the value of our x will be, the way our logistic function is defined will always assure the results being included are within zero and one. Moreover, you should keep in mind that the logistic function is defined as a monotonic function, that is, a function that always grows when the explanatory variable grows.

Putting it in that way, you could think that not that much is left to model, since we already have a function and it respects our desires. But, how do we express the level of influence that the x has on the y?

If you look back at the plot I showed you before, you can see that the *s-shape* in the middle has its own inclination. How steep the shape is is a matter of how strong the relationship is between x and y—if the relationship is strong a small increase in x, which is a small move on the right, will produce a relevant increase in the level of y, and we will reach the value of one sooner.

How do we express this within our model? We can easily do this by introducing coefficients within the model itself:

$$f(x) = \frac{e^{\beta_0 + \beta_1 x}}{1 + e^{\beta_0 + \beta_1 x}}$$

As you are surely observing, this coefficient closely resembles the one we have seen for the linear regression. This is actually not causal, and is related to the origin of the logistic function, which was the study of population growth. Nevertheless, we will not focus on this.

Let me show you instead how we estimate the coefficients.

Maximum likelihood estimator

The most common technique employed for a coefficient estimate within the logistic regression model is the maximum likelihood estimator. The main intuition behind this concept is to find the coefficients that are better able to produce probability close to the actual event observed for the given record.

In other words, we want to find a set of coefficients able to produce a probability closer to one when a one is actually observed, and a zero when instead a zero is observed.

This is formalized through the likelihood function:

$$L(\theta|x) = p_\theta(x) = P_\theta(X = x)$$

Not making it too technical, you should just notice that it expresses the trust of a given parameter being equal to θ, considered that the response variable assumes the value x. In the case of the logistic model, this can be translated as— the likelihood of θ being equal to one considering that x is equal to one.

The actual task of finding the value of coefficients that maximize this probability is usually solved by the means of consequent iterations, that is, consequently trying a different set of coefficients and finally evaluating which is the best one in terms of likelihood value.

Model assumptions

Let's see what the assumptions behind the logistic regression are and how they are usually checked.

Absence of multicollinearity between variables

We have already talked about this attribute for the conclusions of our model being reliable and sound that we should avoid multicollinearity between explanatory variables employed, and we should be sure that our explanatory variables prove to be independent among each other.

As we have discussed before, having variables too correlated within your set of explanatory variables could lead to our coefficient estimates being unreliable or unstable.

Two common ways to check for collinearity among variables is to compute the related value of tolerance and the **variance inflation factor**. I am not going to bore you again by discussing these two new concepts. Nevertheless, we are going to check for the assumption in a moment when actually estimating our model.

Linear relationship between explanatory variables and log odds

One more assumption, even if it would be better to call it a requirement, is the presence of a linear relationship between the explanatory variables and the log odds. *What on the sacred heart are log odds?* I can see this question bumping up in your mind. Log odds are actually closely related to what we have already seen about logistic regression. First of all, we have to define what an odd is supposed to be. Odds are formally defined as the ratio between the probability of an event showing up and its opposite, that is, the probability of the event not showing up:

$$\frac{p}{1-p}$$

It turns out that the odds of a logistic regression are simply constituted by:

$$e^{\beta_0 + \beta_1 x}$$

Which actually is the term composed of the numerator and part of the denominator of our logistic function. What are log odds then? Simply the log of the odds! Let's try to find them out, resorting to the properties of logarithms:

$$log(e^{\beta_0 + \beta_1 x}) = \beta_0 + \beta_1 x$$

And here we are, you have your assumption explained, a logistic regression is characterized from the linearity between the explanatory variables and the log odds of the outcome.

How do we test for if this assumption holds true? This can be done by fitting one more model, other then the plain logistic one, including quadratic and cubic terms, so to understand if those terms produce a significantly better performance for our model, and we can, therefore, infer that a non-linear relationship is taking place.

We are going to check for this through the likelihood ratio test. I am going to be more explicit about this while actually applying it, since we need to know a bit about hypothesis testing to understand it, and we will talk about hypothesis testing in a second.

Large enough sample size

There is one more relevant requirement that should be satisfied when talking about logistic regression—the dimensions of the estimation sample. We are not going to make this too technical, you should just consider that for a good logistic regression to be estimated for the maximum likelihood estimator to work properly, at least 30 records should be available, meaning that for each explanatory variable at least 30 non-missing observations should be found. This is clearly not a problem for our sample, which encompasses way more than 30 records. Nevertheless, you should keep this requirement in your mind when dealing with logistic regression.

How to apply logistic regression in R

As is often the case with R, the heavy task of estimating a fairly complex model, as the logistic model is, can be easily accomplished by just running a function, which in this case is the `glm()` one. Let's take a closer look at this function, which is actually a powerful one.

The `glm()` function, which comes with the base version of R (even if it is actually packed within the `stats` package), was originally developed to estimate a wide range of models, and specifically the whole family of generalized linear models.

We are not going to talk widely about generalized linear models now, but you should be aware at least of the intuition behind this family of models.

The first model we talked about was the simple linear regression model. Even if we didn't stress the point too much when talking about it, this model assumes the residuals being normally distributed around their mean. This means that if we get a large enough sample of records, if we fit a linear model and compute the histogram of the residuals, we find a shape similar to the following:

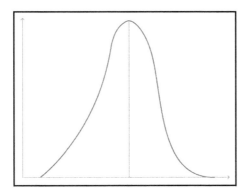

This is exactly what a normal distribution, also named Gaussian distribution, looks like. This distribution is what the simple linear regression expects the distribution of residuals to be like. This is usually a good expectation, but we have already seen that this simple linear regression can be inaccurate when estimating the value of a specific kind of response variable.

Which kinds of variables are we talking about? Yes, we are talking about binary variables. For those kinds of variables, which can assume either the value of zero or the value of one, the assumption of a normal distribution doesn't hold true at all, and we have to assume a rather different distribution.

The answer we find with the logistic model we are talking about now, is to assume as a response variable distribution the binomial distribution. This distribution formally represents the number of successes in a sequence of n independent experiments under the same conditions.

We are not going to look at this too closely; just consider that you consider here exactly a binary outcome—success or failure. Similarly to the binomial distribution for binary outcomes, a whole range of different distributions is available for different phenomena. The models behind this range are part of the generalized linear models.

Getting back to our `glm` function, how do we tell the function which of the generalized linear models we want to fit on our data? This is done through the *family* argument, which can get the following values:

- `binomial`
- `gaussian`
- `Gamma`
- `inverse.gaussian`
- `poisson`
- `quasi`
- `quasibinomial`
- `quasipoisson`

As you can see, we have there both the Gaussian and the binomial distributions.

Fitting the model

To fit a logistic model on our data, we will need to run the `glm()` function, passing as arguments a formula indicating which variable we want to consider as independent, which are to be considered explanatory, and binomial as a family of generalized linear models:

```
logistic <- glm(as.numeric(default_numeric)~ . ,data = training_data,
family ="binomial")
```

As usual, we can see the output of our estimating activity by employing the `summary` function:

```
summary(logistic)
```

Reading the glm() estimation output

We have here a lot of information, haven't we? But let's just focus on the most relevant part. First of all, we find the coefficients associated with each of the explanatory variables. They are shown under the **Estimate** column, and are exactly the beta we find within the logistic function. As you can see, they have different signs, some of them are positive while others are negative. As is the case for linear regression, the sign of the coefficients expresses what kind of relationship there is between the given explanatory variable and the response one:

```
Call:
glm(formula = as.numeric(default_numeric) ~ ., family = "binomial",
    data = training_data)

Deviance Residuals:
    Min      1Q   Median      3Q      Max
-2.1462  -0.6464   0.7251   0.7274   2.2308

Coefficients:
                                    Estimate Std. Error z value Pr(>|z|)
(Intercept)                        1.086e+00  7.730e-02  14.049  < 2e-16 ***
corporation                       -1.637e+01  1.243e+02  -0.132 0.895177
previous_default                   5.681e-01  1.414e-01   4.017 5.91e-05 ***
multiple_country                  -8.244e-02  1.603e-01  -0.514 0.607183
cost_income                        5.872e-08  5.858e-08   1.002 0.316136
ROE                                5.486e-07  2.586e-07   2.122 0.033848 *
employees                          1.990e-08  9.277e-09   2.145 0.031957 *
economic_sector                   -2.856e-08  9.979e-09  -2.862 0.004212 **
ROS                                1.873e-07  5.355e-08   3.498 0.000468 ***
company_revenues                  -1.977e-06  1.045e-07 -18.919  < 2e-16 ***
commercial_portfoliomass affluent  7.714e-01  5.148e-01   1.498 0.134015
commercial_portfoliomore affluent -1.372e+00  7.316e-01  -1.875 0.060782 .
business_unitretail_bank           1.312e-01  7.476e-02   1.756 0.079146 .
---
Signif. codes:  0 '***' 0.001 '**' 0.01 '*' 0.05 '.' 0.1 ' ' 1

(Dispersion parameter for binomial family taken to be 1)

    Null deviance: 13230  on 11522  degrees of freedom
Residual deviance: 12335  on 11510  degrees of freedom
AIC: 12361

Number of Fisher Scoring iterations: 14
```

- A positive sign expresses a positive relation between the two, meaning that an increase in the explanatory variable is expected overall to produce an increase in the response variable, and for sure will produce an increase in the forecasted value of the response variable. We can observe here a positive sign, for instance for the `previous_default` variable, which means that having experienced a default in a previous period increases the probability of going into default in a subsequent period.
- A negative sign expresses a negative relationship between explanatory and response variables. As an example, you can take the `company_revenues` variable, which reasonably shows a negative coefficient, meaning that having a higher level of revenues lowers the probability of going into default.

Do you think this information can be considered of interest to our overall purpose of discovering which type of customer is more inclined to go into default? It could actually be the case, and we will come back to this later. At the moment, before drawing any kind of conclusion, we first of all have to understand if our model satisfies the previously listed assumptions and requirements, and if we can therefore rely on its conclusions.

In the `summary()` output, you will find some other relevant information. Let us focus on two points:

- The level of statistical significance of the association between the explanatory variable and the response variable, shown in the column labeled `Pr(>|z|)`
- The AIC performance metric

The level of statistical significance of the association between the explanatory variable and the response variable

We get here into a fairly complex topic, but I will try to make it as clear as possible to help you understand the main concepts of it.

The topic here is statistical inference and hypothesis testing. Behind these words, there are a lot of techniques employed to assess if results obtained from statistical analyses can be considered significant or not, that is, if the results can be considered due to some structural True relation or simply by chance.

This main objective is pursued by setting a test. A test is usually composed of two hypotheses:

- H0, or the *null hypothesis*, which can equally be the one we want to be true or the one we want to be false
- H1, or the *alternative hypothesis*, which will be the opposite of H0

Once you are done with defining your testing hypothesis, you have to define how to actually test them. This is usually where the hypothesis testing actually comes into life, and basically is constituted from:

- A test statistic related to the observed value we want to test
- A p-value, that is the probability of finding the t-statistic (and therefore, the observed value) in case the null hypothesis is true

Let's imagine for example, that you want to test if the difference between two means, such as the one from a sample and the one from another sample, is significantly different. How do you do this? You can set the following test:

- **H0**: The two means are not significantly different
- **H1**: The two means are significantly different

You then compute the **t-statistic**, which is the one usually employed for comparing proportions. You can now check your t-statistics on a table, which is conveniently name **t-label**, and find out what the probability is of finding the value of the t-statistic in the hypothesis of the two means not being significantly different.

Let's say for instance, that you get a probability of 0.03%, is it high or low? Well, it is for sure a low probability, but how can you tell if it is low enough to exclude the hypothesis of a non-significant difference? It turns out that by setting a level of significance to 95%, it is possible to set this threshold to 0.05, and it is possible to say that if we find a p-value lower than 0.05 we can reject the null hypothesis and accept the alternative one.

This brief explanation is surely not enough to let you understand how to set and perform hypothesis testing on your own. Nevertheless, it is enough to let you understand the output of logistic regression estimation and the vast majority of similar measures you will find in your model estimation. The call of the `glm()` function, besides estimating the coefficient of our logistic function, also performs a test of the hypothesis on the statistical significance of the level of association between the y and each of the x. What we find on the $Pr(>|z|)$ is exactly the p-value we were talking about.

If the p-value is below 0.05, we can be reject the null hypothesis of the association not being significant, while we cannot do this in the opposite case. What are the small stars on the right of this column? I know you are understanding it on your own—the number of stars is proportional to the p-value, and therefore to the level of statistical significance of the association. We therefore see that `previous_default`, `company_revenues`, and the `ROS` index are the variables, results in being the most significant one.

You should notice that the level of significance is in no way related to the level of the coefficient, but just with the statistical significance of the association found between the y and the explanatory variable.

The AIC performance metric

At the very bottom of the output from the call to `summary` you can spot *AIC: 12361* token. What does *AIC* stand for?

First of all, let's explain the acronym. It stands for **Akaike information criterion (AIC)**. Hirotugu Akaike was a Japanese statistician that, around 1974 developed the AIC as an attempt to provide a unique number able to compare the relative performance of alternative models on the same estimation sample.

This AIC is actually quite simply defined as:

$$AIC = 3k = 2ln(\hat{L})$$

Having k as the number of estimated parameters and L as the maximum value assumed from the likelihood function of the given model.

You then have a component, *2k*, that is a penalty component introduced to discourage overfitting. Why do we say that? Because the typical way to produce an overfitted model is to introduce a higher number of parameters able to fine-tune our predicted value.

We then have the value assumed from the likelihood function. As said before, this function expresses in a way how probable it is that our model will predict a given output (which in our case was the default) given that this output is actually observed. In this sense, a greater value of this function expresses a better fit for the model.

We can summarize all that we've just learned by saying that the AIC expresses the relative performance of a model both in terms of the level of overfitting and goodness of fit. Why do we say relative level of performance? Because the AIC doesn't have a fixed range of variation and we can't therefore say absolutely that this is the best possible model.

Nevertheless, when comparing two or more models, we will be able to employ the AIC value to say which of them is better in terms of fitting. From what we have said until now about the AIC criterion, what do you think is better: a higher or a lower AIC value?

If we take a moment to think about it, we discover that, since the overfitting term has a positive sign and the likelihood term has a negative sign, a lower AIC value will be associated with a higher estimated overfitting or a lower likelihood, while a lower AIC value will be associated with the opposite situation.

We can therefore conclude that a lower AIC value is preferable to a higher one. What about that 12,361 we found as the AIC for our model? Is that a good or a bad value? Again, we can't say, but when looking at our model's performance we will compare this with an alternative model, yes, our multiple regression, to find out if it is a better or a worse model.

Validating model assumptions

But before looking at our model's performance, it's time to validate our model assumptions. We will actually validate only the assumption related to the linear relationship between explanatory variables and log odds, since the one about multicollinearity was already checked when dealing with linear models, and the adequacy of sample size is definitely satisfied from our quite large estimation sample.

Now then, how do we check for linearity? We have already seen this: fitting one more logistic model including quadratic and cubic terms. Let's see the rationale behind this and how to actually do it.

Fitting quadratic and cubic models to test for linearity of log odds

If you recall what we have said about log odds and their relationship with explanatory variables, you can see that in the presence of non-linearity, a logistic model including quadratic and cubic terms would show performance better than that of the linear model.

This is the rationale behind the kind of test we are going to perform through the `likelikhood-ratio` test. We take as a null model the quadratic one and confront it with the alternative `linear` model. We then compute a test statistic and get a p-value. This is similar to what we have already seen about significant of statistical significance association of the associations between x and y.

If the p-value is lower than a given threshold, which we will set as usual to 0.05, we can accept here the null hypothesis and therefore conclude that non-linearity of log odds is observed and the assumption is not respected.

But don't panic, we do not have to perform directly all that I have described: we just have to run the `lrtest()` function.

First of all, let's train one more model besides the linear one. We want this model to also include the quadratic term of our variables. At least it will include the quadratic term of continuous variables, since raising a binary variable to the second power would be meaningless.

Let's do this:

```
logistic_quadratic <- glm(as.numeric(default_numeric) ~ . +
cost_income^2 +
ROE^2 +
employees^2 +
ROS^2 +
company_revenues^2 ,
data = training_data, family = "binomial")
```

We now want to compare the resulting model, which we will employ as the *null model*, with the original one. Employing the `lrtest()` function from the `lmtest()` package, we can easily do it. We just have to pass to this function both the `logistic_quadratic` and the `logistic` objects. Just be aware that the first passed object will be the one employed as the null model:

```
lrtest(logistic_quadratic,logistic)
```

```
Likelihood ratio test

Model 1: as.numeric(default_numeric) ~ corporation + previous_default +
    multiple_country + cost_income + ROE + employees + economic_sector +
    ROS + company_revenues + commercial_portfolio + business_unit +
    cost_income^2 + ROE^2 + employees^2 + ROS^2 + company_revenues^2
Model 2: as.numeric(default_numeric) ~ corporation + previous_default +
    multiple_country + cost_income + ROE + employees + economic_sector +
    ROS + company_revenues + commercial_portfolio + business_unit
  #Df  LogLik Df Chisq Pr(>Chisq)
1  13 -6167.5
2  13 -6167.5  0     0          1
```

As you can see, we have here a first recap of the two compared models, followed by two lines of output where the `Pr(>Chisq)` column shows us the p-value associated with the performed test. As you can see, we have a sound one, which lets us reject the null model and therefore conclude positively about the respect of our assumption.

Visualizing and interpreting logistic regression results

We have our model fitted now, and we have concluded that its conclusions can be considered reliable. What's next? We need to visualize its results and draw a conclusion from the model.

Visualizing results

How would you visualize results coming from a logistic regression? We are dealing here with multiple explanatory variables against one response variable. Trying to visualize all of the involved dimensions, equal to the number of $x's$ plus a dimension for y, wouldn't be feasible.

One thing we can definitely do is to choose one, and even two relevant variables, and visualize how the observed and predicted values vary as they seem varies.

Since our main aim is always to define which type of customers are more likely to default, I would select among the variables showing significant relationships in terms of p-values, the ones with the higher beta coefficients. Those variables will be the ones for which a one-unit variation will produce a higher increase in terms of probability of defaulting.

Let's have a look again at our variables and coefficients:

```
Coefficients:
                                 Estimate Std. Error z value Pr(>|z|)
(Intercept)                     1.086e+00  7.730e-02  14.049  < 2e-16 ***
corporation                    -1.637e+01  1.243e+02  -0.132 0.895177
previous_default                5.681e-01  1.414e-01   4.017 5.91e-05 ***
multiple_country               -8.244e-02  1.603e-01  -0.514 0.607183
cost_income                     5.872e-08  5.858e-08   1.002 0.316136
ROE                             5.486e-07  2.586e-07   2.122 0.033848 *
employees                       1.990e-08  9.277e-09   2.145 0.031957 *
economic_sector                -2.856e-08  9.979e-09  -2.862 0.004212 **
ROS                             1.873e-07  5.355e-08   3.498 0.000468 ***
company_revenues               -1.977e-06  1.045e-07 -18.919  < 2e-16 ***
commercial_portfoliomass affluent  7.714e-01  5.148e-01   1.498 0.134015
commercial_portfoliomore affluent -1.372e+00  7.316e-01  -1.875 0.060782 .
business_unitretail_bank        1.312e-01  7.476e-02   1.756 0.079146 .
```

Looking at coefficient significance, we can select the following three variables:

- `previous_default`
- `ROS`
- `company_revenues`

Among those three, the ones that are associated with the higher coefficient values (taken into their absolute term) are:

- `previous_default`
- `company_revenues`

Just to let you familiarize yourself with the object resulting from a `glm()` call, let's observe the value of these two coefficients, isolating them from the whole vector of the estimated coefficient.

We can do this directly from the `logistic` object. This object is actually really similar to the one resulting from the `glm()` function—it is a list of different elements resulting from the estimation activity. Among these elements, there is one named coefficients, which conveniently stores all of the estimated coefficients. It is a named vector, meaning that every number stored is paired with a name that is equal to the name of the corresponding variable.

To extrapolate the coefficient it is therefore sufficient to select the `coefficients` element within the `logistic` list and filter this element, employing the name of the variable you are interested in:

```
logistic$coefficients['previous_default']

previous_default
 0.5680765

logistic$coefficients['company_revenues']

company_revenues
 -1.976669e-06
```

Which is a number that considered in its absolute value, is way lower than the previous 0.56. We can therefore conclude that the most relevant element when evaluating a customer to predict how probable it is that they will repay their bill, is to look at their previous default history. After that, the second most relevant character will be its size: the smaller they will be, the more probable it is that it will be difficult for them to pay their bills.

Let's try to actually visualize the relationship between company_revenues and the predicted probability of default.

First of all, we have to obtain a dataset showing our two explanatory variables together with the estimated probability of default. We can do this directly from the results of the glm() call, selecting and slicing the model data frame stored in the resulting logistic object, and binding it with the fitted.value object stored within the same logistic object:

```
logistic$model %>%
  select(company_revenues) %>%
  cbind(probability = logistic$fitted.values, .)-> dataviz_dataset
```

Now that we have the dataset read, visualization is just a matter of passing to the ggplot() function, specifying company_revenues as x and probability as y:

```
dataviz_dataset %>%
  ggplot(aes(x = company_revenues, y = probability)) +
  geom_point()
```

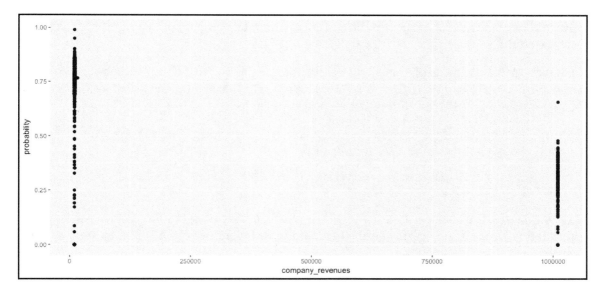

What can you see from the plot? You surely notice that the increased level of company revenues is associated with an overall lower value of predicted probability. This is coherent with the negative sign of our coefficient. Why we do not have all probability on the same level for a given level of company_revenues?

Because there are also other explanatory variables that for the different predicted values show different observed values.

Interpreting results

It seems we finally have a first relevant answer to our question. The customers most inclined to default within our portfolio are the smallest ones and the ones that have already experienced a previous default.

One final question is coming into my mind before moving to another model, the so-called support vector machine—are we sure that the logistic regression is providing us better results?

For sure it is at least satisfying the related requirements, but how does it perform compared to our multiple linear regression?

One way we could actually answer this would be by computing the AIC criteria for the linear model as well and then comparing it to the one obtained for the logistic model.

Unfortunately, our `glm()` function didn't return any AIC value. Have you got any idea of how we could fix this?

Yeah, we can fit our multiple linear model through the `glm()` function, and obtain our AIC value. How would you do it? If you remember, we said that the linear model assumes a normal or Gaussian distribution of the response variable.

No surprise then that if we specify `gaussian` as the `family` argument of the `glm()` function, we get a linear model as an output:

```
linear_glm <- glm(as.numeric(default_numeric)~.,data = training_data,
family = "gaussian")
```

I know that you are curious to know if this model is exactly equal to the one we previously estimated with `lm()`. Just print out the estimated coefficient of both of them to see the answer:

```
multiple_regression_new$coefficients
linear_glm$coefficients
```

```
> linear_glm$coefficients
                 (Intercept)                    corporation              previous_default
                7.441154e-01                  -6.676497e-01                  9.265625e-02
            multiple_country                    cost_income                           ROE
               -1.072549e-02                   1.131387e-08                  9.515206e-08
                   employees                economic_sector                           ROS
                2.943640e-09                  -4.615894e-09                  3.397692e-08
           company_revenues commercial_portfoliomass affluent commercial_portfoliomore affluent
               -4.298078e-07                   1.357221e-01                 -3.084859e-01
     business_unitretail_bank
                2.747193e-02
> multiple_regression_new$coefficients
                 (Intercept)                    corporation              previous_default
                7.441154e-01                  -6.676497e-01                  9.265625e-02
            multiple_country                    cost_income                           ROE
               -1.072549e-02                   1.131387e-08                  9.515206e-08
                   employees                economic_sector                           ROS
                2.943640e-09                  -4.615894e-09                  3.397692e-08
           company_revenues commercial_portfoliomass affluent commercial_portfoliomore affluent
               -4.298078e-07                   1.357221e-01                 -3.084859e-01
     business_unitretail_bank
                2.747193e-02
```

Great, they are exactly identical. It's now the moment of truth—is the logistic model better than the linear one?

If you remember, we discovered from the `summary` that for the logistic model the AIC value was *12360*, which is the AIC value for the linear model. We have here an AIC element within the `linear_glm` list, that conveniently stores our AIC value. Let's just print it out:

```
linear_glm$aic
```

```
[1 ] 12754.22
```

Which is higher. Since, as we said, the higher the AIC the worse the model in term of goodness of fit and overfitting, we can conclude that moving from the linear to the logistic model gave us a performance boost.

Not too bad for a model created nearly two hundred years ago! And I have also found the cheat sheet for this model. Let me show it to you before moving on to support vector machines.

Logistic regression cheat sheet

The following image shows the logistic regression cheat sheet:

Logistic Regression cheatsheet

intuition and maths

logistic regression is a model developed to describe a process influenced from one or more explanatory variables and having a possible outcome enclosed within an upper and a lower bound. It is based on the following formula:

$$f(x) = \frac{e^{\beta_0 + \beta_1 x}}{1 + e^{\beta_0 + \beta_1 x}}$$

in case of a binary response variable is possible to interpret its prediction as the probability of one of the two outcomes showing up

kind of data

as X:
- categorical variables
- continuous variables

as Y:
- boolean/binary variables
- continuos variables included with and upper and a lower bound (opportunely rescaled on the 0-1 range)

how to fit in R

glm(y ~ ., family = 'binomial') fits y against all variables

assumptions

1. absence of autocorrelation in model residuals
2. absence of multicollinearity between variables
3. linear relationship between explanatory variables and log odds

how to test them in R

1. DurbinWatsonTest(glm_object): 0 positive correlation (ko). 2 absence of positive correlation (passed) 4 negative correlation (ko) - *applicable to time series data only*
2. vif(): <=10 passed, >10 ko
3. fitting alternative model showing cubic and quadratic explanatory variables: if this shows being statistically significant the assumption is broken

Support vector machines

It is now time to move on to support vector machines, to see if they help us better define the profile of those customers more inclined to get into default status.

First of all, you should notice that support vector machines are way more recent models since they where developed around the 1990s. Secondly, you should notice that when we talk about SVMs, we are actually talking about a family of models rather than a single one.

I am going to show you now just what you need to know to understand the main concepts behind this model, but I will point out to you some good references in case you want to deepen your knowledge of the topic.

The intuition behind support vector machines

There are three main concepts you have to bear in mind when talking about support vector machines:

- The hyperplane
- The maximal margin classifier
- The support vector

The hyperplane

The hyperplane can be considered as the first brick to be employed when building a support vector machine.

Have you ever played with one of those tanks full of coloured solid plastic balls? Yeah, it actually is a game for children, but you should at least know what I am talking about.

OK, let's perform some mental experiments with one of those tanks. First of all, let's imagine it being filled only with red and yellow balls. We take the empty tank, we first fill half of it with the yellow ones and then with the red ones. They don't mix up since we fill the tank carefully, and in the end we should have something similar to the following:

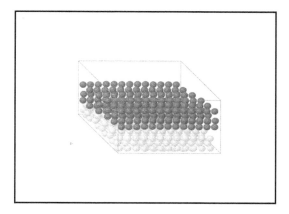

Let's imagine now that we take a really big blade and insert it into the tank from one side (don't worry, it is a mental experiment, you won't have to repay the tank's owner), at a height which is approximately half of the tank:

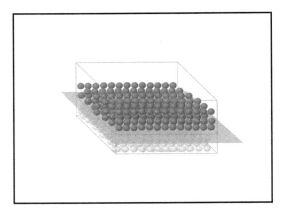

You see? The blade divides the tank into two groups. The balls on the top of the blade are the yellow balls, while on the bottom are the red ones.

Congratulations! You have just understood what a hyperplane is. We will make it more formal in a minute, but at the moment just understand that a hyperplane is some kind of plane (we will talk more about this later) able to exactly separate our data into two groups depending on the response variable we are looking at.

In a 3D space, this hyperplane is actually represented by a solid plane like our blade is, while in two dimensions it will be a line, and in more then three dimensions it will be hardly imaginable even if still formally defined.

Nevertheless, just take a second to focus on the main point of our first experiment: there is a plane that crops the tank and divides the balls into two groups based on their colours.

We are now going to make our experiment even more mental. Let's imagine that our balls start to levitate in the air. Let me show you how:

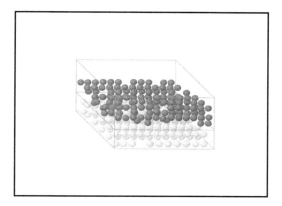

You see? They are still divided into two groups but are now placed apart from each other. Is there still a plane able to divide the balls into two groups?

For sure there is, and we can even draw it:

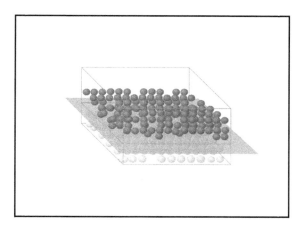

If we look at it carefully, we can actually see more than one possible plane. Moving the first one we drew just a bit will produce a nearly infinite number of other planes. Which is the best one?

Answering this question introduces the concept of the maximal margin classifier, which was the first classification algorithm based on a hyperplane to be introduced.

Maximal margin classifier

A desirable property of our best possible hyperplane could be the one of being the furthest possible from our balls, maximising the distance from our data. We can call this distance the margin between the hyperplane and the observation point.

Intuitively, the further this point the surer the classification will be. This intuition is the basis for the maximal margin classifier, which is simply an algorithm able to identify and estimate the hyperplane corresponding to the maximum possible margin.

It all went smoothly until now, but what if we shake our tank up a bit? Let's imagine that we shake it up a bit. Not that much, just enough to make our balls start to mix up, especially in the region where the plane was previously placed.

Let's look at the result now:

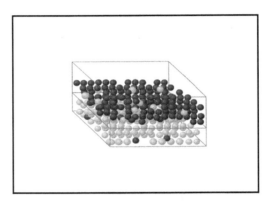

Uhm... not the same setting we were looking at before, is it? What if I now ask you to place your blade so that all of the yellow balls stay on one side of the blade and all of the red on the opposite one? Yeah, we cannot accomplish this task, there is no plane able exactly divide our points into two homogeneous groups.

That is why we have to move from the maximal margin classifier to support vector machines.

Support vector and support vector machines

Trying to overcome the issue of no perfect hyperplane, we place our blade somewhere within the tank, trying to place it in a way that allows us to put most of the yellow balls on one side and most of the red balls on the opposite side.

Moving from *all* to *most* is what the support vector machine is about, but let's first see what these support vectors are. You have now placed your blade somewhere. I see it, and I can tell you that there is a better position for the blade, and I invite you to find it out by placing it differently. What would you do?

After thinking about it carefully, you discover that what makes the difference in the performance of your classifier are not the balls that are far from the plane, which we can consider as safely classified from nearly every position of the blade but are rather the more next to the plane itself. You would actually discover that the most relevant ones are the points lying on the margin we have described before. Those points are the so-called support vectors, and they are the most relevant for the algorithmic procedure that produces the final selection of the best possible plane.

But, what is now the best possible plane? It is the one that maximizes the number of yellow balls on the yellow side, or alternatively the one that minimizes the number of red balls on the yellow side.

A final step to finally arrive to support vector machines is to remove the idea of the hyperplane being linear. Support vector machines are a group of algorithms defined to find out the best possible hyperplane, defined with different functional forms, from the simple linear to the non-linear and even radial one.

Model assumptions

I think you have now understood that one of the relevant points when applying any kind of data mining model is to know and test its assumptions, in order to understand how significant and reliable the conclusions you can draw from it are.

When talking about support vector machines, the only assumption usually cited to be relevant is the presence of independent and identically distributed random variables.

Independent and identically distributed random variables

First of all, it should be noticed that this assumption is not specifically related to support vector machines, but rather to the vast majority of data mining models, and especially to the family of generalized linear models we have dealt with before.

That said, another warning arises: the independent and identically distributed assumptions do not tell us anything about the relationship among the independent variables, but just about the behavior of each single variable.

As you can imagine, we can further split this assumption into two basic components:

- Independent variables
- Identically distributed variables

Independent variables

We have actually already seen this kind of assumption when talking about linear regression. If you carefully think about what assumption was considered there, you should remember the one about the absence of auto-correlation within residuals, which basically said that no clear trend should be noticed within residuals coming from our modeling. Of course, we were talking there about residuals of the dependent variables, and specifically about time series data. Generally speaking, the independent variable assumptions mean that no correlation should be noticed within the couples of (X_i, y_i), X being the explanatory variable and y the dependent one. We can formalize this assumption as follows:

$$(X_i, y_i) \quad independent \quad of \quad (X_j, y_j), \forall i \neq j \in \{1, \ldots, N\}$$

Having i and j as two different records and N the total number of records.

Identically distributed

Let's move on to the second sub-requirement, the one regarding the distribution of independent variables. First, we need to understand the proper meaning of this distribution. We mean here frequency distribution or probability distribution. You can understand it easily by resorting to the classic example of a dice.

You take a dice and ask yourself, *What are the possible outputs of this action?* We will exclude the possibility of the dice getting lost or eaten by your dog for the sake of simplicity, taking therefore as a list of possible outputs one number from one to six. We formally define this as follows: the random process of throwing a dice has a sample space composed of all real positive numbers from one to six.

You now ask yourself, *Is it more probable to get a one or a three?* As you already know, there is an equal probability of getting a one or a three, and there is actually the same probability of getting every number from one to six when rolling a (fair) dice. What is the probability distribution of this random process? Let's first compute the probability associated with every possible outcome. Considering that the total probability of a sample space is conventionally assumed to be equal to one, and that every possible outcome has the same probability, we can compute this as one divided by the total number of possible outcomes, that is one divided by six, and therefore a number around 0.16. We can then describe the probability distribution as follows:

Number	Probability
1	0.16
2	0.16
3	0.16
4	0.16
5	0.16
6	0.16

You get a sense of what a probability distribution is. Let's now apply it to our context. What is the probability distribution of our independent variable? There are two possible ways to answer this question:

- You already know the answer from some outside knowledge of the variable, such as the sex variable that is overall equally distributed between males and females, having therefore a probability distribution equal to 0.5 for both of the possible values
- You don't know the answer and you try to get it from your data

This latter answer can be considered for sure as the easiest one, nevertheless, it requires you to answer some more questions:

- Is your data a sample from an originating population or is it the populated by itself?
- If a sample, is your sample of the independent variable representative of the population from which it was drawn?

While the first question should usually get an easy answer, since we should know how our data was generated, the second question requires a careful analysis of sampling methodologies applied and an overall evaluation of the dimension of the sample, usually based on some formula defining the minimum sample size required to obtain representatives. I will point you to some resources on this topic.

OK then, let's imagine that you now know what the probability distribution of your dependent variable should be, what should you look for now? Well, you should compare the actual probability distribution you can observe in your data with the one you know should be the right one.

Let's go back to our dice example and imagine we now have a sample of outcomes drawn from a population of 1,000 tosses. *Imagine that we have already checked for the sample being representative; what should you look for now?* You should definitely look for the probability distribution of your sample, computing the number of occurrences for each outcome. The desired final output of this computation should resemble the table we have seen above, showing an equal probability of occurrence for each possible outcome.

Should they be exactly equal? No, we are not dealing here with physics or chemistry, a reasonably similar probability distribution will do the job.

Two final caveats:

- We are not assuming here that all outcomes should have the same probability of occurrence. If we know that our coin is tossed and will therefore give a higher probability of occurrence to two as an outcome, we will look for a probability distribution within our sample with a higher probability for two, and this will be completely correct.
- We are checking here for this assumption computing the observed probability distribution with the theoretical one, considering that if all observations are drawn from the same theoretical distribution and the sample is representative of the population, the final observed distribution should be equal to the theoretical one. What if there are some observations that are not drawn from the same theoretical distribution, such as some record coming after some structural break in the process? We have two answers here. One, if your sample is large enough you should check for the drawing of small sub-samples and look at their theoretical distribution. Two, if these anomalous records are in a small number, this should not let you conclude that the assumption is not satisfied and you should go on with your modeling activity.

Applying support vector machines in R

Let's get our hands dirty and model a support vector machine on our data. Within the R environment, this activity can be easily performed through an `svm` function, provided by the e1071 package.

The svm() function

First, let me give you a quick assignment, you know there is a function you are going to apply to your activity called `svm()`, and you don't know too much about this function, what are you supposed to do first? Take a second to answer.

Yeah, you should first of all check the function's documentation by using:

```
?svm
```

In doing so, you will be confronted with a quite well structured piece of documentation showing you the arguments of the function and a bit of context for it. Let's focus on the arguments we are going to consider here:

- `formula`, which is as usual the equation of the model you want to train, and looks exactly equal to what we have already seen for linear and logistic models
- `data`, which is the training dataset we are going to estimate our model on
- `type`, which is the type of task we want to accomplish. We will set it to C for classification
- `kernel`, which can be thought of as the type of hyperplane we want to model (things are a bit more complex since this kernel is a part of the objective function optimized for SVM estimation, but this goes beyond our purposes). This argument can assume one of the following values:
  - Linear
  - Radial
  - Polynomial
  - Sigmoid

Let me show you the difference between these hyperplanes, by employing once again paper and markers. If we think about a simple dataset having one explanatory variable and one response variable, we have the following:

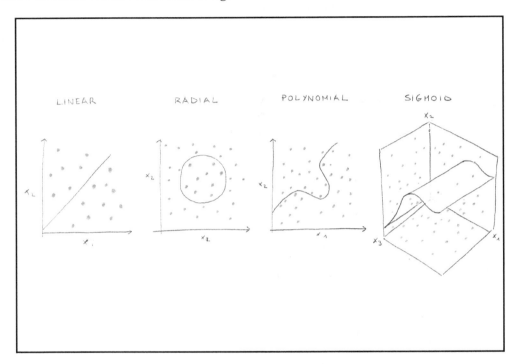

Applying the svm function to our data

We are now done with this, and we are ready to actually train our model. As an initial step, let's employ a linear kernel, even if our population is quite far from the two dimensions we have seen in the sketches, and therefore linear here does not mean that our hyperplane will be a line, but rather that it will be estimated by employing a linear equation in its parameters.

Let's actually apply the function, as follows:

```
support_vector_machine_linear <- svm(default_numeric ~ .,
                                     type = "C",
                                     data = training_data,
                                     kernel = "linear")
```

Interpreting support vector machine results

We now have a support vector machine fitted; what should we do next? Well, let's think about the final objective here: we want to understand which features are the most influential in defining the probability of a customer going into default by not repaying their bills.

We can do this by looking at the coefficients defining our hyperplane. Unfortunately, we do not have these coefficients directly stored within the `support_vector_machine_linear` object, but we indeed have in this object all of the elements of the list of support vectors and their coefficients, that is, a way to measure their position relative to the hyperplane.

It turns out that starting from these two groups of values, we can compute the weights of features as a matrix multiplication of the two, as follows:

```
weights <- t(support_vector_machine_linear$coefs) %*%
support_vector_machine_linear$SV
```

I'm not expecting all of this to be clear to you, but you should just keep in mind that it is possible from `svm()` output to get the final weights determining the hyperplane. Let's take a look at those weights and try to figure out their meaning. We could actually also start comparing them with the messages coming from the logistic regression.

Understanding the meaning of hyperplane weights

First of all, let's visualize our weights:

```
weights
```

corporation	**-0,204619**
previous_default	-0,000002
multiple_country	0,000008
cost_income	0,000024
ROE	-0,000016
employees	0,000011
economic_sector	-0,000096
ROS	0,000013
company_revenues	-0,443589

`commercial_portfolioless.affluent`	0,691648
`commercial_portfoliomass.affluent`	0,691678
`commercial_portfoliomore.affluent`	-1,383325
`business_unitretail_bank`	-

As you can see, some of them are positive and some are negative. Moreover, the order of magnitude varies quite a lot within the series. You can get a sense of this by computing the standard deviation. I will let you do it on your own just to recall the concept. Done?

Let's do it together now:

```
weights %>% sd()
```

Which prints out 0.506351. This is a lot, since we have a minimum equal to -1.383325 and a maximum equal to 0.6916776.

But, what is the meaning of these numbers? They are the actual coefficients that we estimate to define the hyperplane to employ as a classifier. Keeping it simple, in a linear context, we can say that the higher the absolute value of the coefficient, the more relevant a feature can be considered. You should not worry too much about the sign of the coefficient, since these are not coefficients employed to compute a final y value (as was the case for logistic regression), but just to define a blade to be inserted within our tank to divide balls of different colors.

OK then, what are the higher coefficients in the absolute value? We can figure this out by computing the absolute value, sorting the data frame, and looking at the first, let's say, five features:

```
weights %>% abs() %>% as.data.frame() %>%  sort(decreasing = TRUE)
```

As you can see, we first take the absolute value of our weights, pass it to a data frame to preserve the features' names, and finally sort it, specifying through the `decreasing` parameter that we want to see greater coefficients first. Let's see now the first five features:

```
commercial_portfoliomore.affluent commercial_portfoliomass.affluent commercial_portfolioless.affluent company_revenues corporation economic_sector
                        1.383325                        0.6916776                        0.6916476       0.4435888  0.2046195      9.552785e-05
  cost_income          ROE          ROS    employees multiple_country previous_default business_unitretail_bank
2.376661e-05 1.643502e-05 1.312615e-05 1.135139e-05      8.262641e-06     2.366936e-06              1.638474e-08
```

As you can see, we have all the `commercial_portfolio` modalities on the first three positions, and we then find `company_revenues` and `corporation`. We can then conclude that the inclusion within a given commercial portfolio is considered generally relevant, and that equally relevant are the company revenues and the nature of the company.

Is this the same message we were getting from the logistic regression? Not quite, since the only feature resulting relevant for both models is the `company_revenues` one. Nevertheless, we will handle this in the end, when trying to get a final list of possibly defaulted customers for the Middle East area. Before moving on this, let me show you the cheat sheet I have found for Support Vector Machine fitting:

Support Vector Machine cheat sheet

Support Vector Machine cheatsheet

intuition and maths

SVM is classificarion algorithm based on the concept of hyperplane. This hyperplane, which in 2D population can be considered as common plane, is employed to divide into two groups the population of response variable so to minimise the number of observations grouped with the wrong group.

Beside a linear version of linear hydroplane it is also possible to define non linear and even radial hyperplanes, which usually shows better level of performance.

kind of data

as X:
- categorical variables
- continuous variables

as Y:
- boolean/binary variables

how to fit in R

svm(y ~ ., data= data.frame, kernel = 'linear') fits y against all variables. alternative kernels:
- radial
- polynomial
- sigmoid

assumptions

1.IID : indipendent and identically distributed variables

how to test them in R

1.indipendente should be verified looking to the nature of variables, verifying that the different outputs are not influenced one from each other. A classical example is dice rolling, when the records represented from the sequence of rolling are independent
2.identically distribution should be checked looking at frequency distribution: is it coherent with the expected one? is there any structural change that could interfere with this distribution?

References

- *The Origins of Logistic Regression*, J.S. Cramer `https://papers.tinbergen.nl/02119.pdf`. This interesting paper explains when and why logistic regression was developed and how it evolved into the currently employed model.
- Introduction to probability theory on `brilliant.org`, a really well-crafted interactive course on probability, from basic probability theory to continuous variables and experiments: `https://brilliant.org/courses/probability/`.
- An online sample size calculator to define the minimum sample size needed for statistical significance: `http://www.nss.gov.au/nss/home.nsf/pages/Sample+size+calculator`, a useful explanation about the significance of sample size and related terms is also provided.
- `http://www.di.fc.ul.pt/~jpn/r/svm/svm.html#svm-for-regression`, a good vignette showing in great detail the content of the `svm()` output and its meaning.

Summary

Here I am again. You just took another major leap on your journey to machine learning discovery. If you took the right time to acquire and practice what Andy just showed you, you should have now added to your toolbox two of the most employed classification models: logistic regression and support vector machines. Both of them are employed to perform classification exercises.

The logistic regression predicts the probability of a given outcome occurring, estimating the level of contribution to this output provided by all of the explanatory variables. This makes this model quite useful when interpretability is one of the objectives of the analysis.

On the other side, you have support vector machines, which are based on the concept of a hyperplane, a sort of blade of different possible shapes able to divide our population into two or more groups, and by that, mean perform the desired classification task. This algorithm shows pretty high performance, especially with a non-linear hyperplane, but on the other side also shows a lower level of interpretability.

For both models, you have also learned what the relevant assumptions are and how to test them. Among these assumptions, one that should be considered as really relevant is the one about the independent and identically distributed variables, which is considered a requisite for the vast majority of machine learning methods.

Finally, you have acquired new elements to solve our mystery, since both of the models have shown acceptable performance and significance, and could be employed to derive the final list of the probability of defaulted companies to focus subsequent internal audit analyses on.

11
The Final Clash – Random Forests and Ensemble Learning

I am not saying you reported to Mr. Leveque about this investigation, I am just saying that I got to know about it! You suddenly hear the unpleasant and unusually loud voice of Mr. Clough shouting out. Next to him is your head, Mr Sheene, looking quite intimicated.

Mr. Clough, I do not know who revealed this investigation to Mr. Leveque, and I sincerely hope you are not even supposing that me or one of my collaborators did it.

I am an auditor and I do not suppose anything, I only draw conclusions from evidence, and at the moment I don't have any evidence, except that Mr. Leveque is aware of our investigation. What we have to do now is close our analyses as quick as possible to avoid him or anyone that could be involved in this strange episode adopting some kind of counter move.

We are fairly collaborating to the analyses and we are close to being able to provide you with the list of customers we promised. I will tell you more, you will find it in your inbox in two hours!

We will probably never know if this was the actual purpose of Mr. Clough's intimidating approach, nevertheless, he surely met a great objective in obtaining from Mr Sheene the reassurance of the customer list being provided within two hours.

And you surely know what it means for you and Andy: you have to hurry up completing your analyses, discovering what kinds of customers are more likely to default, and create a customer list on the basis of this information.

Random forest

Hey there, did you hear the discussion between Mr. Clough and Mr Sheene? And who do you think was the next person Mr. Sheene talked to after Mr. Clough? Yeah, you are guessing right, it was me: Andy, I want the list on my desk in two hours. Mr. Sheene was actually quite upset by Mr. Clough suggesting that one of us spread the word about the analyses.

That said, what we have to do now? Well, first of all, we still have to fit random forest on our data, in order to complete our data modelling strategy. Finally, we will employ all of our estimated valid models on the full list of customers pertaining to the Middle East area.

The result of this application will be the list of customers enriched with our model prediction.

What? How are we going to merge predictions from our different models? We are going to leverage ensemble learning techniques for that. But let's keep things in their order—we still have to fit two more models, and time is running out.

Time to hurry up now and fit our last model: random forest. As usual, I will first of all show you the intuition behind it, then go into the math, and finally show you how to apply it. But before doing this, we need to start from the basic building block of any random forest: decision trees.

Random forest building blocks – decision trees introduction

You have already seen a classification algorithm, which employed a hyperplane to classify records among categories. Decision trees are indeed another way to meet the same objective. What you do with decision trees is split your records into groups based on the values of explanatory variables, seeking the grouping able to minimize the residual sum of squares we have already talked about.

As is often the case, the devil is in the details, and with decision trees, the relevant detail is how we define the grouping. This is actually obtained through **recursive binary splitting**. I will help you understand how it works with a set of my wonderful sketches. It all starts with a blank sheet. You have a response variable and a set of predictors, let's say three:

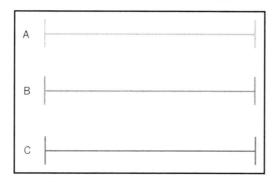

You then perform a first iteration, where you take each predictor, and for each predictor you:

- Try to split the population into two halves based on the value of the predictor. For instance, you take predictor **A** and split the response variables into two groups, the first including all records having **A** less than six and one including all records showing attribute **A** greater or equal to six.

- For each possible split you compute the corresponding RSS, employing as a predicted value the mean of the observed values within the two halves. If for instance a group having **A** less than six has a mean response variable of five, you take this value as the predicted one. You then compute the RSS for that combination of explanatory variables and cutoff.

- For each variable, you choose the cutoff resulting in the lower RSS.

- You finally compare the RSS obtained with every variable and choose the variable and the cutoff associated with the lower value of RSS. Let's say for instance you take variable **A** and cutoff three, that is, the first split is into two halves: all records having **A** less than three and all records having **A** greater or equal to three:

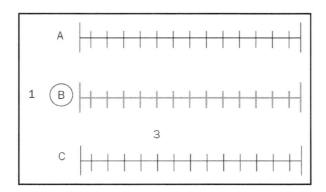

You now find the first limitation of this approach. You have your population divided into two groups, but which group do you take to further proceed with the split? It turns out that this is a completely random choice performed by the algorithm, and we have no assurance that the best choice in terms of RSS is made. Nevertheless, the algorithm makes a choice and the show can go on:

- You take one of the two halves, and for each of the remaining variables you try every possible cutoff, computing the associated RSS
- You choose the combination of variable and cutoff, minimizing the RSS
- You further split the selected half into two halves based on the cutoff selected for the given variable

I am sure you get the point. There is now one more variable. Once again, for the remaining variable, you try all possible values of cutoffs, finally selecting the one associated with the lower value of the RSS:

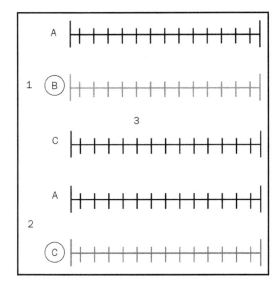

Things are now mature, and to put all parts together, you have got three consecutive splits and you have therefore split your population into four subgroups. This can be conveniently represented as a tree, having the split depicted as branches:

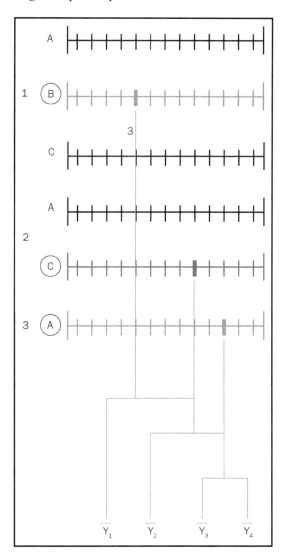

You can now understand the second limitation of this model: our final combination is obviously associated with an RSS, but who could tell us that this RSS is the smallest one we could obtain for that set of predictors and explanatory variables? The procedure we have just seen makes every decision without taking into consideration the possible effects on the effect of the final value of the RSS, and we can therefore legitimately infer that some better combination is waiting for us out there.

All of the limitations we just described are exactly the reasons why random forest was developed by Leonard Breiman in 2001.

Before going into details with this, let me give you a non-trivial warning, decision trees can be applied both to regression and classification models. The main difference here is the way the predicted value is computed. We have seen in our description that the mean value of the group is taken as a predicted value. This is the case for regression applications. For classification problems, the records pertaining to a specific group are assigned to the category showing up the higher number of times within the group, that is the mode of the population.

The intuition behind random forests

Random forests actually solve all of the issues in a very basic way, they fit a great number of decision trees and define a final result as an average result of all decision trees. The only tricky part you have to understand here before calling random forests trivial is the way those decision trees are obtained.

Let's have a closer look at how it works. We can divide the process into two main phases:

- Estimation of multiple decision trees
- Joining of the multiple decision trees' results

Within the first phase, the following steps are iterated for a given number of times:

- We select a subsample of predictors from the p total available predictors
- A subsample of the total population is drawn on which to perform the decision tree estimation
- The decision tree estimation is performed

In the second phase, a majority vote technique is employed to join the results:

- For every record it is observed to which category it is assigned within very of the estimated decision trees
- The record is assigned to the category to which it was assigned from the majority of the decision trees

As you can easily understand, this process removes or at least mitigates the main limitation we saw when talking about decision trees, that is, the problem of not considering alternative splitting and the final effects on the RSS of the partial splitting adopted during each phase of the recursive binary splitting.

How to apply random forests in R

To apply the random forests algorithm in R, we are going to use the randomForest package that was directly developed employing code written by Leo Breiman himself.

The main function within this package is the randomForest() one, which is employed to fit the algorithm itself.

Let's have a look at the main argument and some specifications before actually applying it to our data:

- formula: As usual, this is the formula employed to describe which is the response variable and which are the explanatory ones. The relevant point here is that if the response variable is a factor, the algorithm will be applied with a classification setting, otherwise it will perform a regression task.
- data: I don't really need to explain this to you after working with all these models.
- ntree: The number of random trees you want to fit before computing the final result.
- importance: This is a relevant argument. It tells the function if you want to take note of the relative importance of the predictors on the final outcome. We will see how to resonate about importance in a second.

As usual, there are a lot of other arguments you can use to fine-tune the model. You can find them by looking at the function's documentation:

```
?randomForest()
```

A general warning here is to be considered about categorical variables: they have to be passed as factors. This is why we will have to transform our `commercial_portfolio` and business unit into factors by applying the `as.factor()` function we learned about some time ago:

```
training_data %>%
  mutate(commercial_portfolio = as.factor(commercial_portfolio),
  business_unit = as.factor(business_unit))-> training_data_factor
```

Here we are, now we can fit the model, specifying all of the relevant parameters we described earlier:

```
set.seed(11)
random_forest <- randomForest::randomForest(formula =
as.factor(default_numeric)~.,
data = training_data_factor,
ntree = 400,
importance = TRUE)
```

Can you see that `set.seed(11)` in the preceding code? Why do you think we employed it? You are right, it is because the algorithm iteratively performs random subsampling, and to make our results reproducible we have to set a seed.

Depending on the number of trees specified via the `ntree` argument, the algorithm will take a bit of time before converging to a final result.

Once this is done, we will be ready to visualize and interpret its work.

Evaluating the results of the model

We will now look at random forest fitting results, and particularly at the performance of the model and the importance of predictors.

Performance of the model

How would you measure the performance of our classification model? Yeah, I know we already talked about that: employing a confusion matrix. This is the right answer, or at least part of the right answer, since in the case of random forest classification algorithms you can also check another metric, the **out-of-bag error rate** (**OOB error rate**). We can actually find both of them directly through the print method of the function. Let's check this by simply printing out the `random_forest` object:

```
random_forest
```

```
> random_forest

Call:
 randomForest(formula = as.factor(default_numeric) ~ ., data = training_data_factor,    ntree = 400, importance = TRUE)
               Type of random forest: classification
                     Number of trees: 400
No. of variables tried at each split: 3

        OOB estimate of  error rate: 14.31%
Confusion matrix:
     0    1 class.error
0 1951 1056  0.35118058
1  593 7923  0.06963363
```

As you can see, we have here a summary of the relevant parameters and then the two really useful pieces of information we were looking for:

- OOB estimate of error rate
- The confusion matrix

OOB estimate error rate

The idea behind this metric is actually quite simple, yet really powerful: since in order to create every decision tree composing the forest we make a subsample of records, we can employ the remaining records to test the resulting tree and compute the error rate. The OOB error rate will therefore be a synthetic measure of the level of accuracy of the model.

The `randomForest()` function comes out of the box with a dedicated `plot` method to depict the effect of the number of trees increasing on the final OOB error rate. We can show it in action by simply calling `plot()` on the `random_forest` object:

```
plot(random_forest)
```

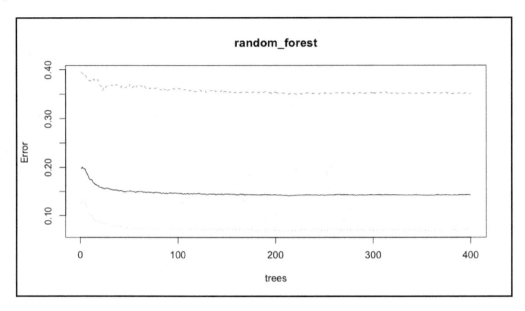

We see the OOB overall error as a black solid line, the error rate related to misclassification of zero as a red line, and the error rate related to misclassification of one as a green line. A first bold message you can get here is that, except for some little incoherence along the way, increasing the number of trees always increases the level of accuracy. You can then observe that the final level of the black line is around 0.14, and it turns out that is actually equal to 0.1431, that is, the 14.31% you find printed out when printing the `random_forest` object.

What about the red and green line? We said they are the error rates related to the misclassification of zero and one respectively. Can we find this information in some other way? Of course we can, and we are talking about a confusion matrix.

Confusion matrix

As we were saying, the default print method for randomForest objects produces a really convenient confusion matrix of our model. We are actually quite familiar with this object, so you can see in the output that we find 1,056 occurrences over 11,523 total records where the actual response variable was zero and our model predicted one, and just 593 cases of one prediction in the presence of a zero response variable. You then conveniently compute the zero and one classes' error rates, shown as a third column on the confusion matrix. As you can see, the error rate related to zero misclassifications is way higher than the one related to one misclassification. This means that our model is better at detecting true default events than it is at detecting true performing counterparts, that is, it may overestimate the real number of defaults.

Before moving on, let me ask you a question: do those two numbers, *0.35118058* and *0.06963363*, remind you of anything? No? Take a look at the plot we just looked at, and particularly at the red and green light. Any ideas? Yeah, the red and green light exactly represent the misclassification rate we can find from our confusion matrix, and particularly its evolution at the increase of the number of trees. To be sure of this, we can explore the random_forest object, inspecting the err.rate object included in it. This is actually the data frame employed to produce the plot, and we can, therefore, see the values corresponding to the last data point by looking at its tail:

```
random_forest$err.rate %>% tail()
```

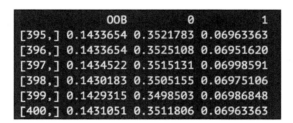

As you can see, we find at the bottom:

- The final OOB error rate
- The final misclassification rate of the zero class
- The final misclassification rate of the one class

Importance of predictors

As we have already said, interpretability is a relevant topic when talking about data mining models. If you think about it, decision trees are highly interpretable since you can describe them as a sequence of decisions on the different response variables you perform to come to a final prediction. *What about random forests? How would you describe the conjoint effect of 400 random decision trees on the final prediction?* From similar concerns, two measures were defined to evaluate the importance of every explanatory variable:

- The mean decrease in accuracy
- The Gini index

As you know, starting from a confusion matrix you can derive a great variety of metrics, such as sensitivity, accuracy, and similar. But how do we establish if this model is a good one? What value of every possible metric is a good value? There is no universal answer; it always depends on the specific problem we are addressing.

For instance, for the problem we are facing, since we are employing different models to solve the same problem, one relevant point could be comparing the performance of all models in terms of classification. We will get back to this when dealing with ensemble learning.

Mean decrease in accuracy

A mean decrease in accuracy measures the increase in misclassification produced on average by removing the given predictor. For instance, a value of 15 for predictor A means that on average removing A from the set of predictors leads to 15 more records being misclassified. The higher this number is, the more relevant the associated predictor has to be considered.

Gini index

The Gini index is alternatively described as a measure of variance and a measure of purity. Let's start with its definition to get its meaning:

$$G = \sum_{k=1}^{K} \hat{p}mk(1 - \hat{p}mk)$$

The $\hat{p}mk$ is the number of records pertaining to the k class within the given group. Let's take for instance, a decision tree with a first split on variable A. You now take one of the halves and compute for that half how many records pertaining to the k class (for instance, default) are within that half. If you think about it, this proportion is a measure of purity within that half: a number of p close to one means that this group is mainly composed of records pertaining to a single class, that is, it means that the given variable and cutoff are well discriminating our population.

Once you understand this, it is easy to understand the meaning of the whole index. The sum of $\hat{p}mk(1 - \hat{p}mk)$ will be low if all, or a great part of, $\hat{p}mk$ is either close to zero or close to one. This is reasonable, since if a decision tree is able to well discriminate, this will translate into halves having one k class with a $\hat{P}$ close to one and the other classes with a $\hat{P}$ close to zero.

The final take away is: the smaller the Gini, the better the model.

Plotting relative importance of predictors

A convenient plotting method is available to immediately get the relative importance of predictors. It is wrapped within the `varImpPlot()` function:

```
varImpPlot(random_forest)
```

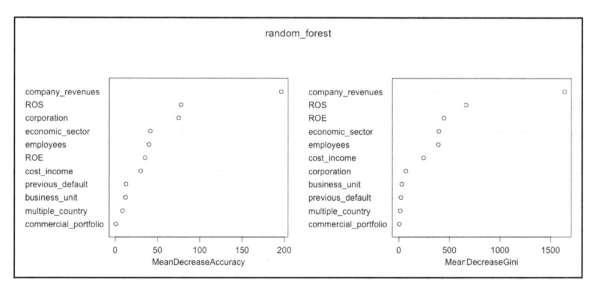

As you can see, we get two relevant messages here, one related to the general behavior of our metrics and one specific to our data:

- Accuracy and the Gini index tend to behave in a really coherent way, since if you derive a ranking of variable importance employing the two of them, you will come close to the same rank
- Random forest is confirming conclusions drawn from other models, that is, that company revenues and the ROS index are relevant variables to predict if a customer will default or not

We are now done with random forests, and it is time for the final clash: defining a list of probably defaulted counterparts combining results from different models. But first, I want to share with you the random forest cheat sheet, as done for all of the other models.

Random forest cheat sheet

Following is the Random Forest cheat sheet

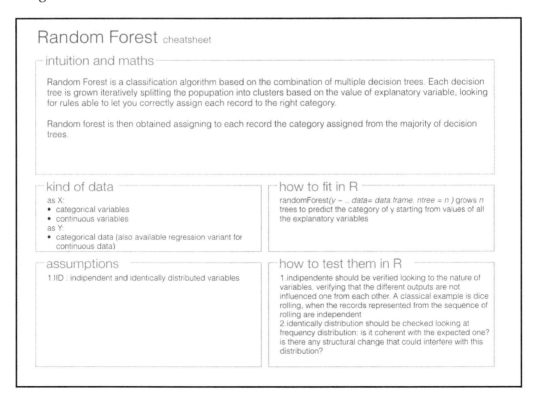

Ensemble learning

What we have to do now is gather signals we can draw from different models into one final prediction, so we can select from Middle East customers a list of probably defaulted customers to be sent to the internal audit team.

How would you seek this objective? Imagine you are chilling out with your friends at a pub when you suddenly start talking about your next vacation. You tell them that you are probably going to choose Austria as a destination, even if you don't know if your are going to like it.

Your friends, who really care about your well-being and love you, start sharing their opinions with you. One of them says you are not going to have a good time there because of the cold, one says you are not going to like it because of the humidity, and this goes on until all of your friends have shared their opinion with you. You now know that five of your friends think you are not going to have good time in Austria, while three think you are going to have a great vacation. *What would you conclude?*

The first possible idea could be to conclude that you are not going to love Austria because the majority of your friends think so. But then, you could probably start thinking that not all of your friends know you in the same way. There are some that really know your tastes, while others do not. Should you evaluate equally the opinion of both groups of friends, or give more relevance to the friends that know you better? Those reasonings are the foundations of ensemble learning techniques. Let's now have a more formal view of them.

Basic ensemble learning techniques

Ensemble learning techniques are basically solutions developed to join together predictions coming from different models. The three most basic techniques to accomplish this task are:

- **Averaging prediction**: Which applies to regression problems and basically involves computing a final prediction equal to the average of predictions coming from single models.
- **Majority vote**: Which is applicable to classification problems involving the definition of a final prediction equal to the prediction expressed from the higher number of models, that is, the mode within the available predictions.

- **Weighted average or weighted majority vote**: Which are applicable to both regression and classification problems, involving the computation of a weighted average for the case of regression problems or the determination of a different computed mode assigning different relevance to votes **expressed** from different models. The weight assigned to each model is usually proportional to the accuracy shown from the models themselves.

You should be aware that other, more advanced techniques are available that sometimes are needed to obtain better results. For the sake of completeness, I will list the most popular of them here:

- **Bagging**, which is basically equal to a majority vote, except for the fact that different models are fitted on random subsets of the whole estimation population
- **Boosting**, which involves iteratively building an ensemble model, each time starting from the misclassification produced from the previous model
- **Stacking**, which involves training a new model starting from the outputs produced from the other models

I will provide you with some good references as usual, in case you want to deepen your knowledge of the topic. Let's now apply basic ensemble learning techniques to our data.

Applying ensemble learning to our data in R

As you know, we are dealing here with a classification problem. We can, therefore, employ the majority vote or the weighted majority vote. Nevertheless, before actually implementing it, I would like to summarize here the results obtained from different models, to let us finally evaluate the obtained improvement in classification performance. To perform this task we are going to introduce one more relevant R package, called caret.

The R caret package

Let's start from the very beginning—*What does this strange name mean?* It turns out that the package's author, Max Kuhn, defined its name by employing the first letters of classification and regression training.

This package can actually be considered as a precious toolbox storing an infinite number of tools for data mining activities. It contains functions to be employed for:

- Data splitting
- Preprocessing
- Feature selection
- Model tuning using resampling
- Variable importance estimation

Just to give you an idea of how rich it is, I will just tell you that this package currently encompasses 238 classification and regression algorithms.

Computing a confusion matrix with the caret package

It is now time to get a sense of how useful this package is, by computing the confusion matrix for all of the models we have previously fitted:

- Logistic regression
- Support vector machine
- Random forest

The function we are going to employ here is the `confusionMatrix()` function, which basically takes the vector of predicted values and the vector of observed values (order here is not irrelevant) and produces as an output an appropriate confusion matrix. Moreover, it produces a whole set of metrics commutable from confusion matrices, as shown within the pertaining documentation, given the following confusion matrix:

	Reference	
Predicted	Event	No Event
Event	A	B
No Event	C	D

The following metrics are computed:

$$Sensitivity = A/(A + C)$$

$$Specificity = D/(B + D)$$

$$Prevalence = (A + C)/(A + B + C + D)$$

$$PPV = (sensitivity * prevalence)/((sensitivity * prevalence) + ((1 - specificity) * (1 - prevalence)))$$

$$NPV = (specificity * (1 - prevalence))/(((1 - sensitivity) * prevalence) + ((specificity) * (1 - prevalence)))$$

$$Detection\,Rate = A/(A + B + C + D)$$

$$Detection\,Prevalence = (A + B)/(A + B + C + D)$$

$$Balanced\,Accuracy = (sensitivity + specificity)/2$$

$$Precision = A/(A + B)$$

$$Recall = A/(A + C)$$

$$F1 = (1 + beta^2) * precision * recall/((beta^2 * precision) + recall)$$

The main warning when trying to apply this function is that variables passed to it should be encoded as factors. We, therefore, have to transform our predicted and observed variables from all of the estimated models. Moreover, since some of the employed models produced a continuous predicted value ranging from zero to one, in order to produce a confusion matrix, we will have to transform each of the predictions either to zero or one. We can do this by establishing a threshold and forcing to zero everything below this threshold, and to one everything equal or above this threshold.

For logistic regression, we get:

```
logistic_df <- data.frame(y = logistic$y, fitted_values =
logistic$fitted.values)

logistic_df %>%
 mutate(default_threshold = case_when(as.numeric(fitted.values)>0.5 ~ 1,
 TRUE ~ 0)) %>%
 dplyr::select(y, default_threshold)-> logistic_table
```

For the support vector machine, we get:

```
support_vector_data <- data.frame(predicted =
support_vector_machine_linear$fitted,
 truth = as.numeric(training_data$default_numeric))

support_vector_data %>%
 mutate(predicted_treshold = case_when(as.numeric(predicted)>0.5 ~ 1,
 TRUE ~ 0))-> support_vector_table
```

Let's now actually compute a confusion matrix for the logistic support vector and random forest models, remembering that employed vectors have to be of the `factor` type:

```
confusionMatrix(as.factor(logistic_table$default_threshold),
as.factor(logistic_table$y))

confusionMatrix(as.factor(support_vector_table$predicted_treshold),
as.factor(support_vector_table$truth))

confusionMatrix(as.factor(random_forest$predicted),
as.factor(random_forest$y))
```

From which we respectively get:

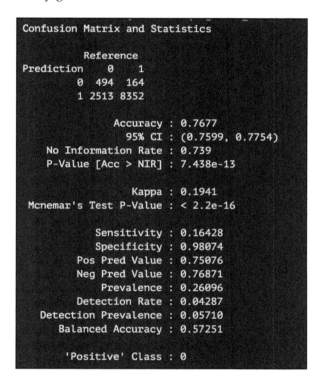

And also:

```
Confusion Matrix and Statistics

            Reference
Prediction   0    1
         0  487  160
         1 2520 8356

               Accuracy : 0.7674
                 95% CI : (0.7596, 0.7751)
    No Information Rate : 0.739
    P-Value [Acc > NIR] : 1.188e-12

                  Kappa : 0.1919
 Mcnemar's Test P-Value : < 2.2e-16

            Sensitivity : 0.16196
            Specificity : 0.98121
         Pos Pred Value : 0.75270
         Neg Pred Value : 0.76830
             Prevalence : 0.26096
         Detection Rate : 0.04226
   Detection Prevalence : 0.05615
      Balanced Accuracy : 0.57158

       'Positive' Class : 0
```

And finally:

```
Confusion Matrix and Statistics

            Reference
Prediction   0    1
         0 1951  593
         1 1056 7923

               Accuracy : 0.8569
                 95% CI : (0.8504, 0.8632)
    No Information Rate : 0.739
    P-Value [Acc > NIR] : < 2.2e-16

                  Kappa : 0.6095
 Mcnemar's Test P-Value : < 2.2e-16

            Sensitivity : 0.6488
            Specificity : 0.9304
         Pos Pred Value : 0.7669
         Neg Pred Value : 0.8824
             Prevalence : 0.2610
         Detection Rate : 0.1693
   Detection Prevalence : 0.2208
      Balanced Accuracy : 0.7896

       'Positive' Class : 0
```

Interpreting confusion matrix results

How do you think you could interpret those results? Looking at all of the computed metrics, we generally see that random forest is performing better than the other two models, but which metrics should we focus on? As is always the case, to answer this question, we should focus on the objective of our analysis, we want to predict from a list of customers which ones have probably defaulted. Since our output will then be employed by the internal audit department to perform further analyses, we could also afford the inconvenience of selecting a counterpart and then discovering that it is not actually defaulted. On the other hand, not selecting a counterpart that is actually a defaulted one could constitute a serious problem for the following steps of analyses.

We are saying here that we care more about type II errors, that is, false negatives, than about type I errors, that is, false positives, where positive here is the prediction of a default. That is why simply considering accuracy, which overall measures how good a model is at avoiding type I and II errors, wouldn't be the best possible way. Going back to the list of computed metrics, which do you think is the best one to correctly take into consideration type II errors? Among the most relevant for us, we should necessarily include precision, which exactly measures how many of the real positives were detected from the model, and by that way also how many were not detected.

Looking at the printed out confusion matrix, we can now produce a simple plot to compare the three models on these metrics:

```
data <- data.frame(model = c("logistic",
 "support_vector",
 "random_forest"),
 precision = c(8352/(164+8352),
 8356/(160+8356),
 7923/(7923+593)))

ggplot(data = data, aes(x = model,y = precision, label =
round(precision,2)))+
 geom_bar(stat = 'identity')+
 geom_text()
```

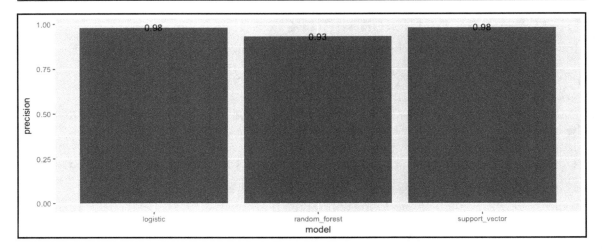

As you can see, on the precision index, our random forest is performing slightly worse then the other models, even if they overall perform quite well. Let's now see if employing results together from all of these three models will lead to an increase in performance in terms of precision.

Applying a weighted majority vote to our data

As said, since we are dealing here with a classification problem, we can apply the majority vote technique, assigning to each record the prediction it received from the greatest part of the models. To do this, first of all, we have to merge in one unique data frame:

- Observed data
- Prediction from logistic model
- Prediction from support vector machine model
- Prediction from random forest model

Let's do this, starting with the objects we created for our confusion matrix computation:

```
ensemble_dataset <- data.frame(svm =
(support_vector_table$predicted_threshold),
logistic = (logistic_table$default_threshold),
random_forest = as.numeric(as.character(random_forest$predicted)),
observed = as.numeric(training_data$default_numeric))
```

What would you do now? First of all, we can try to perform our majority vote in the most simple and linear way, that is, creating a new attribute to our ensemble dataset, which takes a value of one if the majority of models predicted one, and zero in the opposite case:

```
ensemble_dataset %>%
 mutate(majority = case_when(svm + logistic + random_forest >= 2~ 1,TRUE ~
0))-> ensemble_dataframe
```

Let's have a look at the resulting confusion matrix:

```
confusionMatrix(as.factor(ensemble_dataframe$majority),
as.factor(ensemble_dataframe$observed))
```

```
Confusion Matrix and Statistics

          Reference
Prediction    0    1
         0  452   82
         1 2555 8434

               Accuracy : 0.7712
                 95% CI : (0.7634, 0.7788)
    No Information Rate : 0.739
    P-Value [Acc > NIR] : 9.508e-16

                  Kappa : 0.1917
 Mcnemar's Test P-Value : < 2.2e-16

            Sensitivity : 0.15032
            Specificity : 0.99037
         Pos Pred Value : 0.84644
         Neg Pred Value : 0.76749
             Prevalence : 0.26096
         Detection Rate : 0.03923
   Detection Prevalence : 0.04634
      Balanced Accuracy : 0.57034

       'Positive' Class : 0
```

As you can see, we actually found out that our ensemble model performs worse than the best of the single models. Let's also try to compute precision metrics again to see if for the number of our interests, things are going differently:

precision = true positive /(true positive + false negative) = 8434/(82 + 8434) = 0.99

As you can see, we actually obtained a result even higher than the already great results obtained from every single model. How do we apply this to the Middle East customer list? We can apply the three composing models to the new data and finally compute the majority vote on the resulting prediction.

Applying estimated models on new data

Formally, our problem is the following, applying the estimated models to new, unlabeled data, in order to get a prediction of the response variable.

To do this, we are going to leverage the `predict()` function, which basically takes the following arguments:

- `object`, that is, the object resulting from estimation activity
- `new_data`, pointing to a data frame storing the new data on which to perform the prediction activity

The function will return a vector storing the obtained new predictions.

All good then, but on which data do you think we are going to apply our models? I have got here the customer list of the Middle East area, as of one year ago. We are going to apply our models to it. Let's assume that it is a `.xlsx` file, so first of all we have to import it, employing our well-known `import` function:

```
me_customer_list <- import("middle_east_customer_list.xlsx")
```

Let's have a look at its attributes via the `str()` function, as you should be used to doing by now:

```
str(me_customer_list)
'data.frame': 115 obs. of 15 variables:
 $ corporation : num 0 0 0 0 0 0 0 0 0 ...
 $ previous_default : num 0 0 0 0 0 0 0 0 1 ...
 $ multiple_country : num 0 0 0 0 0 0 0 0 0 ...
 $ cost_income : num 9.84e-01 1.00 1.00 -1.00e+06 6.65e-01 ...
 $ ROE : num 2.13e-01 9.77e-02 4.85e-02 2.08e-05 5.82e-02 ...
 $ employees : num 2866452 122287 277979 188 313 ...
 $ economic_sector : num 351 2515 48808 188 313 ...
 $ ROS : num 6.61e-01 9.73e-01 5.55e-01 -1.00e+06 -1.00e+06 ...
 $ company_revenues : num 10000 10000 10000 10000 10000 ...
 $ commercial_portfolio: chr "less affluent" "less affluent" "less
affluent" "less affluent" ...
 $ business_unit : chr "retail_bank" "retail_bank" "retail_bank"
"retail_bank" ...
 $ company_name : chr "ExoBiotic" "Cocoa Clasp" "Doggy Due" "Carnival
Coffee" ...
```

As you can see, we have here all common attributes plus a `company_name` attribute. Therefore, it shouldn't be difficult to apply our models to them.

Just for the sake of clarity, let's select only attributes that resulted as relevant for our models. Moreover, we are going to apply a factor transformation to the commercial portfolio and business unit attributes, since we are going to need these attributes as a factor in order to apply random forest, as seen before.

Finally, we are going to set levels of those two attributes equal to the one of the data employed for estimation purposes. This is also needed in order to apply random forest, since when performing prediction the `predict.randomForest()` function is going to look for all levels, raising otherwise an error:

```
me_customer_list %>%
select(corporation,
previous_default,
multiple_country,
cost_income,
ROE,
employees,
economic_sector,
ROS,
company_revenues,
commercial_portfolio,
business_unit) %>%
mutate(commercial_portfolio = as.factor(commercial_portfolio),
business_unit = as.factor(business_unit))->wrangled_me_customer_list

levels(wrangled_me_customer_list$commercial_portfolio) <-
levels(training_data_factor$commercial_portfolio)
levels(wrangled_me_customer_list$business_unit) <-
levels(training_data_factor$business_unit)
```

Let's now try to apply our models to new data, starting with the logistic one.

predict.glm() for prediction from the logistic model

As introduced a while ago, the main arguments of the `predict.*` functions are the `object` and `newdata` ones. Let's therefore call the `predict.glm()` one, passing `logistic` as an object and `wrangled_me_customer_list` as `newdata`. We are going to add the result of this computation directly to the `me_customer_list` object to have them handy when applying the majority vote technique:

```
me_customer_list$logistic <- predict.glm(logistic,newdata =
wrangled_me_customer_list)
```

If you now try to look at our prediction through the `head()` function, you will discover that zero to one predictions were obtained. We can therefore move on to the `predict.randomForest()` function.

predict.randomForest() for prediction from random forests

The same seen for the logistic model applies to the `predict.randomForest()` function. When calling this function on our new data, it will scan the provided dataset in order to find the attributes that resulted as relevant during the estimation phase. Once these are found, the splitting rules contained within the `random_forest` object will be applied in order to estimate the prediction of the `default` attribute:

```
me_customer_list$random_forest <-predict(random_forest,newdata =
wrangled_me_customer_list)
```

predict.svm() for prediction from support vector machines

Finally, let's apply the `predict.svm()` function to our data, which, based on the hyperplane described within the `support_vector_machine_linear` object, will define which customer will default and which will not:

```
me_customer_list$svm <- predict(support_vector_machine_linear,newdata =
wrangled_me_customer_list)
```

A more structured approach to predictive analytics

We near to finally draw conclusions from our predictive analyses, so I think it is the right moment to make you clear that the one we have followed here is a simplified approach to such kind of analyses.

We already talked before about the difference between training and testing dataset, let me place this into the context of predictive analysis.

When you estimate a model for the purpose of gaining prediction about the future, you are basically assuming that the relative importance of variables and all the other circumstances observed in your estimation sample will be found as well in future data and that therefore we can draw prediction about the future from past data.

What if this is not true? In this case, we would have a model able to describe the past but not to predict the future.

In a similar way, if we specify our model in a way which is too much related to the actual data available within our estimation sample, we are going to incur in the so-called phenomenon of overfitting, which we already mentioned before.

Which are the possible solution for those kinds of problems?

It turns out that the most common solution employed for those problems is related to subsampling of the estimation sample.

Particularly, and this is where our previous discussion about training and testing samples comes to help, we distinguish between:

- A training sample, where our model is actually estimated
- A testing sample, on which our estimate model is applied in order to measure its performance on data different from the ones employed to define the model specification.

This actually means that in order to estimate a new model we actually take the estimation sample we have at our disposal and further divide it into two subsamples. There are at least three main techniques employed to perform this task:

- **Simple subsample**: Which basically splits the sample into two sub samples. The relevant decision here is about the proportion between records in training and testing dataset.

- **k fold cross-validation:** Which requires you to split the complete sample into k subsample and iteratively perform the estimation of your model on a sample composed from the sum of k-1 subsamples. The testing activity will be then performed on the remaining kth subsample.
- **Leave one out cross-validation:** Which is exactly equal to the k fold cross-validation, except for the size of the kth subsample, which is always equal to just one record.

Both in k fold cross-validation and leave one out cross-validation the final parameters to be employed for your predictive activity will be obtained as an average of the parameters estimated within each iteration.

The approaches described have shown to be relevant and effective in increasing the level of performance of final predictions.

Know that you have a more clear picture of predictive analyses and how is possible to perform them, let's move on with our predictions, applying ensemble learning techniques to our data.

Applying the majority vote ensemble technique on predicted data

It is now time to finally draw our list, applying the majority vote technique we learned previously to our predictions. As done before, we are going to apply a threshold on values predicted from the logistic and SVM models, to map the original predictions on the [0,1] domain. Finally, with a piece of code really similar to the one we have seen before, let's create an `ensemble_prediction` attribute, storing a final prediction defined from results coming from the three estimated models:

```
me_customer_list %>%
mutate(logistic_threshold = case_when(as.numeric(logistic)>0.5 ~ 1,
TRUE ~ 0),
svm_threshold = case_when(as.numeric(svm)>0.5 ~ 1,
TRUE ~ 0)) %>%
mutate(ensemble_prediction = case_when(logistic_threshold+svm_threshold+
as.numeric(as.character(random_forest)) >=2 ~ 1,
TRUE ~ 0)) -> me_customer_list_complete
```

Is this the list the internal audit team needs from us?

Not quite; there is one more computation required: we have to share the list of the defaulted companies, which means we need to filter for predictions equal to one:

```
me_customer_list_complete %>% filter(ensemble_prediction == 1) ->
defaulted_companies
```

We have got the list! Without losing any more time, let's export this in an .xlsx file and share it with the internal audit department:

```
defaulted_companies %>% export("defaulted_companies.xlsx")
```

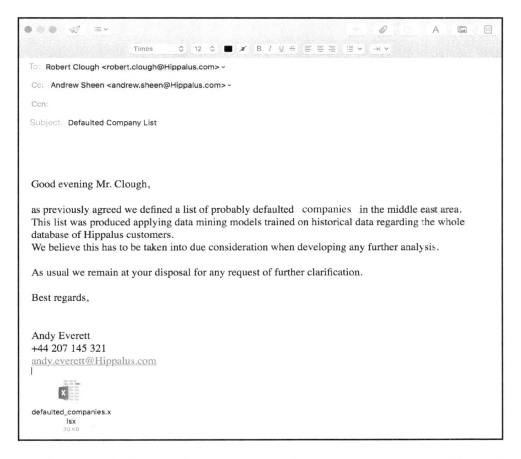

My dear colleague, I think our task is complete, and so too is your training with me. You have been a really good apprentice, and it was a pleasure to work with you!

Further references

- *Random Forest* by Leonard Breiman: https://www.stat.berkeley.edu/~breiman/randomforest2001.pdf
- *Ensemble Methods in Data Mining: Improving Accuracy Through Combining Predictions*, by Giovanny Seni, John F. Elde, Nitin Agarwal and Huan Liu: https://doc.lagout.org/Others/Data%20Mining/Ensemble%20Methods%20in%20Data%20Mining_%20Improving%20Accuracy%20through%20Combining%20Predictions%20%5BSeni%20%26%20Elder%202010-02-24%5D.pdf
- **Official caret package website**: http://topepo.github.io/caret/

Summary

Match point! You and Andy finally got the list Mr Clough requested. As you may be guessing from the simple fact that there are still pages left in the book, this is not the end.

All you know at the moment is that the companies that probably produced that dramatic drop in Hippalus revenues are small companies with previous experiences of default and bad ROS values. We could infer that those are not exactly the ideal customers for a wholesale company such as Hippalus. Why is the company so exposed to these kinds of counterparts?

We actually don't know at the moment: our data mining models got us to the entrance of the crime scene and left us there. What would you do next? You can bet Mr Clough is not going to let things remain that unclear, so let's see what happens in a few pages.

In the meantime, I would like to recap what you have learned in this chapter. After learning what decision trees are and what their main limitations are, you discovered what a random forest is and how it overcomes those limitations. You also learned how to apply this model to your data with R, through the randomForest() function within the randomForest package.

Employing the objects resulting from `svm()`, `glm()`, and the `randomForest()` package, you learned how to obtain a confusion matrix and a lot of related metrics such as accuracy and precision. To do so, you employed the `confusionMatrix()` function contained within the `caret` package.

You also learned what ensemble learning is and why it is so useful. Applying it to the estimated classification models, you discovered how effective it can be in improving your final performance.

Finally, you learned how to perform predictions on new data by employing trained models, through the `predict.something` function.

12

Looking for the Culprit – Text Data Mining with R

I would like to personally thank you, Mr Shine, for your support. We have received the list and my guys are already working on it.

Mr. Clough's voice sounds a lot more pleasant now that your office has provided the long-awaited list. *Nevertheless, I am here to ask for your help once more. We need the support of the team that performed the analysis to get some more detail on it.*

I am afraid we can not help you this time because Andy, the guy who did the analysis, is now involved with another task that came directly from our CEO.

What about him? Wasn't he involved in the analysis as well? Yeah, Mr Clough is pointing at you. How does he know that you collaborated with Andy on the analysis? He does not actually know, but he is from internal audit, and being informed is one of his main tasks.

Well, he actually helped Andy with the analysis, but he is quite new to the job and you should consider that when dealing with him. Mr. Shine is definitely trying to protect you, lowering the expectations about what help you can provide.

That is not a problem. We just need someone who is aware of what has been done, and he is perfect. Could you kindly follow me? I will take you to Albert, the guy performing the analysis. You know this is actually a rhetorical question, and that's why you immediately start following Mr. Clough, who leads you to a new office where Albert, at his desk, is waiting for you.

Hi, nice to meet you, I'm Albert. Please take a seat here. I was just looking at the customer cards of the defaulted companies.

Extracting data from a PDF file in R

I don't know whether you are aware of this, but our colleagues in the commercial department are used to creating a customer card for every customer they deal with. This is quite an informal document that contains some relevant information related to the customer, such as the industry and the date of foundation. Probably the most precious information contained within these cards is the comments they write down about the customers. Let me show you one of them:

BUSINESSCENTER business profile

Information below are provided under non disclosure agreement. date of enquery: 12.05.2017

date of foundation: 1993-05-18

industry: Non-profit

share holders: Helene Wurm ; Meryl Savant ; Sydney Wadley

comments

This is one of our worst customer. It really often miss payments even if for just a couple of days. We have problems finding useful contact persons. The only person we can have had occasion to deal with was the fiscal expert, since all other relevant person denied any kind of contact.

My plan was the following—get the information from these cards and analyze it to discover whether some kind of common traits emerge.

As you may already know, at the moment this information is presented in an unstructured way; that is, we are dealing with unstructured data. Before trying to analyze this data, we will have to gather it in our analysis environment and give it some kind of structure.

Technically, what we are going to do here is called text mining, which generally refers to the activity of gaining knowledge from texts. The techniques we are going to employ are the following:

- Sentiment analysis
- Wordclouds
- N-gram analysis
- Network analysis

Getting a list of documents in a folder

First of all, we need to list all the customer cards we were provided from the commercial department. I have stored all of them within the `data` folder on my workspace. Let's use `list.files()` to get them:

```
file_vector <- list.files(path = "data")
```

Nice! We can inspect this looking at the head of it. Using the following command:

```
file_vector %>% head()
```

```
[1] "banking.xls" "Betasoloin.pdf" "Burl Whirl.pdf" "BUSINESSCENTER.pdf"
[5] "Buzzmaker.pdf" "BuzzSaw Publicity.pdf"
```

Uhm... not exactly what we need. I can see there are also `.xls` files. We can remove them using the `grepl()` function, which performs partial matches on strings, returning TRUE if the pattern required is found, or FALSE if not. We are going to set the following test here: give me TRUE if you find `.pdf` in the filename, and FALSE if not:

```
grepl(".pdf",file_list)
```

```
  [1] FALSE  TRUE  TRUE  TRUE  TRUE  TRUE  TRUE  TRUE  TRUE FALSE  TRUE  TRUE  TRUE  TRUE
 TRUE  TRUE  TRUE
 [18]  TRUE  TRUE  TRUE  TRUE  TRUE  TRUE  TRUE  TRUE  TRUE  TRUE  TRUE  TRUE  TRUE  TRUE
 TRUE  TRUE  TRUE
 [35]  TRUE  TRUE  TRUE  TRUE  TRUE  TRUE  TRUE  TRUE  TRUE  TRUE  TRUE  TRUE  TRUE  TRUE
 TRUE  TRUE  TRUE
 [52]  TRUE  TRUE  TRUE  TRUE FALSE  TRUE  TRUE  TRUE  TRUE  TRUE  TRUE  TRUE  TRUE  TRUE
 TRUE  TRUE  TRUE
 [69]  TRUE  TRUE  TRUE  TRUE  TRUE  TRUE  TRUE  TRUE  TRUE  TRUE  TRUE  TRUE  TRUE  TRUE
 TRUE  TRUE  TRUE
 [86]  TRUE  TRUE  TRUE  TRUE  TRUE  TRUE  TRUE  TRUE  TRUE  TRUE  TRUE  TRUE  TRUE  TRUE
 TRUE  TRUE  TRUE
[103]  TRUE  TRUE  TRUE  TRUE  TRUE  TRUE  TRUE  TRUE  TRUE  TRUE  TRUE  TRUE  TRUE  TRUE
FALSE FALSE  TRUE
[120]  TRUE
```

As you can see, the first match results in a FALSE since it is related to the `.xls` file we saw before. We can now filter our list of files by simply passing these matching results to the list itself. More precisely, we will slice our list, selecting only those records where our `grepl()` call returns TRUE:

```
pdf_list <- file_vector[grepl(".pdf",file_list)]
```

Did you understand `[grepl(".pdf",file_list)]`? It is actually a way to access one or more indexes within a vector, which in our case are the indexes corresponding to `".pdf"`, exactly the same as we printed out before.

If you now look at the list, you will see that only PDF filenames are shown on it.

Reading PDF files into R via pdf_text()

R comes with a really useful package that's employed for tasks related to PDFs. This package is named `pdftools`, and beside the `pdf_text` function we are going to employ here, it also contains other relevant functions that are used to get different kinds of information related to the PDF file into R.

For our purposes, it will be enough to get all of the textual information contained within each of the PDF files. First of all, let's try this on a single document; we will try to scale it later on the whole set of documents. The only required argument to make `pdf_text` work is the path to the document. The object resulting from this application will be a character vector of length 1:

```
pdf_text("data/BUSINESSCENTER.pdf")
```

```
[1] "BUSINESSCENTER business profile\nInformation below are provided under
non disclosure agreement. date of enquery: 12.05.2017\ndate of foundation:
1993-05-18\nindustry: Non-profit\nshare holders: Helene Wurm ; Meryl Savant
; Sydney Wadley\ncomments\nThis is one of our worst customer. It really
often miss payments even if for just a couple of days. We have\nproblems
finding useful contact persons. The only person we can have had occasion to
deal with was the\nfiscal expert, since all other relevant person denied
any kind of contact.\n
1\n"
```

If you compare this with the original PDF document you can easily see that all of the information is available even if it is definitely not ready to be analyzed. What do you think is the next step needed to make our data more useful?

We first need to split our string into lines in order to give our data a structure that is closer to the original one, that is, made of paragraphs. To split our string into separate records, we can use the `strsplit()` function, which is a base R function. It requires the string to be split and the token that decides where the string has to be split as arguments. If you now look at the string, you'll notice that where we found the end of a line in the original document, for instance after the words `business profile`, we now find the `\n` token. This is commonly employed in text formats to mark the end of a line.

We will therefore use this token as a split argument:

```
pdf_text("data/BUSINESSCENTER.pdf") %>% strsplit(split = "\n")
```

```
[[1]]
 [1] "BUSINESSCENTER business profile"
 [2] "Information below are provided under non disclosure agreement. date
of enquery: 12.05.2017"
 [3] "date of foundation: 1993-05-18"
 [4] "industry: Non-profit"
 [5] "share holders: Helene Wurm ; Meryl Savant ; Sydney Wadley"
 [6] "comments"
 [7] "This is one of our worst customer. It really often miss payments even
if for just a couple of days. We have"
 [8] "problems finding useful contact persons. The only person we can have
had occasion to deal with was the"
 [9] "fiscal expert, since all other relevant person denied any kind of
contact."
[10] " 1"
```

`strsplit()` returns a list with an element for each element of the character vector passed as argument; within each list element, there is a vector with the split string.

Isn't that better? I definitely think it is. The last thing we need to do before actually doing text mining on our data is to apply those treatments to all of the PDF files and gather the results into a conveniently arranged data frame.

Iteratively extracting text from a set of documents with a for loop

What we want to do here is run trough the list of PDF files and for each filename found there, we run the `pdf_text()` function and then the `strsplit()` function to get an object similar to the one we have seen with our test. A convenient way to do this is by employing a `for` loop. These structures basically do this to their content: *Repeat this instruction n times and then stop.* Let me show you a typical `for` loop:

```
for (i in 1:3){
 print(i)
}
```

If we run this, we obtain the following:

```
[1] 1
[1] 2
[1] 3
```

This means that the loop runs three times and therefore repeats the instructions included within the brackets three times. What is the only thing that seems to change every time? It is the value of i. This variable, which is usually called counter, is basically what the loop employs to understand when to stop iterating. When the loop execution starts, the loop starts increasing the value of the counter, going from 1 to 3 in our example. The for loop repeats the instructions between the brackets for each element of the values of the vector following the in clause in the for command. At each step, the value of the variable before in (i in this case) takes one value of the sequence from the vector itself.

The counter is also useful within the loop itself, and it is usually employed to iterate within an object in which some kind of manipulation is desired. Take, for instance, a vector defined like this:

```
vector <- c(1,2,3)
```

Imagine we want to increase the value of every element of the vector by 1. We can do this by employing a loop such as this:

```
for (i in 1:3){
 vector[i] <- vector[i]+1
}
```

If you look closely at the loop, you'll realize that the instruction needs to access the element of the vector with an index equal to i and modify this value by 1. The counter here is useful because it will allow iteration on all vectors from 1 to 3.

Be aware that this is actually not a best practice because loops tend to be quite computationally expensive, and they should be employed when no other valid alternative is available. For instance, we can obtain the same result here by working directly on the whole vector, as follows:

```
vector_increased <- vector +1
```

If you are interested in the topic of avoiding loops where they are not necessary, I can share with you some relevant material on this.

For our purposes, we are going to apply loops to go through the `pdf_list` object, and apply the `pdf_text` function and subsequently the `strsplit()` function to each element of this list:

```
corpus_raw <- data.frame("company" = c(),"text" = c())

for (i in 1:length(pdf_list)){
print(i)
 pdf_text(paste("data/", pdf_list[i],sep = "")) %>%
 strsplit("\n")-> document_text
data.frame("company" = gsub(x =pdf_list[i],pattern = ".pdf", replacement =
""),
 "text" = document_text, stringsAsFactors = FALSE) -> document

colnames(document) <- c("company", "text")
corpus_raw <- rbind(corpus_raw,document)
}
```

Let's get closer to the loop: we first have a call to the `pdf_text` function, passing an element of `pdf_list` as an argument; it is defined as referencing the `i` position in the list. Once we have done this, we can move on to apply the `strsplit()` function to the resulting string. We define the `document` object, which contains two columns, in this way:

- `company`, which stores the name of the PDF without the `.pdf` token; this is the name of the company
- `text`, which stores the text resulting from the extraction

This `document` object is then appended to the `corpus` object, which we created previously, to store all of the text within the PDF.

Let's have a look a the resulting data frame:

```
corpus_raw %>% head()
```

```
    company                                                                       text
1 Betasoloin                                                  Betasoloin business profile
2 Betasoloin Information below are provided under non disclosure agreement. date of enquery: 12.05.2017
3 Betasoloin                                                  date of foundation: 2000-09-05
4 Betasoloin                                                  industry: Metal ard Mineral Wholesalers
5 Betasoloin                          share holders: Demetra Mcnary ; Lauri Baysinger ; India Lanasa
6 Betasoloin                                                  comments
```

This is a well-structured object, ready for some text mining. Nevertheless, if we look closely at our PDF customer cards, we can see that there are three different kinds of information and they should be handled differently:

- Repeated information, such as the confidentiality disclosure on the second line and the *date of enquiry (12.05.2017)*
- Structured attributes, for instance, *date of foundation* or *industry*
- Strictly unstructured data, which is in the *comments* paragraph

We are going to address these three kinds of data differently, removing the first group of irrelevant information; we therefore have to split our data frame accordingly into two smaller data frames. To do so, we will leverage the `grepl()` function once again, looking for the following tokens:

- `12.05.2017`: This denotes the line showing the non-disclosure agreement and the date of inquiry.
- `business profile`: This denotes the title of the document, containing the name of the company. We already have this information stored within the *company* column.
- `comments`: This is the name of the last paragraph.
- `1`: This represents the number of the page and is always the same on every card.

We can apply the `filter` function to our `corpus_raw` object here as follows:

```
corpus_raw %>%
filter(!grepl("12.05.2017",text)) %>%
filter(!grepl("business profile",text)) %>%
filter(!grepl("comments",text)) %>%
filter(!grepl("1",text)) -> corpus
```

Now that we have removed those useless things, we can actually split the data frame into two sub-data frames based on what is returned by the `grepl` function when searching for the following tokens, which point to the structured attributes we discussed previously:

- `date of foundation`
- `industry`
- `shareholders`

We are going to create two different data frames here; one is called information and the other is called comments:

```
corpus %>%
filter(!grepl(c("date of foundation"),text)) %>%
filter(!grepl(c( "industry"),text)) %>%
filter(!grepl(c( "share holders"),text)) -> comments

corpus %>%
filter(grepl(("date of foundation"),text)|grepl(( "industry"),text)|grepl((
"share holders"),text))-> information
```

As you can see, the two data treatments are nearly the opposite of each other, since the first looks for lines showing none of the three tokens while the other looks for records showing at least one of the tokens.

Let's inspect the results by employing the head function:

```
information %>% head()
comments %>% head()
```

```
> information %>% head()
          company                                                       text
1      Betasoloin                              date of foundation: 2000-09-05
2      Betasoloin                      industry: Metal and Mineral Wholesalers
3      Betasoloin share holders: Demetra Mcnary ; Lauri Baysinger ; India Lanasa
4      Burl Whirl                            industry: Data and Records Management
5      Burl Whirl                    share holders: Omid Tahvili ; Debora Welter
6 BUSINESSCENTER                                            industry: Non-profit
> comments %>% head()
          company                                                                                    text
1      Betasoloin Difficult company to do business with. We should definitely revise agreements since an unjustified discount
2      Betasoloin                                                                               was accorded.
3      Burl Whirl   Small company quit unknown on-the-market. It usually places small orders with 30 days payments schedules.
4      Burl Whirl   we should reconsider agreements since an high discount value was placed given the small company dimension
5 BUSINESSCENTER This is one of our worst customer. It really often miss payments even if for just a couple of days. We have
6 BUSINESSCENTER       problems finding useful contact persons. The only person we can have had occasion to deal with was the
```

Great! We are nearly done. We are now going to start analyzing the comments data frame, which reports all comments from our colleagues. The very last step needed to make this data frame ready for subsequent analyzes is to tokenize it, which basically means separating it into different rows for all the words available within the text column. To do this, we are going to leverage the unnest_tokens function, which basically splits each line into words and produces a new row for each word, having taken care to repeat the corresponding value within the other columns of the original data frame.

This function comes from the recent `tidytext` package by Julia Silge and Davide Robinson, which provides an organic framework of utilities for text mining tasks. It follows the `tidyverse` framework, which you should already know about if you are using the `dplyr` package.

Let's see how to apply the `unnest_tokens` function to our data:

```
comments %>%
  unnest_tokens(word,text)-> comments_tidy
```

If we now look at the resulting data frame, we can see the following:

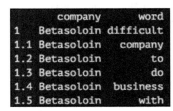

As you can see, we now have each word separated into a single record.

Sentiment analysis

The first kind of analysis is called **sentiment analysis**. It basically involves trying to understand the mood expressed in a piece of text. We are therefore going to look for the overall sentiment of each of the comments to see whether the general sentiment is mainly good or bad for those companies.

A common technique employed to perform this analysis is based on the use of a lexicon, which is a dataset that stores a wide list of words, with each word paired with an attribute that expresses the sentiment of the given word. The `tidytext` package provides three different lexicons to choose from:

- `afinn` : Assigning the sentiment as a score from -5 (negative) to 5 (positive)
- `bing`: Denoting the sentiment as either positive or negative
- `nrc`: Assigning various levels of sentiment, such as *joy* and *fear*

We can easily explore them by calling the `get_sentiments()` function . Let's inspect `bing`:

```
get_sentiments("bing")
```

```
# A tibble: 6,788 x 2
             word  sentiment
            <chr>      <chr>
 1        2-faced   negative
 2        2-faces   negative
 3             a+   positive
 4       abnormal   negative
 5        abolish   negative
 6     abominable   negative
 7     abominably   negative
 8      abominate   negative
 9    abomination   negative
10          abort   negative
# ... with 6,778 more rows
```

What do we do now to understand the sentiment of our documents?

The most straightforward way to perform such a task is by merging our data frame with the lexicon, using the word as a key. We will finally have our original data frame enriched with an extra column, which shows its sentiment. Finally, we will be able to count how many positive and negative words are there within the document and even draw a distribution showing whether our companies are perceived in a good or bad way.

Let's actually do this:

```
comments_tidy %>%
  inner_join(get_sentiments("boing")) %>%
  count(company,sentiment) %>%
  spread(sentiment, n, fill = 0) %>%
  mutate(sentiment = positive - negative)
```

This gives the following output:

```
# A tibble: 115 x 4
              company negative positive sentiment
                <chr>    <dbl>    <dbl>     <dbl>
 1          Betasoloin        2        0        -2
 2          Burl Whirl        1        0        -1
 3      BUSINESSCENTER        4        1        -3
 4           Buzzmaker        4        1        -3
 5    BuzzSaw Publicity        1        0        -1
 6            CareWare        2        0        -2
 7     Carnival Coffee        2        0        -2
 8          Cascadence        4        1        -3
 9    Casinoville, Inc.        2        0        -2
10       Castlewatchers        2        0        -2
# ... with 105 more rows
```

We first merged the two data frames by leveraging the `inner_join` function. The result of this merge was then passed to the `count` function, which basically groups by the two variables passed as arguments (`company` and `sentiment`) and summarizes the number of occurrences of each sentiment for each company.

Lastly, the `sentiment` column, which is basically composed of `positive` and `negative` tokens, is spread and a new `sentiment` column is created, subtracting positive from negative. So, a negative number means negative sentiment while the opposite holds true for a positive number.

Let's now try to visualize this. We can conveniently do it with a histogram showing the frequency of each sentiment score:

```
ggplot(comments_sentiment, aes(x = sentiment)) +
  geom_histogram()
```

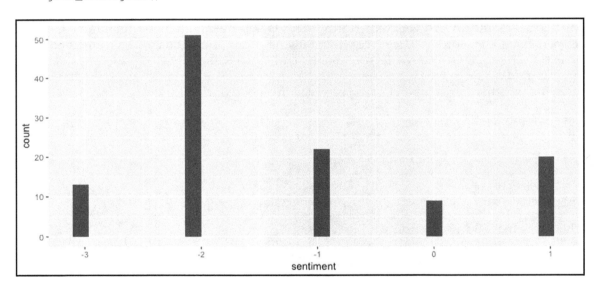

Uhm...what would you conclude? We are not in an idyllic situation with these customers, which is coherent with our model's prediction; it seems that our commercial colleagues use negative words in the comments about the companies we predicted as defaulting.

This is encouraging; nevertheless, we don't know enough about those negative words. What are they talking about? Let's try to figure this out.

Developing wordclouds from text

We can make our first attempt to look at these words using the `wordcloud` package, which basically lets you obtain what you are thinking of: wordclouds.

To create a wordcloud, we just have to call the `wordcloud()` function, which requires two arguments:

- `words`: The words to be plotted
- `frequency`: The number of occurrences of each word

Let's do it:

```
comments_tidy %>%
count(word) %>%
with(wordcloud(word, n))
```

Reproduced in the plot are all the words stored within the `comments_tidy` object, with a size proportionate to their frequency. You should also be aware that the position of each word has no particular meaning hear.

What do you think about it? Not too bad, isn't it? Nevertheless, I can see too many irrelevant words, such as *we* and *with*. These words do not actually convey any useful information about the content of the comments, and because they are quite frequent, they are obscuring the relevance of other, more meaningful, words.

We should therefore remove them, but how do we do this? The most popular way is to compare the analyzed dataset with a set of so-called *stop words*, which basically are words of the kind we were talking about earlier—they have no relevant meaning and high frequency. `Tidytext` provides a built-in list of `stop_words` that we can use.

Let's have a look at it:

```
stop_words
```

```
# A tibble: 1,149 x 2
          word lexicon
         <chr>   <chr>
1            a   SMART
2          a's   SMART
3         able   SMART
4        about   SMART
5        above   SMART
6     according  SMART
7   accordingly  SMART
8        across   SMART
9      actually   SMART
10        after   SMART
# ... with 1,139 more rows
```

We can now filter our `comments_tidy` object based on the `word` column:

```
comments_tidy %>%
filter(!word %in% stop_words$word) %>%
count(word) %>%
with(wordcloud(word, n))
```

The wordcloud is now a more useful instrument for our analysis. What would you conclude by looking at it? Beside the quite obvious *company*, we find *contact* and *person*, which probably show up together as *contact person*. We find even more relevant words such as *delay, discount, difficult, unjustified*, and *revise*.

Those words confirm that something bad is going on with these companies, even if they fail to provide the relevant context. Looking at the wordcloud, we can conclude that the topics of the discussions relate to the contact persons, discounts, and delays in payments.

How do we obtain more context? We are going to look at n-grams for that.

Looking for context in text – analyzing document n-grams

What was the main limitation of our wordclouds? As we said, the absence of context. In other words, we were looking at isolated words, which don't help us to derive any meaning apart from the limited meaning contained within the single words themselves.

This is where n-gram analysis techniques come in. These techniques basically involve tokenizing the text into groups of words rather than into single words. These groups of words are called n-grams.

We can obtain n-grams from our `comments` dataset by simply applying the `unnest_tokens` function again, but this time passing `"ngrams"` as value to the token argument and 2 as the value to the n argument:

```
comments %>%
unnest_tokens(bigram, text, token = "ngrams", n = 2) -> bigram_comments
```

Since we specified 2 as the value for the n argument, we are extracting here what are called `bigrams`, couples of words that appear adjacent to each other in a text. Let's try to count the frequency of our `bigram` now. We are also removing the `stop_words` from our dataset:

```
bigram_comments %>%
separate(bigram, c("word1", "word2"), sep = " ") %>%
filter(!word1 %in% stop_words$word) %>%
filter(!word2 %in% stop_words$word) %>%
count(word1, word2, sort = TRUE)
```

```
# A tibble: 30 x 3
              word1       word2      n
              <chr>       <chr>  <int>
1           contact      person     45
2        unjustified    discount     26
3           contact     persons     21
4               bad    customer     19
5         difficult     company     17
6            revise  agreements     17
7            fiscal      expert     13
8              miss    payments     13
9            person      denied     13
10         relevant      person     13
# ... with 20 more rows
```

Since we specified `sort = TRUE` within the `count` function, what we are looking at is a sorted list of n-gram weights based on their frequency in the whole dataset.

What can you conclude from this? There are some messages that are now starting to become evidences in some manner:

- Our colleagues are complaining of unjustified discounts being given to the companies
- There are problems with the relevant contact persons
- There are problems with payments related to this company

Is this enough? What if we now try to perform the same kind of analysis but employ three rather than two words? Let's try this, moving from `bigrams` to `trigrams`:

```
comments %>%
unnest_tokens(trigram, text, token = "ngrams", n = 3) -> trigram_comments
```

We now have a group of three words for each line. Let's split this into three columns, named `word1`, `word2`, and `word3`, and leave the rest as before in order to obtain the frequency count:

```
trigram_comments %>%
separate(trigram, c("word1", "word2","word3"), sep = " ") %>%
filter(!word1 %in% stop_words$word) %>%
filter(!word2 %in% stop_words$word) %>%
filter(!word3 %in% stop_words$word) %>%
count(word1, word2, word3, sort = TRUE)
```

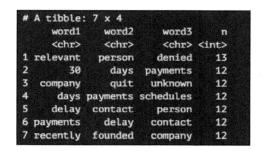

```
# A tibble: 7 x 4
       word1     word2      word3     n
       <chr>     <chr>      <chr> <int>
1 relevant    person     denied    13
2       30      days   payments    12
3  company      quit    unknown    12
4           days payments schedules  12
5    delay   contact     person    12
6 payments     delay    contact    12
7 recently   founded    company    12
```

This is definitely adding context. We now know that a relevant and common problem is related to contact persons not being easily reachable and payments getting delayed. I think we can consider our analysis of the unstructured part of the text concluded. Let's move to the information data frame to see if the information contained within that dataset can further highlight the commonalities between these companies.

Performing network analysis on textual data

One hypothesis we could make is that these companies, or at least a good part of them, are from the same industry. Is that true?

We actually have the data to figure this out. If we look back at our `information` dataset, we can easily see that some of the records start with the `industry` token. These are the records reproducing the line related to the customer's industry, which is contained within every customer card.

Let's filter out all the other records to retain only those records that specify the industry of the company:

```
information %>%
  filter(grepl("industry", text))
```

	company	text
1	Betasoloin	industry: Metal and Mineral Wholesalers
2	Burl Whirl	industry: Data and Records Management
3	BUSINESSCENTER	industry: Non-profit

This is fine; nonetheless, we still have that `industry:` token, which is meaningless. Let's remove it by using the `gsub()` function. This function basically substitutes a pattern with a *replacement* within a *character vector*. Therefore, to apply it, you have to specify the following:

- The pattern to look for, through the argument pattern
- The replacement to put where the pattern is found
- The vector where the pattern has to be searched

```
information %>%
filter(grepl("industry", text)) %>%
mutate(industry = gsub("industry: ","",text))-> industries
```

We can now easily visualize the result in a nice bar plot. To obtain a readable result, we will filter out the industries occurring less than twice:

```
industries %>%
count(industry) %>%
filter(n >1) %>%
ggplot(aes(x = industry, y = n)) +
geom_bar(stat = 'identity')+
coord_flip()
```

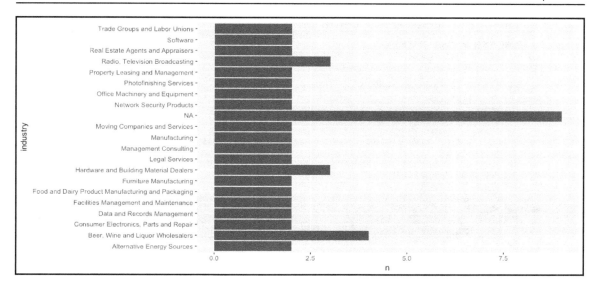

It looks nice and the industry labels are easily readable. Yet there is not much insight in it; nearly all industries have the same frequency, meaning that this attribute is not what correlates the companies we are analyzing. Let's hope for a better result with the shareholders list.

First of all, let's isolate all the records related to shareholders from the `information` data frame, also removing the `share holders` token:

```
information %>%
  filter(grepl("share holders", text)) %>%
  mutate(shareholders = gsub("share holders: ","",text))
```

What is the problem now? I guess it is that we have at least two different shareholders for every record, which makes it impossible to perform further analysis on them. We have to fix it by separating the shareholders into columns and then gathering the result into a single column. If you know a bit about the tidy data framework, we are going to make our data wide at the beginning here and then make it long by employing the `gather` function.

Let's start with the widening phase, which we can perform by employing the `separate` function from the `tidyr` package:

```
information %>%
  filter(grepl("share holders", text)) %>%
  mutate(shareholders = gsub("share holders: ","",text)) %>%
  separate(col = shareholders, into = c("first","second","third"),sep = ";")
```

We specify here that we want to take the `shareholders` column and split it into three new columns, named `first`, `second`, and `third`. To make the function understand when to split, we specify `;` as a separator.

	company	text	first	second	third
1	Betasoloin	share holders: Demetra Mcnary ; Lauri Baysinger ; India Lanasa	Demetra Mcnary	Lauri Baysinger	India Lanasa
2	Burl Whirl	share holders: Omid Tahvili ; Debora Welter	Omid Tahvili	Debora Welter	<NA>
3	BUSINESSCENTER	share holders: Helene Wurm ; Meryl Savant ; Sydney Wadley	Helene Wurm	Meryl Savant	Sydney Wadley
4	Buzzmaker	share holders: Omid Tahvili ; Terri Keep	Omid Tahvili	Terri Keep	<NA>

This is close to what we were looking for, even if there are still some NAs to be dealt with in the third column. It comes from some companies having two rather than three shareholders.

Let's now make our data long using the `gather` function. We specify that we want to create a new key column to store the labels of columns `first`, `second`, and `third`, and a value column to store the names of the shareholders:

```
information %>%
  filter(grepl("share holders", text)) %>%
  mutate(shareholders = gsub("share holders: ","",text)) %>%
  separate(col = shareholders, into = c("first","second","third"),sep = ";")
%>%
  gather(key = "number",value ="shareholder",-company,-text)
```

	company	text	number	shareholder
1	Betasoloin	share holders: Demetra Mcnary ; Lauri Baysinger ; India Lanasa	first	Demetra Mcnary
2	Burl Whirl	share holders: Omid Tahvili ; Debora Welter	first	Omid Tahvili
3	BUSINESSCENTER	share holders: Helene Wurm ; Meryl Savant ; Sydney Wadley	first	Helene Wurm
4	Buzzmaker	share holders: Omid Tahvili ; Terri Keep	first	Omid Tahvili
5	BuzzSaw Publicity	share holders: Leia Crupi ; Chastity Klink ; Scottie Upham	first	Leia Crupi
6	CareWare	share holders: Felica Sinner ; Chris Mellin ; Natashia Haider	first	Felica Sinner

Because we specified -company and -text, the two corresponding variables are used as grouping variables. The very last step is to select only the columns we are interested in, the company and the shareholder columns:

```
information %>%
  filter(grepl("share holders", text)) %>%
  mutate(shareholders = gsub("share holders: ","",text)) %>%
  separate(col = shareholders, into = c("first","second","third"),sep = ";")
%>%
  gather(key = "number",value ="shareholder",-company,-text) %>%
  filter(!is.na(shareholder)) %>%
  select(company,shareholder)-> shareholders
```

Nice! What's next? We have a list of companies and shareholders. Shouldn't we try to check if there are common shareholders? We can simply do this with another bar plot, but this could make us miss some relevant information, *Industries where exclusive among each other, meaning that a company could pertain to only one industry at the time*. This is not true for shareholders. Since every company can have one to three shareholders, we should try to find out a convenient way to visualize this information without losing its richness and complexity.

A great way to do this is via network analysis.

Obtaining an hedge list from a data frame

Network analysis involves producing a network plot with a point for each statistical unit observed and a hedge between two points for each relationship between the points. The relationship can be of almost any kind, from point A being in the same country as B to two companies having the same shareholder, as in our case.

The object storing these relationships is called a edge list, and you can imagine it as follows:

from	to
A	B
B	C
A	C
C	D

If you now look at this table, you notice that A has a relation with B, B with C, and A with C. Finally, D will be related only with C.

We can easily represent this as a network, as follows:

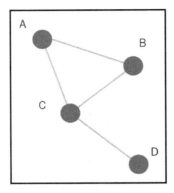

This is exactly what we are going to do now: create an edge list from our `shareholders` data frame. This data frame already contains an edge list, since it has the name of a company in the first column and the name of a shareholder related to that company in the second column.

To actually transform this into a proper edge list to be later visualized as a network, we will employ the `graph_from_data_frame()` function from the `igraph` package. This package is a must-have package when dealing with network analysis in R. If you are interested in deepening your knowledge of the topic, I will share with you a tutorial on this, which greatly explores the potential of the package itself.

Visualizing a network with the ggraph package

At the moment, all you need to know is that we are going to apply this function to our data to obtain a proper edge list, which will then be passed to the `ggraph()` function. This is a function from the `ggraph()` package, which basically constitutes an interface between the `igraph` package and the `ggplot` one. Once this is done, we will be able to add geoms as is usually done in `ggplot`, by using the `geom_edge_link,` `geom_node_point and` `geom_node_tect` functions:

```
graph_from_data_frame(shareholders) -> graph_object
graph_object %>%
 ggraph() +
 geom_edge_link() +
 geom_node_point() +
```

```
geom_node_text(aes(label = name), vjust = 1, hjust = 1, check_overlap =
TRUE) +
  theme_graph()
```

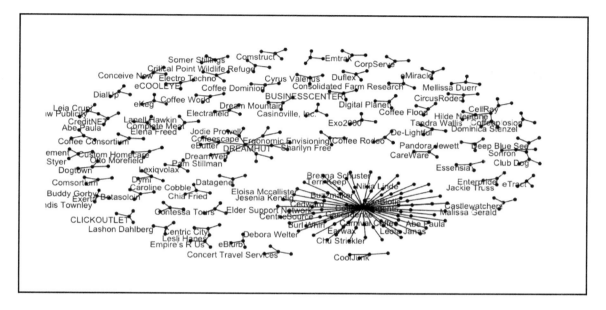

Well, this is definitely a network plot, but I am not sure whether it is a useful one. What do you think is missing from it?

At least two things:

- The names are unreadable due to the node labels on them
- It is not easy to visualize which nodes are the most relevant ones

As you may have guessed, we can fix both.

Tuning the appearance of nodes and edges

In order to make labels stand out, we can change the colors of both nodes and edges, giving to both a level of transparency via the `alpha` parameter:

```
graph_object %>%
ggraph() +
geom_edge_link(alpha = .2) +
geom_node_point(alpha =.3) +
geom_node_text(aes(label = name), vjust = 1, hjust = 1, check_overlap =
TRUE)+
theme_graph()
```

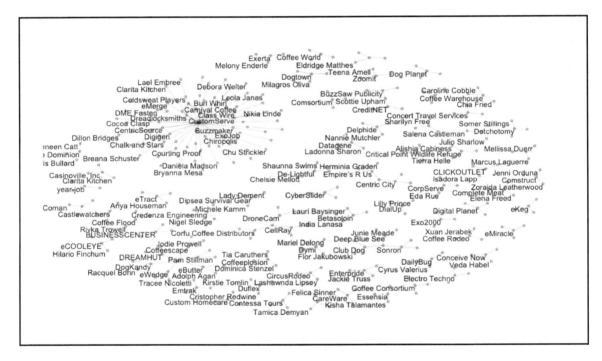

This is now a lot more readable. But what about the relevance of the nodes?

Computing the degree parameter in a network to highlight relevant nodes

The degree is a useful number when dealing with networks. It is basically defined as the number of edges related to a given node. For instance, we can compute the degree for every node of the previous example as follows:

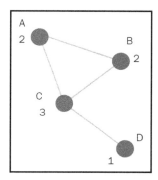

As you can see, the node with the highest degree is *C*, which is an important node in the network. Without *C*, *D* would be completely isolated from the rest of the network. This is exactly what the degree measure tries to express: the relevance of a node in a network.

Now that we have an `igraph` object obtained from the `graph_from_data_frame` function, we can easily compute the degree of each node through the `degree` function, as follows:

```
deg <- degree(graph_object, mode="all")
```

To employ it now as an attribute when representing the network with `ggraph`, we have to add it to the list of attributes that `igraph` associates with nodes and edges:

```
V(graph_object)$size <- deg*3
```

What we are saying here is take all the nodes (vertices) of our `graph_object` and add to them an attribute named `size` that is equal to the degree of that node taken three times.

The final step is to employ this attribute to set the dimension of each node in the plot so that the most relevant one will be highlighted:

```
set.seed(30)
graph_object %>%
ggraph() +
geom_edge_link(alpha = .2) +
geom_node_point(aes(size = size),alpha = .3) +
geom_node_text(aes(label = name,size = size), vjust = 1, hjust = 1,
check_overlap = FALSE)+
theme_graph()
```

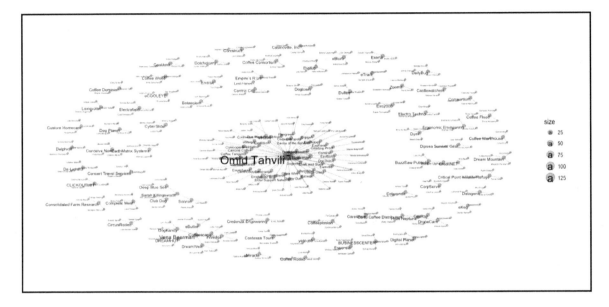

Wow!

That's really surprising. I thought it was going to be useful, but not *that* useful. Omid Tahvili is like a sun in our network, and a lot of companies are rotating around him. I think we have got something useful now, and all that is left to do is to share it with Mr. Clough.

Further references

- https://www.datacamp.com/community/tutorials/tutorial-on-loops-in-r.
- *Network Analysis and Visualization with R and igraph* by *Katherine Ognyanova*, available at http://kateto.net/networks-r-igraph.

- A great book to deepen your knowledge of text mining stuff is *Text Mining with R* by Julia Silge and Davide Robinson. You can find an online version at http://tidytextmining.com/.

Summary

As usual, this is the author speaking at the end of the chapter. How was your first experience with internal audit? It seems you actually got a lot out of those PDFs.

You first learned how to iteratively read text from PDFs and store it in a single data frame.

Then you discovered how to prepare the data frame for text mining activities, removing irrelevant words and transforming it from a list of sentences into a list of words. Finally, you learned how to perform sentiment analysis, wordcloud development, and n-gram analysis on it.

From these analyses, you discovered that the companies you predicted being defaulted are actually considered bad customers by your colleagues in the commercial department.

This helped you gain knowledge from unstructured data.

Moving to more structured data contained in the same PDFs, you learned how to transform the data into an edge list in order to perform network analysis, which mainly consisted of the computation of the nodes' degrees. This resulted in highlighting the relevant node, represented by Omid Tahvili, very effectively.

The mystery is coming close to the end. You just have to move on to the next chapter to discover more.

13
Sharing Your Stories with Your Stakeholders through R Markdown

I don't know what your thoughts are about our discoveries, but I think they mark a clear point to our investigations: we now know that those companies are involved in some bad relationship with our company, that they were probably granted an unjustified discount, and that the greatest part of them are related with this Omid Tahvili.

This is definitely enough to catch the interest of Mr Clough. But he is quite a demanding boss, and we need to prepare a well-crafted report, one able to effectively convey our messages while providing enough evidence on the correctness of the adopted approach of analysis.

To do this, we are going to employ R markdown and shiny, two powerful instruments made available within the RStudio ecosystem.

Principles of a good data mining report

I have written quite a lot of reports, highlighting results from a wide range of activities. Based on the feedback received and from the requests of changes intervened from the first version to the definitive one, I can tell you the following basic principles for producing a good data mining report:

- Clearly show the objectives and questions that initiated the analyses performed
- Explicitly highlight the assumptions made when performing the analyses

- Enumerate and get into the details with data treatment applied to analyzed data
- Always verify that the reproduced data is consistent
- Provide data lineage to the maximum possible extent

Let's get a bit deeper into these principles before we actually develop our report.

Clearly state the objectives

When I was a newbie in the field, I got really excited at the idea of applying all the data mining techniques I knew by then to real data. You can imagine my happiness when I was first provided with a bunch of data. I was literally thrilled. At that time, we were looking at the inventory process and related stuff. After nearly two weeks of munging and visualizing the data, I wasn't still able to conclude that much. That was the moment when I realized that even the greatest set of data, paired with the most advanced data mining technique, is nothing without a real purpose in your analyses.

You should always have in mind the questions you are trying to get answered when performing data mining activities. And those questions should be clearly stated in your reports in the form of objectives. This will let your stakeholders clearly understand why you performed the analyses you are talking about and evaluate whether the answered questions are the same as they were asking.

Clearly state assumptions

We all make assumptions whenever we open our mouth. Have you ever experienced a dialogue where, after quite a long period, your interlocutor pops out with an, *Oh, you are talking about him, not me!* or *wow! You thought I already knew this, didn't you?* Well, those are cases when you were making assumptions while talking with someone. Moreover, those are examples of occasions where not clearly stating these assumptions made the conversation harder, if not impossible.

Such examples make you clearly see why it is important to explicitly state assumptions. In the realm of data mining, a typical example of assumptions is applied proxies. For instance, in a study about absenteeism at work, you can assume that all absences from work longer than 2 days but shorter than 6 are to be considered episodes of absenteeism due to some in-depth analysis you performed on a sample of employees that showed this pattern being true. It is an assumption that can be considered reasonable, or cannot, but not explicating it to your stakeholder will seriously compromise their understanding of the report.

Make the data treatments clear

Similar to the principle related to assumptions is the one related to data treatment. It is really uncommon to employ a dataset exactly as it comes out of the box. You always have to perform data cleaning and validation.

Quite common results of this activity are exclusions of records or substitutions of missing data. Both of them are examples of data treatment to be communicated within your report. Why?

First of all, because this will increase the level of reproducibility of your work; that is, it will make it clear how to reperform the analysis you conducted. This will provide assurance on the quality of your analysis and make your stakeholders more confident at drawing conclusions from it.

Moreover, documenting these treatments and their rationales will be of great help for you as well in the eventuality of a future need to reperform the same analysis with updated data.

Show consistent data

Do you know the first activity a statutory auditor performs on a financial statement before actually starting to audit it?

They check whether the closing balances of the previous year match with the one reported on the previous financial statement. This a good way to get the point raised from this principle: you should always verify that the data shown within your reports is consistent within them and if needed also with external sources.

Let's say, for instance, you have a table showing a three cases A, B, and C found in a population, which sums up to 1,436 cases. You then show in two separate tables how cases A and C can be further split into subclusters. A check you should always do is that the total shown within these two tables is consistent with the one shown as a raw total in the first table.

Missing these checks, which could also appear as trivial, and sharing documents with inconsistent data, will dramatically decrease the level of trust in your analyses and thus increase the effort needed to convince your stakeholders of the validity of your results.

Provide data lineage

This last principle also proved to be true in my professional life. I was still a newbie when I prepared my first report. It showed some robust but rather counter-intuitive result about a phenomenon widely known in the office. Everyone was expecting a given result, but the data actually showed the opposite.

My report was packed with nice-looking plots that clearly showed the surprising result and also with text supported by means of reasoning the result itself.

When I first shared this with my boss, he was reasonably surprised and he started being inquisitive about my approach: *How do you get there? What is this plot made of? Can you show me the data behind? What's the name of the employee behind this red point here? Is he still in that office or not?*

As you can imagine, I was able to answer just a small number of those questions and this made me more nervous as time passed. In the end, he frankly told me: *I think you have to review this analysis, the result is really strange and I cannot share it with my bosses if we are not able to explain it in detail.*

It was a hard lesson for me, but as it always happens with hard lessons, I learned it well: I have to provide the maximum possible extent of data lineage in my analysis.

Data lineage is broadly considered as the possibility to trace back a number to the records it was generated from. A really basic example is the one of an average for which you are able to show from which vector of numbers it was computed.

Adding data lineage to your report means adding an instrument to investigate the raw data lying behind the final results you are showing. Moving on with the episode... Adding data lineage that my report would have meant being able to show for each point in the plot who the represented employee was and how the raw list of employees was aggregated to obtain the surprising result my boss was looking at.

Set up an rmarkdown report

No more chatting now! Let's move to the actual production of our report. We are going to use RStudio, so let's open it and create a new R markdown report:

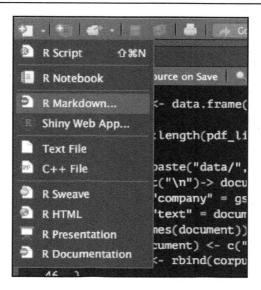

We can now specify what kind of document we want to create, which in our case is a **Shiny Document**. I write down the title and my name as the author:

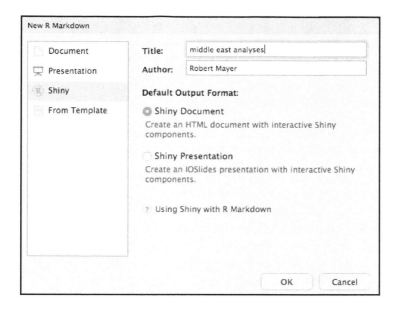

A non-empty template with a file extension as `.rmd` was just created for us:

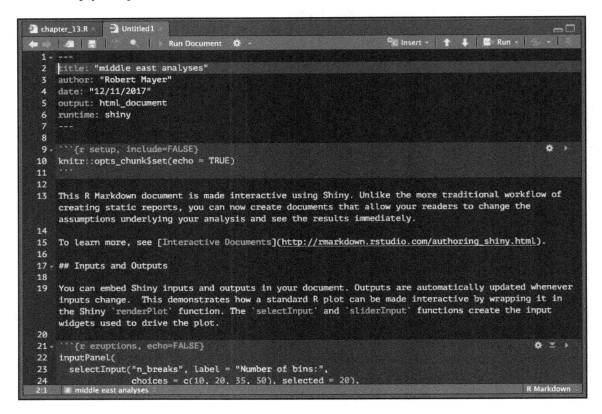

I will tell you a bit more about Shiny later when we actually use it, but let me give you just a quick intro to it and R markdown so that you can feel more comfortable in going ahead:

- R markdown is basically an R package that provides functions to create various kinds of documents hosting both text and R code outputs. It was a father of a prolific family, which nowadays encompasses packages for writing books directly from R to packages for building websites.
- `shiny` is an R package that provides functions to build web applications through R codes. It takes care of generating from the R code the needed Javascript and HTML without the user worrying about this.

Once you have taken a careful look at the non-empty template, you can go on and delete the most part of it except for the first part, which is actually made of `.yaml` code:

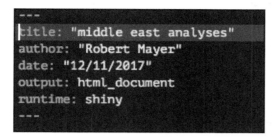

Let's now see how we are going to build our report.

Develop an R markdown report in RStudio

There are three kinds of basic contents of an R markdown document:

- Text chunks
- Inline R code
- Code chunks

A brief introduction to markdown

Now that you have deleted all of the content originally provided within the template, you actually find yourself in some kind of text field where it is possible to write down characters as in a common `.txt` file. To be more precise though, what you are going to write here will not be interpreted as common text but rather as Markdown code. Behind this name, there is a really convenient technical solution developed by John Gruber to provide people with a way to write in plain text documents that could lately be rendered as LaTeX, `.pdf`, or even `.html`.

Basically, when you write in markdown, you don't have to worry about formatting or alignment anymore, since this will be eventually handled from subsequent rendering instruments, such as the `rmarkdown` functions in this case. All you have to worry about is specifying the headings and their levels, the need for some word or sentence being rendered as bold or italic, and some other stuff, such as hyperlinks and tables.

Let me give you a really small guide on how to deal with the most common elements, as follows:

Format	Markdown
H1, first level heading	`#`
H2, second level heading	`##`
H3, third level heading	`###`
bold	`**word**`
italic	`*word*`
hyperlink	`[title](http://)`

Let's lay down the structure of our report, which will show the following main paragraphs:

- Activity objectives
- Analyzed data
- Performed analyses
- Results

We can go on defining each of these paragraphs within the document:

```
## activity objectives


## analysed data

## performed analyses

## results

## data lineage tool
```

Let's, for the moment, skip the first paragraph, which will be the most descriptive one. Move on to the first code chunk, namely the setup chunk.

Inserting a chunk of code

Chunks of code can be considered as R islands in a sea of markdown. A code chunk is opened with the following token:

```
```{r}
```

And it is closed with:

```
```
```

Within these signs, the PC knows that everything has to be taken as R code, and everything has to be interpreted accordingly. The most prominent example to understand what the implications are is this one, within a code chunk, the ## token will not be taken as the start of an h2 headline, but rather as the start of a commented line.

It is quite a common practice when developing `rmarkdown` documents to insert the first setup chunk where preliminary operations are performed and general options are defined. These operations are mainly:

- Loading libraries
- Data loading
- Preliminary data treatments
- General variable initialization
- Code chunk options setting

While the first four should not be obscure to you, let me spend some more time on the last one. Code chunks come with a full list of possible options to be set in order to express the behavior we want them to follow with regards to some specific aspects. Let's have a look at the most used ones:

- `name`: Every chunk can have a name, which is useful when dealing with debugging activity and other, more advanced, operations. Be aware that every chunk must be provided with a unique name.
- `eval`: This decides whether the code chunk should actually be run or not.
- `echo`: This specifies whether the code itself should be printed out.
- `warning`: Used to define whether hypothetical warnings coming from code execution should be printed.

- `error`: This is the same as `warning` but is only related to errors.
- `include`: This decides whether the output coming from the code running should be included within the document. This is different from `eval` in that not evaluating a chunk will necessarily result in its output not being in the report, but not including the output will not stop it from being executed.

You can set all of these options in two ways:

- Once for all chunks, usually by writing something like the following within the setup chunk: `knitr::opts_chunk$set(echo = FALSE)`
- Individually for each chunk, by inserting your set within the opening brackets of a specific chunk

In doing so, you should be aware that the nearest command will override the most farthest one; so, writing in the brackets of a chunk `eval=TRUE` will make the code of the chunk run even if a general `knitr::opts_chunk$set(eval = FALSE)` code was stated somewhere earlier.

That said, we can open our first chunk, naming it `setup`, since we are going to employ it to set up the general parameters and load the needed libraries:

```
```{r setup, echo=FALSE}
```

Let's actually write down our setup chunk:

```
```{r setup, include=FALSE}

library(dplyr)
library(ggplot2)
library(tidytext)
library(tidyr)
library(igraph)
library(ggraph)
library(wordcloud)

knitr::opts_chunk$set(echo = FALSE)
load("data/corpus.rdata")

corpus %>%
  filter(!grepl(c("date of foundation"),text)) %>%
  filter(!grepl(c( "industry"),text)) %>%
  filter(!grepl(c( "share holders"),text)) -> comments

corpus %>%
  filter(grepl((("date of foundation+"),
```

```
text)|grepl(( "industry+"),
text)|grepl(( "share holders+"),
text)) -> information
```
```
```

As you see, we basically load our libraries, set the echo option to false, and load the corpus object we have saved from our analyses. We then split it into `comments` and `information` to have those two data frames ready for subsequent chunks.

And this last statement leads us to the last relevant concept I would like to teach you about code chunks, code chunks are like islands but are not isolated. You can imagine some kind of underground system of communication that lets the islands share information among themselves, at least from top to bottom. This means that if I create a data frame or any other kind of object within the first chunk, I will have it available within subsequent chunks. The opposite will not hold true, just as it will not hold true in a regular R script since the code is read and evaluated from the PC from top to bottom.

How to show readable tables in rmarkdwon reports

Before we move on to inline R code, let me show you how to insert readable static tables within an `rmarkdown` code. Here, we are going to leverage the `kable` function from the `knitr` package, which generally makes a relevant number of useful utilities available for interaction between R code and markdown documents.

Employing the `kable` function, add a well-formatted table to your report. This will just imply passing your data frame as an argument of the `kable` function itself. Let's do this for our `ngram` counts tables:

```
```{r}

comments %>%
unnest_tokens(trigram, text, token = "ngrams", n = 3) -> trigram_comments

trigram_comments %>%
separate(trigram, c("word1", "word2","word3"), sep = " ") %>%
filter(!word1 %in% stop_words$word) %>%
filter(!word2 %in% stop_words$word) %>%
filter(!word3 %in% stop_words$word) %>%
count(word1, word2, word3, sort = TRUE) %>%
table()
```
```

Reproducing R code output within text through inline code

Now that our R environment is up and running, we can move on to the *analyzed data* section, which will let me show you how to put inline code within the body of markdown text.

To get how this works, you have to think of your document as a code script. This script is mainly written in markdown language, and when we ask the PC to render it, it will start reading it while looking for markdown code. This will result in the PC reading the `##` token as a need for placing an h2 headline and a `**` as a need to bold the subsequent text until the closing `**` token.

We therefore need to pass some specific token within this code to tell the PC that after that token, there will be some R code and it will have to treat it just as it is used to working on regular R code. There are two ways to do this within an `rmarkdown` document, which are the two remaining ones within the list we previously looked at:

- Inline R code
- Code chunks

Inline R code mean, as you may guess, just reading the name; it's R code placed inline with the markdown text. Imagine we want to tell the reader how many companies we analyzed with our text mining activity. One possible way to do this would be to reopen our R code script, write an `nrow()` function on the `pdf_list` object, copy the result, and paste it within the markdown text. Or, we can ask the PC to do this for us through the inline code. The base token of an R inline code is the following:

```
` r `
```

If you place a token like this within your markdown text, it will tell the PC that all that follows the first `` ` `` token, until the last `` ` `` token, has to be considered as R code and subsequently handled. Let's think, for instance, we want to print out within the text the result of a difficult computation without previously solving it by our own: 2+2. How to do that?

The correct answer is:

```
` r 2+2 `
```

Which, once rendered, will print out just a sound 4; so if you write in your `.rmd` file a line like the following:

The final result is `` ` r 2+2 ` ``, which is not obvious. It will be finally rendered as: the final result is 4, which is not obvious.

We are actually going to use inline code to share some data about the dataset we looked at, especially the total number of companies and the total length of our corpus.

Now that we have the corpus object loaded, to do this, we have just to count the number of unique companies available within the `company` column and the number of words available within our `text` column. The first inline code will therefore look like:

```
`r corpus$company %>% unique() %>% length()`
```

The resulting output will just be a well-rounded 115. Obtaining the second number will rather require us to take the `text` column and `unnest` the word tokens contained within it, leveraging the well-known `unnest_tokens` function:

```
`r corpus %>% unnest_tokens(word, text, token = "words") %>% select(word)
%>% nchar() %>% as.numeric()`
```

Just to let you appreciate the potentiality of the tool you are getting your hands on at its fullest, let me ask you a question, *What if we had more customer cards to our PDFs? What is going to happen to our report?*

Yes, it is going to dynamically change its values so as to always represent the up-to-date situation of our data, without requiring you to copy and paste from here to there, which multiplies the probability of making errors.

Introduction to Shiny and the reactivity framework

To make things even more interesting, we are now going to add a small piece of the Shiny application within our paragraphs.

As we were saying before, the `shiny` package was developed to let people programming in R easily build web applications to share results of their analyses. Well, just to be clear from the beginning: saying that shiny develops web applications doesn't mean that you need a web server to employ the package. It just means that what shiny produces is ready, with some further steps that we are not going to see now—to be published on the Web.

Without looking at all the complexity behind the scenes, we can say that a shiny web app is built of three basic components:

- A user interface : `ui <- fluidPage()`
- A server: `server <- function(input, output, session) {}`
- A function calling the app: `shinyApp(ui, server)`

In the standard setting of a Shiny App, you will have to develop all the data mining and plotting activities in the server function, leaving to the `ui` function the responsibility of disposing their output in the best possible way for the user.

Given this static picture, there is one more layer that adds flexibility to the app--reactivity. The idea behind reactivity is quite simple. Through some controls are available within the user interface specified by the `ui`, the user can select parameters or specify filtering options. Given this, within the server side of the function, these new inputs can be considered to update the data mining and plotting activities previously performed.

As you might expect, this will produce an updated result to be shown within the user interface. What if the user now changes some of the filtering parameters again? You got it! Everything changes again.

Employing input and output to deal with changes in Shiny app parameters

If you now look closer at the `server` object, you can see that the function behind it shows an `input` and an `output` argument. These two arguments are the solution Shiny found to support the kinds of double-sided exchanges of information we were mentioning before:

- `input` is a list that stores all choices coming from the `ui` object, for instance, a selected column among a list of columns or a range of minimum and maximum values to be employed to filter a vector
- `output` is a list of objects representing the result of computation performed from the `server` function

This is the real building block of all of the Shiny world. Let's develop a small example before applying Shiny to our report. Imagine we want to build a small app that is able to create and plot a distribution of *n* numbers, with *n* defined by the user of the app. We need:

- A control that lets the user decide *n*
- A piece of interface to show the resulting plot

- A piece of server to create the distribution and build the plot

In the Shiny, this translates into the following:

```
ui <- fluidPage(
  numericInput("num", label = h3("Numeric input"), value = 100),
  plotOutput("plot")
)

server <- function(input, output, session) {
output$plot <- renderPlot({
  rnorm(input$num) %>% hist() })
}
shinyApp(ui, server)
```

If we now source this code (assuming we have already installed and loaded the library `shiny`), it will produce the following output:

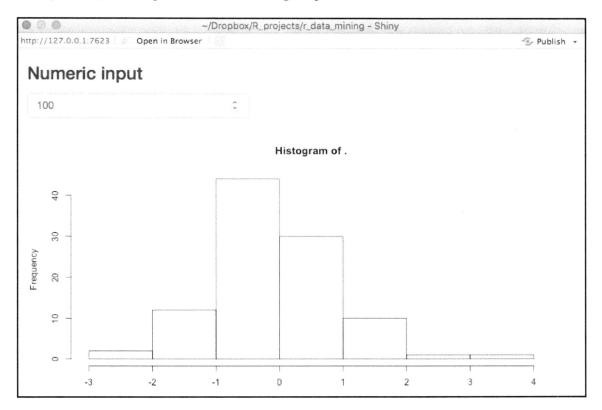

Now that you know a bit of R markdown and the Shiny app framework, we can smoothly complete our report by adding one paragraph for each of the following analyses:

- Sentiment analysis
- Wordcloud
- ngram analysis
- Shareholders network analysis

Given the great integration between markdown and the R language, writing this chapter will simply mean taking the code from the previously performed in the R script and placing it within different code chunks. You will then be easily able to add notes and comments to your analyses while writing text outside your chunks and respecting the markdown conventions. We can therefore obtain the report with the following code:

```
## results reproduced below are results from mentioned analyses.
### sentiment analysis

```{r}
comments %>%
 unnest_tokens(word,text)-> comments_tidy
#sentiment analysis

lexicon <- get_sentiments("bing")

comments_tidy %>%
 inner_join(lexicon) %>%
 count(company, sentiment) %>%
 spread(sentiment, n, fill = 0) %>%
 mutate(sentiment = positive -negative)-> comments_sentiment

ggplot(comments_sentiment, aes(x = sentiment)) +
 geom_histogram()
```

wordcloud

```{r}

comments_tidy %>%
 filter(!word %in% stop_words$word) %>%
 count(word) %>%
 with(wordcloud(word, n))
```
ngram analysis
bigrams
```{r}
```
```

```r
comments %>%
unnest_tokens(bigram, text, token = "ngrams", n = 2) -> bigram_comments

bigram_comments %>%
 separate(bigram, c("word1", "word2"), sep = " ") %>%
 filter(!word1 %in% stop_words$word) %>%
 filter(!word2 %in% stop_words$word) %>%
 count(word1, word2, sort = TRUE) %>%
 head() %>%
 kable()
```
trigrams
```{r}

comments %>%
 unnest_tokens(trigram, text, token = "ngrams", n = 3) -> trigram_comments

trigram_comments %>%
 separate(trigram, c("word1", "word2","word3"), sep = " ") %>%
 filter(!word1 %in% stop_words$word) %>%
 filter(!word2 %in% stop_words$word) %>%
 filter(!word3 %in% stop_words$word) %>%
 count(word1, word2, word3, sort = TRUE) %>%
 kable()
```
network analysis

```{r}
information %>%
 filter(grepl("share holders", text)) %>%
 mutate(shareholders = gsub("share holders: ","",text)) %>%
 separate(col = shareholders, into = c("first","second","third"),sep = ";")
%>%
 gather(key = "number",value ="shareholder",-company,-text) %>%
 filter(!is.na(shareholder)) %>%
 select(company,shareholder)-> shareholders
graph_from_data_frame(shareholders)-> graph_object
#linking the size of a node to its degree
deg <- degree(graph_object, mode="all")
 V(graph_object)$size <- deg*3

 set.seed(30)
 graph_object %>%
 ggraph() +
 geom_edge_link(alpha = .2) +
 geom_node_point(aes(size = size),alpha = .3) +
 geom_node_text(aes(label = name,size = size), vjust = 1, hjust = 1,
check_overlap = FALSE)+
```

```
theme_graph()
```

Let me show you now how to create the final interactive data lineage paragraph part of your report, leveraging the shiny framework we have seen before.

Adding an interactive data lineage module

To add a data lineage paragraph, we can easily add a table showing raw data feeding the computations showed within the report. To maximize the effectiveness of this tool, we can then add inquiry tools to let the final user directly filter the table and, by that means, test the results shown in the previous paragraphs.

To add such a kind of tool, we basically have to introduce two main components within a code chunk:

- An input panel
- One (or more) output objects

These two objects are related but not exactly overlapping with the `server` and `ui` objects we saw earlier. Particularly:

- The input panel can be considered as the `ui` of the traditional Shiny app, including all the controls made available to the user to influence the output shown.
- The various output objects can, to some extent, be compared both to the `ui` and the server. This is because they host both the `ui` logic and the server logic (that is, the data treatment and plotting instructions) for the given output, like a plot for instance.

Let me show you this in detail by trying to develop an interactive data lineage paragraph where the corpus table is made available by means of a filterable table.

Adding an input panel to an R markdown report

The first part we are going to add our data lineage paragraph is the input panel giving the user the possibility to filter the corpus table by industry and shareholders. An input panel is basically represented by a function having inside one argument for each of the controls we want to add. For our purposes, we are going to add two kinds of controls:

- A select box that shows all available industries to choose what to filter on
- A textbox used to give the user the opportunity of inserting a string to look for in the shareholders column:

```
inputPanel(
  selectInput("selected_industry", label = "select the industry you
want to focus on", selected = "",
              choices = unique(data_lineage_data$industry)),
  textInput("name_string", label = "write the name of the
shareholder",
              value = "")
)
```

Let me point you out the first string available within both `selectInput` and `textInput`, which are respectively `selected_industry` and `name_string`. These two strings are the univocal names of the two corresponding object. We are going to use these names to recall the outputs of the user choices on the server side of our app. If you render only this part of the document (we are actually going to see later how to do it), it will result in the following interactive interface:

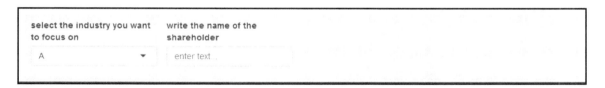

Let's now see how to render our corpus data frame and interactively filter it based on user choices from the controls we just added.

Adding a data table to your report

We now want to render our data frame as a table. We can easily do this by inserting a `renderDataTable` call, passing corpus as an argument. To do this, we have to create a new code chunk within our R markdown report and add the following code:

```
renderDataTable({
data_lineage_data
  })
```

We now have a nice-looking table here, also sortable by different columns and with alternatively colored rows. It will look like the following:

diamonds	mtcars	iris			
Show 5 ▾ entries				Search:	
	Sepal.Length	Sepal.Width	Petal.Length	Petal.Width	Species
1	5.1	3.5	1.4	0.2	setosa
2	4.9	3	1.4	0.2	setosa
3	4.7	3.2	1.3	0.2	setosa
4	4.6	3.1	1.5	0.2	setosa
5	5	3.6	1.4	0.2	setosa
Showing 1 to 5 of 150 entries		Previous 1 2 3 4 5 ... 30 Next			

But, this is still not linked to the input panel. To do this, we just have to pass the choice made from the user as an argument to filter out the data frame. To recall whatever value comes from a choice made within the input panel is sufficient to recall via the token `input$name_of_the_input`.

This token actually tells the PC to access the `name_of_the_input` object from the output coming from the `inputpanel` object. This object, depending on the type of input control, will be a vector of numbers, a string, or some other kind of object.

For both `selected_industry` and `name_string`, we will obtain a string to be employed as an argument within a regular dplyr `filter` function. Let's do this:

```
renderDataTable(
  if (input$selected_industry != "" | input$name_string != ""){
  data_lineage_data %>%
  filter(industry == input$selected_industry,
grepl(input$name_string,shareholders))}else{(data_lineage_data)}
)
```

As you can see, we also place an `if` statement there, given that we want to see all of the table if no filter is provided by the user. Here we are then--a fully functional table to let the user check for themselves and see how good our analyses are. The whole code behind this module will therefore be:

```
```{r}
information %>%
filter(grepl("industry", text)) %>%
mutate(industry = gsub("industry: ","",text))-> industries

industries %>%
inner_join(shareholders) %>%
select(-text)->data_lineage_data
inputPanel(
selectInput("selected_industry", label = "select the industry you want to
focus on", selected = "",
choices = unique(data_lineage_data$industry)),

textInput("name_string", label = "write the name of the shareholder",
value = "")
)
renderDataTable(
if (input$selected_industry != "" | input$name_string != ""){
data_lineage_data %>%
filter(industry == input$selected_industry,
grepl(input$name_string,shareholders))}else{(data_lineage_data)}
)
```
```

Which is the name you think Mr. Clough will check first? *Yeah, I guess the same... Omidi Tahvili.*

Expanding Shiny beyond the basics

Before working on report rendering, let me give you some hints to expand your knowledge of Shiny, which is an always expanding universe, adding features day by day and also giving a hedge to R compared to other data mining languages. If you are interested in building more confidence with this powerful tool, you should definitely look at the following:

- Shiny widgets, that is, a collection of available input controls. See them at: `https://shiny.rstudio.com/gallery/widget-gallery.html`.
- Deepen your knowledge of the reactivity framework to learn how to make your user interact with the data provided: `https://shiny.rstudio.com/articles/#reactivity`.
- The Shiny dashboard is a further expansion of the shiny framework, also available to work on real-time data: `https://rstudio.github.io/shinydashboard/`.

Rendering and sharing an R markdown report

You now have a sense of how flexible and useful this instrument can be in letting you organize and disclose the results from your data mining activity.

Rendering an R markdown report

We are ready to deploy our report and take a look at it. We can easily do this by following two alternative ways:

- Clicking on **Run Document** within the RStudio user interface:

- Rendering the document through the `render()` function, which comes directly from the `rmarkdown` package.

Whichever way you choose, this will be the output obtained:

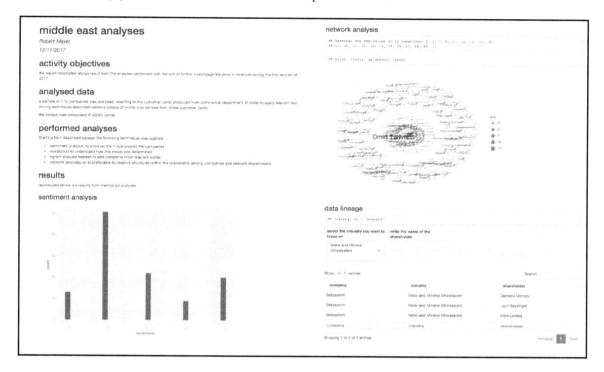

We now have to see how to share this with Mr. Clough.

Sharing an R Markdown report

The alternatives available to share R Markdown documents are basically two:

- **Static R Markdown reports**: If the document encompasses only static elements, you can render it in different file formats, such as .html, .pdf, or even Word. Be aware that in order to create such a kind of document, you need to select **Document** from the **New R Markdown** window. Let me show you how:

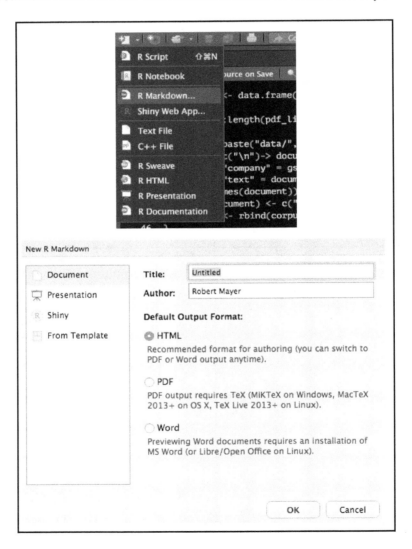

- **Dynamic R Markdown report**: If, like our case, you developed an interactive report, the only way to share it (besides showing it on your PC) will be to upload it on a adequately set online server.

Render a static markdown report into different file formats

The `rmarkdown` package provides three alternatives to render your static document in a shareable form:

- `.html`, as a static HTML document to be embedded in any website
- `.pdf`, through the `pandoc` package and a preliminary latex conversion
- Word, translating markdown headlines into Word headings

All you will have to do is specify which kind of document you are willing to obtain when launching the rendering function. Even more simply, access the *knit* menu and select the right control of the user interface from the following:

This will produce your report in the desired format and a new file in your working directory.

Render interactive Shiny apps on dedicated servers

As we were saying, sharing an interactive R Markdown document developed with `rmarkdown` and `shiny` will require you to upload it onto a proper server.

This server will particularly need a version of *Shiny Server* up and running on it. This is not exactly a painless procedure and you will need some IT knowledge to succeed even if some packages are trying to relieve some of the pain, for instance, `ramazon` for deployment on Amazon S3 servers.

Sharing a Shiny app through shinyapps.io

The other, and easier, alternative you can pursue is to deploy your app on `shinyapps.io`, a dedicated service provided by RStudio to easily deploy and share a Shiny app.

This will require you to just create an account on this platform, choose a pricing plan (yeah, free plans are available as well), and push your app on the `shinyapps.io` server directly from the RStudio IDE.

After having created your account, you will just have to reach the publish control within the RStudio IDE:

Click on it and authenticate it with your credentials to the platform.

Finally, you will be able to select which file you want to publish and actually do it with a final click on the **Publish** button:

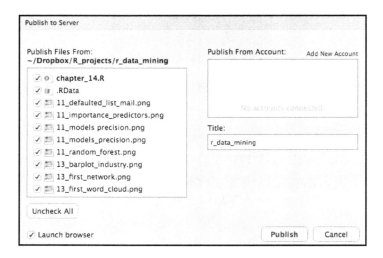

And this is exactly what we are going to do to share our great insights with Mr. Clough. That said, my dear colleague, our analyses comes to an end. All we have to do now is share this report with Mr. Clough and see what's coming next. It was a pleasure working with you, and I hope it will not be the last time.

Further references

- R Markdown website: `http://rmarkdown.rstudio.com/`
- `shinyapps.io` website : `https://www.shinyapps.io/`

Summary

And you just added one more sharp tool into your toolbox! This chapter was surely less intense than the previous one; nevertheless, it gifted you a relevant edge for crafting reports about your data mining activity.

The first relevant point you learned within the chapter is that a report, in order to be effective, has to respect some core principles mainly related with clearness of objectives and assumptions, consistency, and replicability of results.

Furthermore, you learned how to set up and fill down an `rmarkdown` report composed of markdown slices of text and r code chunks. This powerful instrument lets you create reports made on your R code and easily update the results as the data changes.

Finally, you got in touch with the fast-growing world of the Shiny app, a complete ecosystem for web application development and deployment.

Your job is done at Hippalus Inc., but if you look after this page, something interesting is waiting for you. You get closer to discovering the cause of the amazing drop in revenues. Aren't you curious to discover the truth lying behind the data?

14
Epilogue

It's a quiet day at the Hippalus inc. like it was three months ago when the amazing drop in revenues was found. You are sitting at your desk looking at the intranet news when suddenly an email pops-up in your inbox:

Extraordinary meeting @ the main meeting room at 9.00.

You ask some of your colleagues if they know what is going to happen during the meeting. Nobody actually knows, and since the time is getting closer to 9, you decide to get to the meeting room. At the time you get there, a small chat is going on, but as soon as you come into the room the chat almost stops. And it definitely stops once Andy also gets in the room.

Dear colleagues, I have suddenly organized this meeting to share with you some good news. A sound of relief fills the room as soon as Mr. Sheen completes this pleasant sentence.

I was recently notified that the investigations on the revenues drop came to an end, and that end was a bad one. There is actually no great meaning in this talking, nevertheless, the audience is confident that more news will come in the forthcoming words from our boss.

Mr. Clough called me yesterday to provide an update on the status of the investigations and its outcomes. He repeated once more his gratefulness for the effective support we provided during their activities and wished this could be the first episode of a long history of collaboration between our two departments. Well, let's hope this not going to become a soap opera!

The sincere and rigorous laugh welcoming this joke explains, more than a thousand words, how respected and feared at the same time Mr. Clough is.

Nevertheless, we have to admit that on this occasion our collaboration was actually constructive and helpful for the whole company. To those of who are not aware of what the investigation was about, I will briefly summarize it.

Nearly three months ago, we received an alarmed communication directly from the CEO showing an incredible drop in our revenues. It was really a surprise for the CEO and for all the company, and we were immediately engaged to discover the reasons of this epic fail.

Suddenly, it became clear that we could have not leveraged the reconciled data from the company data warehouse, which at the moment was still in the development phase.

We had, therefore, to perform the analyses the hard way: gathering, cleaning, and merging data sources from different legacy systems, trying to get ahead of that mess.

Having cleaned the data, we gained our first win: from the clean series of profit data divided by region, we discovered the drop coming from the Middle East area. This produced a kind of relief and pain at the same time, and also the involvement of the internal audit department.

We commonly agreed that the best possible way to move onward the analyses without raising any suspicion in people possibly involved in the story, was to leverage the existing data on the history of our customers to define a list of Middle East customers more prone to going into default.

And this was what we did: we applied data mining models to our data, to better understand the phenomenon and discover the attributes most predictive of a possible default. If I am right, we applied linear regression, logistic regression, and some other evil stuff... we applied random forest as well, didn't we?

After receiving some kind of confirmation from one of his colleagues, Sheen starts talking again to the small crowd which is now sitting in the meeting room.

Those models, which they say we also combined together by means of ensemble learning techniques, were shown to be quite powerful in explaining the reality we were facing. We, therefore, moved to the next step: predicting which customers from the ones pertaining to the customer list of the Middle East, were more probably in default within the last year.

We shared this list with Mr. Clough's department, who employed it to perform another relevant analysis. To be honest, they have done some cool analysis as well.

The internal audit basically collected customer cards for all companies we predicted being defaulted, and applied, to the text extracted from these documents, some powerful techniques of text mining.

Two big results came from the analyses. The first was related to the soundness of our prediction. The comments from our commercials showed that those companies we predicted as being defaulted were actually experiencing a really bad relationship with us. But the most surprising discovery coming from their analysis was the one obtained by exploring the network of companies and shareholders. After representing this network, the internal audit discovered that the most part of the probably defaulted company was related to a shareholder named Omid Tahvili.

I think some of you already knew this part of the story, but probably none of you knows what comes next.

The mixture of increasing silence and the sound of astonishment produced by this last sentence confirmed to Sheene that no one in the room was actually aware of the final developments in the story he was going to disclose.

After receiving a detailed report on the results of the analyses, Clough decided to break the tie and directly reach our subsidiary in the Middle East, to conduct by person the required file work, gathering evidences and interviewing involved people. What? Was he armed? No, I think he wasn't.

A nervous laugh spread through the audience, but everyone was actually just waiting to discover the final result of this adventurous travel to the Middle East.

The final clash was directly with Mr. Leveque, who in the first days appeared to be open and collaborative, but in the end started to show clear signs of impatience and fear.

In the end, Mr. Leveque decided to confess and fully disclose what was going on: he personally got involved in a bad history of horse betting and blackmail. This was one of his achilles heels and a criminal named Omid Tahvili found an effective way to leverage it. Omid met Mr Leveque when he was in a bad day when he nearly lost a fortune.

Tahvili proposed to help him to reduce by half his gambling debt, asking in return for a particularly favorable treatment for a bunch of companies he was affiliated with. Those companies and this will not surprise anyone, were not flourishing, and actually, we at the Hippalus would have never started doing business with them if it wouldn't be for this sad history.

No surprise then if those bad customers, in the end, weren' t able to honour their debts. Since they were all substantially run by Omid himself, and this was testimoniated by our commercials lamenting a difficulty to find useful contact persons to relate with, as soon as this crimal started losing his grip on the shadow market, the business started to ruin, and we started to see our cash flows dramatically drop. Not to be mentioned, Leveque got fired, but you already know this from company news, and Mr. Sahid took his place.

The silence was not absolute; people within the room were surprised by the amazing story and how incredibly close to the truth the data had led them.

That said, even if for the company it was a hard blow, we are already recovering in that area and in the overall figures. That's why we can now look at this story as a relevant case history. Particularly, this was remembered as a great example of the power of data mining models to discover the story data that can tell. Let me, therefore, call two of the main characters of this story to join me here: Andy and his valorous assistant! We already knew about the great skills of Andy. No one would have bet on such great work from a newbie working on the topic: congratulations!

Yeah, Mr. Sheen is talking to you, and you definitely deserve his congratulations. You made a good job moving from the first uncertain steps in R to conducting a full data mining project.

You now have a powerful tool in your hands, and you know how to you use it. Good look, and do not forget to come and say hello at the Hippalus sometimes!

Dealing with Dates, Relative Paths and Functions

Dealing with dates in R

The code for changing bank records date from Chapter 1, *Why to Choose R for Your Data Mining and where to start?*:

```
movements %>%
mutate(date_new = as.Date(movements$date, origin = "1899-12-30")) %>%
mutate(day_of_week = wday(date_new)) %>%
mutate(month = month(date_new)) -> movements_clean
```

Working directories and relative paths in R

R gives the possibility to the reader to set the so called working directory, which is analogous to the current directory, typical of command-line tools. This working directory has to be intended as the folder where we are going to store the greatest part, if not all the files,. needed for our current analysis. Technically this will result in a different behavior from the interpreter when facing a file path.

To understand how this works, we can try the following experiment, starting from our desktop let us create a subfolder, named `analysis_directory` so that the path of this directory from the desktop will look as follows:

```
/Desktop/analysis_directory
```

We now place a new text file into the subfolder `analysis_directory`, namely `experiment.csv`. Finally, we go to the R console and request to the console to show the current the working directory, as follows: `getwd()`.

This results in the console printing out the absolute path leading to the current working directory. We now try to set it to the desktop folder, running a command like the following: `setwd("/Users/andrea_cirillo/Desktop")`.

If you are working in a Windows OS, just look for the address bar into your file system explorer and you will find the full path to your desktop folder. Now that we have set our working directory to the desktop, we can try, for instance, to import the file `experiment.csv`. Let us try in the most naive way and see what happens: `import(experiment.csv)`.

Unfortunately we will be prompted with an error message similar to the following: `Error in import("experiment.csv") : No such file`.

Why? Because R made the following reasoning: He is asking me to look for the file *experiment.csv*, but where to find it? I am going to look for it within my working directory... oh,no! There is no such file here!

May be this was a bit too much colored version of the reality, nevertheless it gets the point: R define the path where to look for the file attaching to the file name the absolute path from the computer root to the working directory. Within our example it will therefore look at the following path: `/Users/andrea_cirillo/Desktop/experiment.csv`.

What is missing here? The `analysis_directory` folder, we have to submit the relative path from the working directory to our file. This is easily done with a slightly modified version of the previous code: `import("analysis_directory/experiment.csv")`

Conditional statements

Conditional statements in R always follow the logical scheme reproduced as follows:

```
if (condition){then execute} else {execute}
```

This scheme basically means that the instruction enclosed within the first brackets will be executed only in the case of the condition being true, while in the opposite case only the second set of instructions will be executed.

Within the R language it is, moreover possible to concatenate more than one conditional statement leveraging `else if`, like in the example below:

```
if(1>2){print("what a strange world")}else if(1==2){print("still in a
strange world")}else{print("we landed in the normal world")}
```

Index

nodes, appearance tuning 372
performing, on textual data 365
visualizing, with ggraph package 370

O

one-level database 100
Optical Character Recognition (OCR) 96
ordinary least squares (OLS) 200, 246
out-of-bag error rate (OOB error rate) 325
outliers
checking for 179, 180, 181

P

packages
installing 48
loading 48
PDF files
data, extracting in R 350
list of documents, obtaining 351
reading, into R via pdf_text() 352
text, extracting from documents with for loop 353
pdf_text()
used, for reading PDF files into R 352
Pearson correlation coefficient 167, 168, 169, 170, 171, 172
performance measuring, in classification problems
about 233
accuracy 237
confusion matrix 234
performance statistics, selecting 240
sensitivity 239
specificity 239
performance measuring, in regression model
about 220
mean squared error 221, 222, 224, 226
R-squared 226, 228
pipe operator 45, 46
pivot-like tables
data, summarizing with 43
plotting method 330
population distribution
about 154
mean 156, 157
median 155, 156
quartiles 154, 156

skewness 162, 163, 165
standard deviation 161
variance 160, 161
predict.glm()
calling, for prediction from logistic model 342
predict.randomForest()
calling, for prediction from random forest 342
predict.svm()
calling, for prediction from support vector machines 342
predicted data
majority vote ensemble technique, applying on 344
predictive analytics
structured approach 343
techniques used 343
predictors
Gini index 328
mean decrease in accuracy 328
plotting method 329
Random Forest cheat sheet 330
principal component regression 257, 258
principle, user interface
auto-completion 110
clarity and mystery 107
clarity and simplicity 107
consistency 108
efficiency 107
syntax highlight 109
principles, data mining report
about 377
consistent data 379
data lineage 380
data treatments, clearing 379
objectives, stating 378
state assumptions 378
principles, data visualization
about 53
chart type, selecting 56
colors, selecting 59
essential components, using 54, 56
programming languages
about 8
high-level programming languages 8
low-level programming languages 8